Money-Tree Marketing

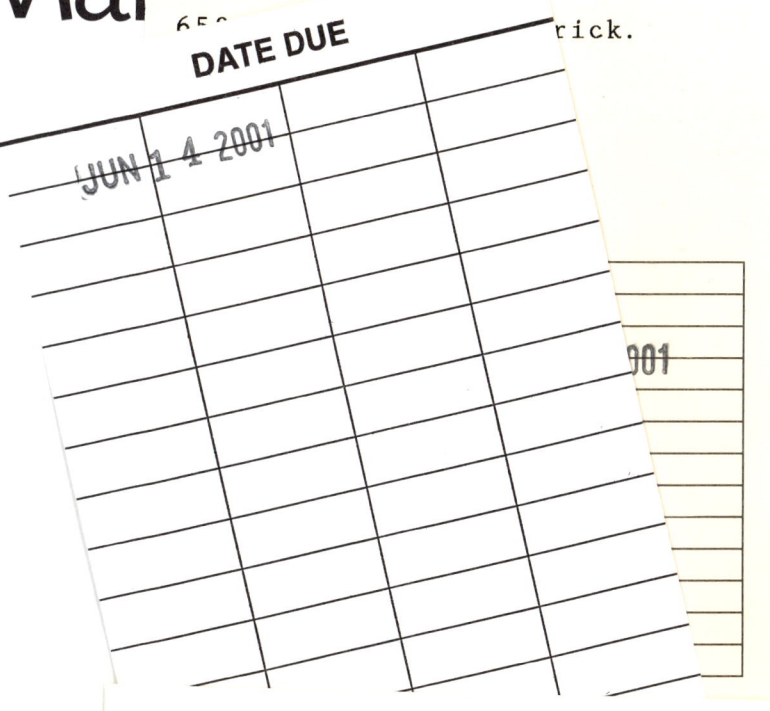

Money-Tree Marketing

Innovative Secrets That Will Double Your
Small-Business Profits in 90 Days or Less

Patrick Bishop
& Jennifer A. Bishop

American Management Association

New York ■ Atlanta ■ Boston ■ Chicago ■ Kansas City ■ San Francisco ■ Washington, D.C.
Brussels ■ Mexico City ■ Tokyo ■ Toronto

*Special discounts on bulk quantities of AMACOM books are available to corporations, professional associations, and other organizations. For details, contact Special Sales Department, AMACOM, a division of American Management Association, 1601 Broadway, New York, NY 10019
Tel.: 212-903-8316 Fax: 212-903-8083
Web site: www. amacombooks.org*

This publication is designed to provide accurate and authoritative information in regard to the subject matter covered. It is sold with the understanding that the publisher is not engaged in rendering legal, accounting, or other professional service. If legal advice or other expert assistance is required, the services of a competent professional person should be sought.

Library of Congress Cataloging-in-Publication Data

Bishop, Patrick, 1958-
    Money-tree marketing: innovative secrets that will double your small-business profits in 90 days or less / Patrick Bishop & Jennifer A. Bishop.
       p. cm.
    Includes index.
    ISBN 0-8144-7055-6
    1. Marketing. 2. Business planning. 3. Small business—Public relations.
I. Bishop, Jennifer A., 1963- II. Title.
    HF5415 B45516 2000
    658.9—dc21

©2001 Patrick Bishop and Jennifer A. Bishop.
All rights reserved.
Printed in the United States of America.
This publication may not be reproduced, stored in a retrieval system, or transmitted in whole or in part, in any form or by any means, electronic, mechanical, photocopying, recording, or otherwise, without the prior written permission of AMACOM, a division of American Management Association,
1601 Broadway, New York, NY 10019.

Printing number
10 9 8 7 6 5 4 3 2 1

Contents

Acknowledgments   ix

Introduction—Money Never Grew on Trees—Until Now   1
You Can Do It • It Works If You Do

Chapter 1—Nonprofit Organizations   7
Sources That Pay to Bring You More Business
How to Set Up Mutually Beneficial Fund-Raising Projects • Teaming Up for Sponsorships • A Recipe for Profit

Chapter 2—Referrals   25
The Key Word for Making Your Business Successful
Models to Follow—or Not • Centers of Influence as Referral Sources • Developing Strategic Referral Alliances • Let the Garden of Customers Grow

Chapter 3—Direct Mail   55
Getting the Postal Service to Deliver Cash and Customers to Your Business
Business Owners' Perceptions of Direct Mail • Consumers' Perceptions of Direct Mail • Preparation Is Vital • How to Develop Lists of Potential Customers • Tips for Using Incentives • Creating Direct Mail Pieces • Your Options • The Four Motivators that Guarantee Success in Direct Mail • Be Irresistible

• Involvement Devices • Increase Your Draw Rate with Personal Packages • Direct Mail Opportunities • Presorted Standard Mail (aka Bulk Mail) • Testing Your Direct Mail Program • Sequential and Nonsequential Mailings • How to Measure Success

Chapter 4—Telemarketing 93
The Personal Connection That Pays Big Profits
Telemarketing Can Make Your Business Successful from Your First Day of Operation • Easy as One, Two, Three

Chapter 5—Print Media 105
How Newspapers and Magazines Will Make Your Business Famous
How to Make the Important Choices • Generate Customers with Free Publicity • Get Paid to Be Published • Expand Your Market Area • Get a Free Yellow Pages Ad • Beat the Competition with Its Own Money

Chapter 6—Television 127
The Medium That Can Make Your Business Successful

Chapter 7—Radio 135
Talk and Make Money

Chapter 8—The Internet 143
The Superhighway to Success
The Web in a Nutshell • What the Internet Can Offer Your Business • How Does a Business Make a Profit from a Web Site? • How to Design Your Web Site • How to Attract Visitors to Your Web Site • Contact Information • Promoting Your Web Site • Get Free Banner Advertising

Contents

Chapter 9—Third-Party Endorsements   **165**
Setting Up Your Own Endorsement Organization to Send You Customers and Increased Profits
What Is a Third-Party Endorsement? • Setting Up a Third-Party Endorsement Program • Mailing Lists—The Key to Third-Party Endorsements • Setting Up the Association Office • Rule for Endorsing Letters—Simple Is Better • How to Boost Results with Customer Follow-Up • Customizing This Program

Chapter 10—Associations and Organizations   **187**
Aligning Your Business with Labor Unions, Credit Unions, and Banks to Make the Business an Overnight Success
What Is an Organization or Association Endorsement? • The Advantages of Marketing to Organizations and Associations • Three Versions of the Association Marketing Program • Examples of Association or Organization Endorsements • Setting Up the Association or Organization Endorsement • Customizing This Program

Chapter 11—Licensing   **209**
The One Technique That Will Triple Your Business and Give You Instant Credibility
What Is Licensing? • When Did Licensing Start? • Benefits to Licensors • Benefits to Licensees • Taking Advantage of Licensing • Getting Paid to Promote Your Company through Licensing • Getting Started in Licensing

Chapter 12—F.A.B.   **225**
How to Put Your Best Foot Forward by Stressing Features, Advantages, and Benefits
How to Add Advantages to Features and Benefits

Chapter 13—Charming Customers Into Your Business   **233**
The Secret to Getting More Business Than You Can Handle
What Is Cobratizing? • How to Go Above and Beyond Customer Service • The Eight Rules for Charming Customers

Chapter 14—Making Your Dreams a Reality   **255**
The One Secret You Must Know in Order to Succeed in Business

Appendix   **261**
Joining the American Small Business Alliance • Win a Free Business • Free Marketing Consulting • Absolutely No Obligation

Index   **263**

Acknowledgments

Our utmost gratitude goes to Hal Bennet, without whom this book would not have been written. Deep appreciation goes to Mark Ryan, our agent at New Brand Agency, who saw our vision and understood it. And we extend our heartfelt thanks to Ellen Kadin, our editor at Amacom, who above all else granted us the gift of patience.

From Patrick:
To our daughters, Amanda, Sara, and Tia, who didn't always like our late nights writing but understood and gave us their constant love and support: We thank you.

This book would not have been possible if I did not have a great support system. I would like to thank Randy Lippert and David Stout, two friends who have always been there for me. I could not ask for better friends.

To my parents, Lawrence and Mae Bishop, who have always given me their unconditional love: Thank you.

To Brandon, an unexpected joy in my life: I wish you the best life has to offer.

Heather Cain, someday you will learn the truth, and it will set you free.

Last, but definitely not least, Jennifer, my partner in business, writing, and life: You are the smartest and most talented person I have ever met. You are the light of my life and my inspiration. This book happened because of you. Thank you.

From Jennifer:
This book is a testament to the fact that persistence brings tangible results. I hope this book helps the people who read it to attain success. It certainly has taught me many things about life and what is valuable.

To my girls: You mean the world to me. I love you all and am filled with joy every day because you chose me to be your mother.

To my mother, Shelly Hawkins: Thank you for always being there to listen. James and Audrey Johnson: No one could ask for a better sister and brother-in-law. Thanks for your honest input and belief in our abilities.

Special thanks go to Gina Gallagher, who opened the door to light. Lil and Dil, my feline friends, where would I be without those tuna kisses? Deep gratitude goes to Pearl Jam for giving me inspiration to follow my dreams and great tunes to listen to at 3:00 A.M.

Patrick, thank you for loving me no matter what. Thank you for showing me the independent road and walking it hand-in-hand with me every day.

Money-Tree Marketing

INTRODUCTION

Money Never Grew on Trees—Until Now

My grandfather was old enough to have been deeply affected by the Great Depression. It was impossible for him to walk past a penny on the sidewalk without stooping over to pick it up. "Money doesn't grow on trees," he used to say. And I believed him, as he'd tell me story after story of his childhood spent in poverty.

I couldn't help but think of my grandfather the night my friend Bernie threw a business-warming party to celebrate the opening of my first business. It was a week before the official opening of Bishop Insurance Group, BIG for short. I had lofty dreams, even at twenty. Bernie brought a "money tree" to the party and started it by pinning a 100-dollar bill to the highest branch. By the end of the night, the tree held over $2000—money I desperately needed to see me through the first few weeks of business.

Like the majority of entrepreneurs starting their first business, I had planned for the rent, employee salaries, supplies, and other miscellaneous items, but the one thing I hadn't planned on or even thought about was marketing. How was I going to get customers to come through my door? I had a disease that I now call the McDonald's Complex. I assumed that if I started a business, customers would flock in just because my doors were open. If you are not opening a McDonald's, it is very unlikely that you will be flooded with customers from your opening day. Even McDonald's has a marketing plan to draw customers to its doors when it opens a new location.

Forget everything you think you know about marketing. This book maps out a brand new road to success.

Amazingly, McDonald's has never had a restaurant fail. But keep in mind that even though McDonald's is the largest fast-food restaurant chain in the world, and everyone knows who McDonald's is, the company still spends several billion dollars every year on marketing. In fact, marketing expenses are one of the biggest expenses McDonald's has. What, then, would make someone who is just starting a business think that he or she can succeed without a plan for generating a strong customer base?

And so I got really lonely the first two weeks after my opening; not even a single customer came into my business. Fortunately, I had the money tree to help me pay for marketing and advertising. If it hadn't been for that, I would have quickly failed and probably never tried to start a business again. The money from the money tree paid for a marketing campaign, but soon I realized that $2000 was not going to last long.

My experiences in this and other businesses led me to develop marketing techniques that were not just low cost or no cost, but that actually put cash in my pocket before the first customer walked through my doors. What I quickly discovered was this: My friend Bernie may have started me off with the money tree he brought to my business-warming that day, but now I was building my own marketing base, one that would help me grow any business I started.

Over the years, my money-tree marketing techniques have not only served me, but allowed entrepreneurs with little or no money for marketing to be successful beyond their wildest dreams. Having enjoyed my own success using these techniques, and having had the pleasure of watching others succeed using those same techniques, I have always felt compelled to share these ideas.

All through my career as an entrepreneur, I've remembered that money tree. It is a symbol of the vision and generosity of each friend who added to it. Of course I didn't see it then, but somehow my friends did. They saw that my businesses, hard work, and plain persistence would give me the experience to approach marketing in a new way.

Years later, some of those same friends told me I should write a book about the marketing ideas that first money tree inspired. Again, I cannot help but think of grandpa and his counsel about money. To some people, marketing simply means spending money on advertising to bring in new customers. But why should anyone pay for advertising or marketing when it is possible to get these things for free or even to make money with your marketing efforts?

To succeed at marketing, you must prepare, have a plan, and implement that plan correctly. Many business owners think that their marketing campaigns are successful if they have a steady flow of customers walking through their doors. This is inaccurate. I have seen many businesses fail because even though they succeeded at getting customers into the business, they failed to make the business customer-friendly.

 *Treat everyone who comes through your door as if that person were your very best customer—even if he or she doesn't spend a dime. You'll be surprised how a welcoming attitude will build a loyal customer base.*

It's vital to attract customers to your business the first time, but it is equally important to make that first experience so enjoyable that they will want to return again and again. If potential customers are walking past your business, you want them to be so enticed that they have to come inside to at least check you out. Several years ago, I realized that any business can do this, and that's one of the things you will discover in this book.

Marketing is a form of charming, of holding attention, of gaining interest. When you market a product or service correctly, it draws people in just as effectively as one of those exotic snake charmers of India. When you have a great marketing campaign, people will stop and listen. All they can do is look at you and blurt out something about how great your product is or how much they appreciate the deal you are giving them. To hear customers say they feel privileged to take advantage of your product or service is one of the best entrepreneurial experiences in the world.

You Can Do It

This book was written for all the business owners who want to experience high yields from their marketing efforts. I am here to tell you that any entrepreneur can generate customers for a business, regardless of budget or marketing experience.

Eighty percent of all businesses fail within five years because their owners do not know how to generate enough customers. Why is this the case? It's a matter of having knowledge. But it's got to be the right knowledge, too. With all the information available today on how to succeed in business, why do so many people fail to keep their businesses profitable and solvent? Well, if you strip away the glitter of any marketing plan, the reality common to them all is contained in one word: motivation.

> A client looking for a new advertising agency called the head of account services at three companies and asked them what time it was. "It's two-thirty in the afternoon," answered the first person. "I'll research that and get back to you," promised the representative at the second company. But the answer that convinced the client that this was the agency for him was, "What time would you like it to be?"

In order to generate customers, a business must motivate potential customers. Isn't the service or product enough to get customers in the door? No. Today's competition is strong, and customers are well informed. A customer wants the same things we all want—quality, a fair price, and your appreciation of the fact that she or he is spending money with you. Most businesses offer the first two things. A business that uses money-tree marketing offers its customers all three.

Entrepreneurs using money-tree marketing do the following:

1. They make their businesses customer-friendly.
2. They increase the number of customers who come into their businesses and treat them well once they get in the door.
3. Everything they put into their marketing campaigns comes back in profits.

When you open a business, you will quickly realize that you are paying for every customer who walks through your door, in advertising, your time, a freebie, or some other incentive. But let's turn that equation around for a moment. What if you were paid to advertise or market your product, service, or business? Sound impossible? I assure you it isn't. In fact, this is the concept behind money-tree marketing. Every time you need more business, you go to the money tree and pull off some money to pay for the marketing that will bring in more customers.

With this book you will learn that, yes, money does grow on trees—at least money for marketing. Is it going to be easy? No. You'll need to have the initiative and persistence to make it work for you. But no business succeeds without those efforts. However, I promise that if you are persistent and you have a good business idea and a plan for marketing, you will succeed.

It Works If You Do

The truth is that no matter how good the techniques in this or any other book are, they will not work unless you do. The format of this book is easy to follow, with step-by-step instructions. You will find several programs here that fit your particular business situation. You will have techniques explained that will help you get customers into your business. You may laugh at some of my unusual approaches to business, but if you take them seriously, you will discover that there are powerful and creative marketing ideas just waiting to be unleashed inside every entrepreneur, and you are no exception.

Marketing ideas are a dime a dozen, but the business owner who puts them into action is priceless.

Consider how successful your business would be if every time you ran an advertisement, were on the radio or television, sent out direct mail, or answered the phone, you were paid from $200 to $2000. This is what money-tree marketing is all about. This book will teach you how to apply the money-tree marketing philosophy to traditional marketing venues, such as television, radio, print media, and direct mail. It will also teach you how to apply it to nontraditional venues, such as marketing to labor unions, credit unions, banks, and nonprofit organizations and establishing your own third-party endorsement associations.

Are all the techniques taught in this book easy to put into action? No. However, if you take one step at a time, you will discover that the road to success is much shorter than you might think. I have operated various businesses, from an insurance agency to a finance company to a department store, a record company, and many others. Not all of them have been successful. Nobody who loves the excitement of creating new businesses succeeds at every one. In fact, that's one of the secrets of success: Taking risks and learning from both success and failure is the most valuable schooling you'll ever get.

I have been a marketing consultant for hundreds of companies during the last fifteen years. One of the first lessons I teach new clients is that failure often has positive effects; it leaves a memorable impression and makes you strive that much harder to be successful.

It is exciting to see my clients attain their goals and dreams. It has been a joy to see hundreds of businesses be born and grow to support so many people. I hope some of the marketing concepts that have resulted will help people who read this book.

I have always believed that if you take a self-made millionaire, take away all of his or her money, and drop that person in any city, within five years he or she will be a millionaire again. Why? Because there is a formula for success that can be repeated again and again. Marketing for business is no different. If you know how to market your product, service, or business, you will succeed at almost any business you try. Every business needs customers, but many business owners don't know how to reach them or feel they can't afford to reach them. With money-tree marketing, lack of marketing capital is no longer an excuse. If you don't have enough cash to make your business succeed, you still have an asset you can use to generate a customer base. It's called "sweat equity." With money-tree marketing, you now have a choice: You can choose between putting out money or sweat.

CHAPTER 1

Nonprofit Organizations
Sources That Pay to Bring You More Business

Through his words and example, my father taught me this: Anything worth having is worth working for. One scorching summer day in Dallas, as I tried to maneuver my car through an obstacle course of highway construction to Mr. B's Restaurant, I thought of this adage. Mr. B's Restaurant is a family-owned business just off Interstate 75. I'd passed it several times, each time promising myself that the next time I was in the area, I'd stop there for lunch. This time I did stop. Once I was inside, my hard work was indeed rewarded; this restaurant had the best chicken-fried steak sandwich and onion rings I had ever eaten. The staff was friendly, and the service was extremely fast.

About halfway through my meal, I looked around the restaurant and noticed that there were only two other people there. I started talking to Joe Bloom, the owner of Mr. B's. He told me that the construction in front of his restaurant had been going on for over six months and the city couldn't even give him an approximate time of completion. "It just seems like it will go on forever," he said with a look of discouragement I've seen many times. I put my sandwich down and gave him my full attention. "Business has dwindled so much that I'm not sure I can hang on much longer," he said.

Now, some people may consider my response as selfish, but if you're a connoisseur of chicken-fried steak sandwiches, you'll understand. I couldn't let

BUSINESS MYTH:	MONEY TREE REALITY:
Business owners cannot afford to hire outside help to promote their products and services.	By affiliating with a charity, you can get paid up front for marketing and have 300 to 1000 people promoting your business.

a restaurant with such good food and great service become another business failure statistic. I offered Joe my services.

Joe's biggest problem was that his cash flow was practically nil, and he couldn't afford to do any marketing. He certainly wasn't in a position to pay me—at least, he didn't think so.

In this chapter you will learn not only how Joe paid me for marketing services but also how you can get charities and other nonprofit organizations to pay you to market your product or service. In addition, you will learn how to get from 300 to 1300 people marketing your business for you.

How to Set Up Mutually Beneficial Fund-Raising Projects

Step 1: Develop a Plan

There are various charities and nonprofit organizations that you can cooperate with to increase the bottom line for both your business and their causes. In Joe Bloom's case, we decided to approach several elementary schools in his area. Most schools do fund-raising twice a year, once in the fall and once in the spring. Fortunately, it was late summer, and school had just started two weeks previously. Our timing was just right.

In addition to schools doing fund-raising projects for the entire student body, there are also many organizations within the school that do fund-raising, such as the band, athletic clubs, the drama club, the choir, booster clubs, and cheerleaders.

As Joe and I discussed some options for his business, he asked how a fund-raising project for a school, or any other organization, would help his business. This is how I explained it to him.

We've all been approached by students selling candy, raffle tickets, or coupon books. Who do you think makes the money from these fund-raising projects? In most cases, the school organization keeps 50 percent or less of the money raised. For most organizations this arrangement works out well, because it helps them bring in the money they need. But the businesses that produce the products being sold are the ones who really benefit.

If you think about it, for every school your business contracts with for a fund-raising project, you get between 300 and 1300 sales representatives selling your product. Now keep in mind, these aren't just any sales reps, these are the best sales reps in the world—children with irresistible smiles and worthy causes. Can you think of any sales force that could be more appealing than kids? From the day they are born, children know how to get what they want. Whether by crying, whining, looking up at us with their big eyes, or just being persistent, they know how to sell us on what they need or want. They instinctively know how to motivate us.

If you want to develop a business relationship with a school organization, you must contact the person who can make a decision, have an enticing offer, and give the school a fair profit.

Step 2: Contact the Decision Maker

Charities and nonprofit organizations are traditionally set up like businesses, meaning that they have a few people who are decision makers and many people who carry out the day-to-day work. Your first contact with an organization will be a phone call to find out the name of the person who makes the decisions regarding fund-raising. In the case of a school, if you want to work with the entire school, the decision maker will usually be the president of the school's Parent-Teacher Organization (PTO). In the case of many other organizations, such as athletic or music groups, the decision maker will be the director or the fund-raising coordinator. Sample 1.1 gives a short but effective script that you can follow to locate the person in charge of fund-raising for an organization.

Sample 1.1 Script to Call a School.

> Hello, could you please tell me the name of the principal? Is (s)he in? Thank you...Good morning, Mrs. Maple. My name is Joe Bloom, and I am the owner of Mr. B's Restaurant. I am calling to personally invite you to my restaurant for a free dinner. I would also like to invite the president of your Parent-Teacher Organization or whoever is in charge of fund-raising for a free dinner. What is the name and phone number of that person? Great! I'll contact him and send both of you a certificate for a free dinner at Mr. B's. Is the correct spelling of your name M-A-P-L-E? And where would you like the certificate mailed? Great! Also, are any school organizations, such as music or athletic clubs, looking for an extremely profitable fund-raising project this year? Good. Whom would I contact to talk to about that? Great. Thank you for your time. I'm looking forward to meeting you when you come for the free dinner.

In some cases the principal may not want to take you up on your offer or may want more information before meeting with you. Don't be offended if this happens. You can either explain things to the person on the phone or ask for permission to send the information by mail. Unfortunately, you will not set up an appointment with every potential contact. Sales and marketing is a numbers game. The more people you talk with, the more appointments you will set up and the more successful you will be.

Keep in mind that some school principals may not be willing to disclose the phone number of the PTO president. In this case, leave a message. At least now you have the PTO president's name, so if you have to call back, you will know specifically whom to ask for and will sound like you know the person. Another way to find the information is to look in the phone book. It is always a surprise when we discover that the information we need is right under our noses.

Donate a percentage of one day's receipts to a local charity. Contact the daily newspaper and radio and television stations about your promotion so that they will publicize it for free. For more on this read Chapter 5, Print Media.

By offering a free gift certificate or a discount at your place of business or at a restaurant, you are giving the PTO president an incentive to call you back. When you talk to the PTO president, be polite and positive. Keep in mind that school fund-raising is extremely profitable, so the PTO president is contacted on a regular basis by dozens of organizations that want to do business with the school he or she represents. However, if your business is local and close to the school, you may have the home field advantage. Most fund-raising companies that approach school organizations are from out of state and have nothing to do with the local community except to use it for making money. Sample 1.2 gives a sample script for your next call.

Sample 1.2 Script for Talking to the PTO/PTA President.

> *Hello. Is Jan Grady in? Jan, this is Joe Bloom with Mr. B's Restaurant. The reason I'm calling is to invite you and your family, along with the vice president and her family, to my restaurant for a free dinner.*
>
> *I would like to discuss some exciting ideas I have about a unique fund-raising project that we would like to do for your organization. It will take*

Nonprofit Organizations | 11

> *only a few minutes, and dinner is on us whether you decide to work with us or not. Would tomorrow evening be a good time for you to stop in for your free meal and discuss my ideas, or would Friday evening be more convenient? Great! I'll see you tomorrow. Be sure to ask for me, Joe Bloom, when you stop in.*

Sample 1.3 gives a script you can use if you want to contact an organization other than a school.

Sample 1.3 Script for Contacting Other Organizations.

> *Hello. Can you tell me who is the president of your organization? Does he handle the fund-raising projects? Is he in?*
>
> *Hello, Mr. Brown. My name is Joe Bloom, and I am the owner of Mr. B's Restaurant. The reason I'm calling is to invite you and your wife to my restaurant for a free dinner. I'd also like to discuss an exciting fund-raising project that we would like to do for your organization. I'm sure that we can help you raise a considerable amount of money. Would tomorrow evening be a good time for you, or would Friday at lunch be more convenient?*

Have customers donate old clothes or toys to give to a charitable organization and give them a credit toward a purchase that day.

Step 3: Prove the Project's Potential

Once you have set up an appointment with the president of the school organization, you must be prepared to show him or her that you represent the company that will be best able to help the school reach its fund-raising goals.

There are various fund-raising projects you can arrange between your business and a school or other community organization. We will cover a few fund-raising plans in this chapter, but the main project we will discuss is a discount card. Fund-raising through discount cards is easy and inexpensive to set up, profitable for your business, and profitable for the school or other organization. Besides that, they are much simpler for the organization to sell than candy bars and cookies. I find it tiresome to be approached 25 times each spring and fall to buy candy bars or cookies. Nonprofit organizations are hungry for something different, for a project that is new and exciting. You are just the person with the plans and project to give it to them.

 *Give gift certificates to nonprofit organizations in exchange for free space in their newsletters.*

What to Emphasize. When an organization makes a decision on a fund-raising project, there are five key things it takes into consideration.

1. The project should be different, but not so different that the organization would be afraid to take a chance on it.
2. The company the organization is working with should have a good reputation, both in business dealings and in other fund-raising projects.
3. The principal people involved should be service-oriented, personable, and ready to help the organization and its president in any way they need.
4. Turnkey programs work best. In other words, all aspects of the project are handled by you. All the organization's representative has to do is pass out the information to the student body or other members and everyone will be ready to get to work.
5. The program must offer high returns! This means that you must offer an above-average commission rate. A minimum of 50 percent is normal. Offer more if you want your company and its project to stand out in the minds of the decision makers.

If you can offer an organization these five things, you will have people clamoring to promote your business. Remember, for every school you sign up, you will have from 300 to 1300 students publicizing your company and bringing in business.

Make every effort to convince the organization that it is making a wise decision by working with you. Personalize your material for the organization.

Nonprofit Organizations | 13 |

Joe Bloom met with five different schools and signed up three. One aspect of dealing with Joe Bloom that impressed the schools was that he had brochures prepared for each school with the name of the school and the town printed on them (Sample 1.4).

Sample 1.4 **Brochure for School Board Members.**

Grimbleton High School
Grimbleton, USA

KEEP UP TO 85% PROFIT FROM YOUR NEXT FUND-RAISING PROJECT!

Are you tired of the same old candy and cookie fund-raising projects for your group?

Are you tired of making a profit of only 50%?

Are you looking for something different?

MR. B'S RESTAURANT WILL GIVE YOU UP TO 85% PROFIT ON A UNIQUE FUND-RAISING PROJECT.

WE OFFER YOUR STUDENTS AN EASY-TO-SELL DISCOUNT CARD ENTITLING BUYERS TO FREE MEALS AT MR. B'S RESTAURANT. THIS CARD SELLS FOR ONLY $10, AND YOU CAN KEEP UP TO $8.50 AS PROFIT.

Private school principals are typically able to decide immediately if they want to do a fund-raising project, without the need to discuss it with school board members.

Joe also had brochures that the president and vice president could take to their next board meeting to discuss the project with the other members. The one downside to this program is that the president, vice president, or fund-raising chairperson normally cannot make a decision without first discussing it with the other members of the school board. In fact, sometimes the board members will decide on a fall fund-raising project the previous spring and the spring fund-raising project the previous fall. Don't let these limitations discourage you. In many cases, organizations have the needs and resources to launch an extra fund-raiser, yours.

 *Contact baseball, football, basketball, and soccer leagues in your area. These have proven to be some of the most successful groups to target for fund-raising projects.*

You should give the organization the option of paying for the discount cards up front. This can be extremely beneficial to the organization, since the price of the cards will be lower, and important for your cash flow and bottom line as well. Some organizations will take the option. In other words, you will actually get paid up front to market your business!

The cost to print up plastic discount cards is usually less than $0.50. Give the organizations you are working with the option of buying a minimum number of cards up front for $1 or $1.50, meaning that you will make between $0.50 and $1 profit per card, not counting the profit you will make from the increased business. If the organization sells the cards for $10 each, it will make 85 to 90 percent commission. If the organization does not want to pay for the cards up front, it can sell the card using a brochure and then order the number of cards it needs. For this second option, the organization pays you a higher rate per card, usually $4 to $5.

The discount card lists one or more merchants and offers special discounts or rates for their merchandise. For example, a discount card could give the cardholder a 10 percent discount on any meal bought at Mr. B's Restaurant and similar discounts at other merchants in the area. You will be more successful with this program if you and other participating merchants give a discount of at least 50 percent. For example, Mr. B's Restaurant gave users of the card a free meal with the purchase of another meal.

Step 4: Contact Other Merchants

Joe Bloom saw the potential in this program. He wanted to give the organizations as much value as possible, so he contacted other businesses about

Nonprofit Organizations

participating in the project. He required that all participating businesses give at least a 25 percent discount or preferably a buy-one-get-one-free. He signed up seven other merchants and charged them $300 each for the opportunity to have their businesses participate. Together, other businesses paid Joe Bloom $2100 before he even signed up the schools or ordered the cards.

Joe showed his wisdom by asking other merchants to participate. When he approached the schools, he had a much stronger program to sell. I usually don't recommend charging other businesses a fee to participate, but it worked in Joe's case. He did it because he needed some working capital in order to proceed.

If you can get merchants to offer extra-special discounts in lieu of a fee, do that. These special discounts are very appealing and make it easier to sell the total program to the organization and easier for their members to sell the cards. You sell the idea of generous discounts by pointing out to the merchant that it will bring in new customers.

 *Be sure to read business-related magazines, such as* Success, Entrepreneur, Small Business Opportunities, *and* Home Business, *along with newsletters and books. One of your best weapons in business is knowledge. A favorite newsletter of mine is* Bottom Line Business. *You can call 1 (800) 234-3834 to request a free copy.*

Step 5: How to Set Pricing

The retail price on the Mr. B's Restaurant discount card was $10. Joe gave the organization two options for buying. For cards paid for up front, he set up a graduated rate schedule, as follows:

Paid Up Front	Organization's Cost per Card	Organization's Profit per Card
100–499 cards	$3.00	$7.00
500–999 cards	$2.50	$7.50
1000–1499 cards	$2.00	$8.00
1500+ cards	$1.50	$8.50

If an organization ordered cards after they were sold, it paid $4 per card, leaving the organization a profit of 60 percent—still much more than it would typically receive.

Of the three schools Joe signed up, two paid up front for 1000 cards each, giving Joe $4000 up front from the schools and $2100 from the seven merchants he signed up for the project. It is easy to get excited by these figures, but let's not forget that the reason Joe used this marketing program was to increase business at Mr. B's Restaurant. He definitely succeeded at his goal. Not only did people come to his business with the discount card, but he also had more than 1000 students promoting his business and getting the word out. Mr. B's also got increased business from people who did not buy a discount card. There was really no way Joe could lose.

When an organization decides to do a fund-raising project with your business, you need to have a contract signed by the responsible party. Sample 1.5 is a sample contract that you can scan into your computer and adapt to fit your business. If several merchants are involved, you may want to do what Joe Bloom did and create a name separate from your business name. As an example, Joe used the name American Discount Card.

Sample 1.5

Sponsor Agreement

This agreement is made at _____ [name of city] _____ this _____ day of _____, 20_____ by and between _____, hereinafter referred to as Company and _____, hereinafter referred to as Sponsor. The Sponsor would like to reserve a starting date on _____ (the "Kickoff"), for its fund-raising project.

Whereas the Company is engaged in advertising, marketing, promotional, and fund-raising programs; and whereas Sponsor wishes to participate for its own benefit in certain programs established by the Company. Therefore, in consideration of the mutual promises and covenants contained herein, the legal sufficiency of which is hereby acknowledged, the undersigned Parties agree as follows:

The Company will contract with participating Merchant(s) to give various offers to be incorporated in Company's discount card program as outlined in this Agreement.

Nonprofit Organizations

The Company further agrees to design, print, and deliver said discount cards.

Sponsor agrees to participate in the discount card program as follows:

_____ Option 1—The Sponsor wishes to sell the discount card using the brochures as a sales tool, collecting the money at the time of sale, and returning the brochures to the Company along with $_____ per card sold.

_____ Option 2—The Sponsor wishes to prepay for the discount cards according to the attached advance payment schedule.

The Company will provide the discount cards ordered before the scheduled Kickoff date. The Company will also provide brochures for each participant. The Sponsor wishes to pay for _____ discount cards at the rate of $_____ per card for a total up front investment of $_____. The Sponsor agrees to send in the brochures with the names of discount card purchasers after the fundraising is over. The Sponsor understands there will be no refunds on unsold cards.

The Sponsor agrees to be responsible for and use its best efforts in the timely promotion and sale of said discount cards and to further perform said functions according to all applicable laws and ordinances. The Company acknowledges the participating Merchant(s) name, address, and logo as well as the name, address, and logo for the Company may appear on the discount cards. Sponsor agrees not to directly or indirectly participate in a program which is in any way similar to the program outlined in this Agreement, with any entity of any type, other than the discount card for a period of 18 months from the Kickoff date.

The conditions and covenants contained herein shall bind the Parties; shall not be assignable except upon written consent of the other Party; and shall be of the terms of the Agreement between the two Parties, with any modification to be in writing and signed by both Parties.

The undersigned hereby acknowledges having read the foregoing Agreement with all blank spaces completed as appropriate, and acknowledges receipt of a completed copy of same. The undersigned also hereby warrants having the authority to commit on behalf of the Sponsor and hereby agrees to the foregoing. Sponsor acknowledges its organization is or is not a tax-exempt organization. Tax-exempt number _____. Number of Participants in Sponsor's organization _____.

_____ YES, our organization would like to participate in the discount card fund-raising program Option 1. Please send us the fund-raising materials before our Kickoff date. We will return the order forms to you along with $_____ per card.

_____ YES, our organization would like to participate in the discount card fund-raising program Option 2. We would like to prepay for _____ discount cards. We have enclosed $_____ as the payment. Please send us the discount cards and fund-raising package.

_____ YES, our organization would like to participate in the discount card fund-raising program Option 2. We would like to prepay for _____ discount cards. We will send in the payment on _____. (This should be at least three weeks before the Kickoff date, the earlier the better so the Kickoff date can be reserved for your organization.)

_____ _____
Sponsoring Organization   Address of Sponsoring Organization

By _____ _____
   Sponsoring Representative   Mailing Address (if different)

Title _____ Phone (____) _____ Alternate (____) _____

Signature _____

If you decide to recruit other businesses to participate in this program, you need to fill out the merchant agreement shown in Sample 1.6 and get them to sign it.

Sample 1.6

MERCHANT AGREEMENT

This agreement is made at _____[name of city]_____ this _____ day of _____, 20_____ by and between _____, hereinafter referred to as Company and _____, hereinafter referred to as Merchant. The Merchant would like to participate in a fund-raising program for ____[name of Sponsor or Organization]____, hereinafter referred to as

Nonprofit Organizations

Sponsor, for a period of _____ months, beginning on _____ and ending on _____ .

Whereas the Company is engaged in advertising, marketing, promotional, and fundraising programs, and whereas the Merchant wishes to participate in certain programs established by the Company. Therefore, in consideration of the mutual promises and covenants contained herein, the legal sufficiency of which is hereby acknowledged, the undersigned parties agree as follows:

The Company will contract with Sponsor to provide the Company's discount card as outlined in this Agreement. The Company further agrees to design, print, and deliver said discount cards.

The Merchant agrees to make the following offer to Buyers of the discount card:

_____

_____

The Merchant agrees to pay _____[amount or no charge]_____ to be a participant in the discount card program of Company. The Merchant understands that the Sponsor agrees to be responsible for and use its best efforts in the timely promotion and sale of said discount cards and to further perform said functions according to all applicable laws and ordinances. The Merchant acknowledges that its name, address, and logo may appear on the Company's discount cards.

The conditions and covenants contained herein shall bind the parties, shall not be assignable except upon written request of the other party, and shall be of the terms of the agreement between the two parties with any modifications to be in writing and signed by both parties.

The undersigned hereby acknowledges having read the foregoing agreement with all blank spaces completed as appropriate, and acknowledges receipt of a completed copy of the same. The undersigned also hereby warrants having the authority to commit on behalf of the Merchant and hereby agrees to the foregoing.

_____   _____
              Merchant   Address of Merchant

By _____   _____
      Merchant Representative   Mailing Address (if different)

Title _____ Phone (___) _____ Alternate (___) _____

Signature _____

Step 6: Get the Cards Printed

If an organization decides to pay up front for the cards, you will need to contact your card printer about forty-five days before the sponsor's kickoff date. You can look in the yellow pages under Credit Card Equipment and Supplies to find a credit card printer.

Step 7: Provide Point-of-Sale Options

Every business that is participating can help the organization and itself by having extra cards it can sell to other customers when they pay for their purchases. Give customers an immediate discount on their present purchase if they buy a discount card to help the organization. This is just one technique to increase your business while at the same time helping charitable organizations in your area. There are many more.

Teaming Up for Sponsorships

"Golf is a sport made in heaven," Sam Purcell said, stepping onto the green of the third hole. "Yep, it's got to be," concurred Vince Rawlins, Sam's business partner. Vince and Sam owned the Desert Pro Shop, a well-known haven for the sports-inclined people of Tempe, Arizona. The sun had just begun to crest over the patch of Sycamore trees to Sam's left.

"Did you look over that packet the Tempe Charity Council left in the office?" Vince asked.

Sam paused, watching his ball sail through the air to land 20 feet from the cup. "Yeah, I looked it over. Seven hundred dollars is a lot to spend on one ad in a charity program."

"That's what I thought," Vince said. Turning to his bag and choosing a three iron, he mulled over the charity's offer. "Seven hundred is quite a bit, but it would be good exposure for the shop. I mean, a charity golf event hits exactly the type of people who would come in and buy."

Sam looked straight at Vince. "Wouldn't it be great if we could sponsor this tournament somehow?" he said.

"Sure, that would be wonderful, but wouldn't that cost more than $700?"

Sam replied, "We could sponsor the charity tournament and offer a $10,000 prize to anyone who shoots a hole-in-one on the tenth. We'd call Lloyds of London and buy an insurance policy to cover the prize, and it would only cost $350. Think of all the free press that would get." Vince stood speechless, in awe of his partner's idea.

We've all heard of these special charity events in which there is a huge cash prize if someone shoots a hole-in-one on a certain hole of the golf course or sinks a 25-foot shot at halftime during a basketball game. I've seen some of the prizes go up to $1 million. Do you think that a nonprofit organization is going to risk losing up to $1 million of its own money? Not a chance! But it will risk a small amount on an insurance policy that will pay off if someone gets extremely lucky.

Today, it's possible to buy insurance for almost anything. Lloyds of London is an organization that provides insurance for some unique things or situations. You can contact an independent agent to find out more about this type of insurance.

If you owned a jewelry store, for example, you could have a promotion in which someone buying an engagement ring from your store would get the purchase free if it rained or snowed on the wedding day. You can apply this type of promotion to almost any business. What is so exciting about this approach is that it's easy to generate publicity for the promotion.

Just send out press releases about your special event and you will get publicity. To find out more about press releases and publicity, read Chapter 5, Print Media.

A Recipe for Profit

Bill Bennet is the deacon of his church and the owner of Bill's Bookshelf, an independent bookstore in Wichita, Kansas. He has always been very civic-minded and has done as much as is humanly possible for his church and the community of Wichita. For three years, the Church of the Good Shepherd had put together a cookbook of church members' recipes that it sold to raise money for various projects. This particular year, however, it looked as if the church would not have enough money to pay for printing the cookbooks. It was definitely a catch-22 situation. The church needed to print the cookbooks to raise much-needed funds, but it needed the funds in order to print the cookbooks.

Bill and I decided to turn the cookbook into a business-sponsored project. Bill belonged to several business organizations, and he approached the members of each organization about being a sponsor and buying ad space in the cookbook. Not every business participated, but quite a few did. As you probably know, business owners are always looking for new ways to market their businesses, and they like to be seen as civic-minded.

Bill sold more than $4000 of ads in the cookbook and got a free ad for himself. One of the advertisers was a printing company, and the church agreed to give this company two free ads in exchange for printing the cookbook. The church made more money by selling the cookbooks for $10 each. This technique also enabled the church to sell more cookbooks than it had ever sold before because every business that was an advertiser also sold the books at its business location.

This concept worked so well that Bill started doing the same thing for other churches and nonprofit organizations. He built up a substantial cookbook advertising business, and his bookstore grew because of all the free marketing he was getting in the cookbooks.

 *Offer to print up weekly bulletins for a local church for free in exchange for a plug for your business in the bulletin.*

Your business can team up with almost any nonprofit organization to apply this technique. Almost everyone buys cookbooks, and it's a great way to promote your business—a way that doesn't have a lot of competition. You can organize the project for an organization in exchange for free ads for your business. You can get more involved by selling ads and handling the printing yourself. Take the money from the sale of ads to pay for the printing and give the cookbooks to the organization. In this way, the organization can keep all the money from the sale of the cookbooks. If you advertise this way, don't rely on a generic ad. Instead, have a coupon that people can use to get a discount.

Nonprofit Organizations

Doing this will benefit the members of the organization and help you gauge the success of the marketing program.

These are just a few ways your business can benefit by teaming up with a nonprofit organization. There is no limit to the different ideas and techniques you can use when your business works with nonprofits. Once again, think of how each of these plans can be a money tree, bringing dollars into your business and into the treasury of your favorite community cause.

CHAPTER 2

Referrals
The Key Word for Making Your Business Successful

John James worked for a large corporation more than fifteen years. He learned early in life the value of loyalty. It's no surprise that John worked for Trinity Lumber, the largest employer in Olympia. His father had worked for Trinity, and John had always counted on the security this local institution offered all its employees. After 40 years, John would have a sizable pension and be able to retire comfortably. John had his life mapped out like the highway from Wichita to Dallas—nothing but straight, smooth sailing for him and his family.

They say bad news travels faster than wildfire, and John knew something was amiss when he came to work one Friday morning. People were standing in small groups, each holding a letter. Some of them were shouting, some were silent, but all of them shared that stunned look that John himself soon came to know all too well.

I doubt it made John feel better about his situation, but he was not alone. Millions of Americans have stood in John's shoes—downsized after decades of loyal service. We all know people who believed that large American corporations were their financial safety net, only to have that security ripped away.

BUSINESS MYTH:	MONEY TREE REALITY:
A business must be in operation for several years to benefit from referrals.	Business owners can get an endless flow of referrals from their first day of operation.

Eventually, John came to accept his new situation, and after six months of unemployment, he decided to do something besides depending on corporate America to give him a job and financial security. As opportunity often comes when we least expect it, when John reached his lowest point, he was given the chance to change his path.

Of course this opportunity could have been offered to anyone in John's situation. The amazing thing is what he decided to do with it: He chose to make a move rather than stay mired in fear and inertia.

John had a chance to be a long-distance service reseller. He had never sold anything in his life, but he did understand the operational end of the business. He had a friend, Mike Seger, who had sales experience. The two friends put together a plan. When Mike and John were alone, they jokingly called their company S.W.L.D.S., which stood for Small World Long Distance Services. Although humor helped them cope with the long hours and frustrations every new business owner knows, they realized that their company could never compete with the giants in the industry, like AT&T, MCI, and Sprint. John and Mike didn't have the budget for a large television ad campaign or even print advertisements, so they found another route to locate customers—referrals.

To illustrate the concept for his partner, Mike took a legal-size pad, put it on the table, and drew a large circle in the middle. "This is one person we know who could tell us about other people who might need long-distance service," he said. Then he drew several lines out from the center circle and made circles at the end of each line. "These are the referrals we can get from one person." Next, Mike drew lines and more circles extending from the second set he had just drawn. "Now these are the referrals we can get from the original referrals. See how quickly we could have hundreds of new customers?" John said nothing; he just gave Mike a wide smile.

The two friends set out to get referrals. They contacted everyone they knew—friends, relatives, business associates, even associations and organizations. Six months later, John and Mike had put in countless late nights and weekends building up their business. The time invested paid off, because eventually their long-distance company was operating in over 200 countries—more than AT&T. To this day, John and Mike don't advertise their business. There's no need.

Referrals

Referrals are a tremendous way to build up a business, for the following reasons:

- Low or no overhead
- The power of compounding to your advantage
- The ease of approaching potential customers because you are a friend of a friend
- Optimum use of time, since you are dealing mostly with people who are already interested in your product or service

The key to an effective and successful referral marketing program is knowing how to find good referral sources and how to treat them as a valuable asset.

Models to Follow—or Not

How would you like to be in an industry that has such a good referral system in place that it produces billions each year in sales from those referrals? How would you treat those referral sources? The airline industry is in this exact situation.

The airline industry receives more than $5 billion annually from travel agency referrals. Apparently, airline company executives do not see these referral sources as valuable assets. The airlines are cutting the commission they pay to travel agents from 10 percent to around 8 percent, with a cap on each ticket of $50. This is not the way to treat the people who refer such a large amount of business to you.

If one of the airlines had an executive with nerve and foresight, it would do the opposite of the other airlines and raise the commission paid to travel agencies from 10 percent to 12 percent. Think about how much business this airline would receive. And this doesn't even take into account the millions of dollars in free publicity the airline would get from stepping away from the industry norm and being an independent leader.

Unfortunately, the airlines don't realize they have the best referral system in the world. The silver lining in this cloud is that you can learn from their mistakes. You can develop a referral system for your business by learning from the examples of the airlines and of John and Mike.

> *No amount of skillful invention*
> *can replace the essential*
> *element of imagination.*
> —Edward Hopper

If you have the advantage of previous sales experience, then you already recognize the value of referrals. One of the first things almost any sales organization will do is ask you to make a list of everyone you know—from your friends to your newspaper carrier to your bowling league partners. The reason sales organizations ask for this list is that they know that referrals are a quick and nearly effortless source of sales. A referral marketing program is also easy to implement and is a cost-effective way to build your business.

In discussing referral marketing programs, we will look at traditional referrals, such as people you know, and we will also cover nontraditional referrals, such as turning people you don't know into referral sources.

Over the last forty years, an entire industry has been created based solely on the idea that referrals are the best source for new customers. What we now call network marketing (we used to call it multilevel marketing) came into existence because a handful of companies realized they could take the concept of referrals and expand their businesses without limit. Today the network marketing industry has revenues of over $85 billion.

I am not suggesting that you take your business into network marketing. What I do suggest, though, is that you stand back a bit from your current referral sources, whether they are existing customers, business associates, friends, relatives, or organizations you belong to, and see the potential for bringing in new customers.

Centers of Influence as Referral Sources

Step 1: Discovering the Potential

Your business is located in a city; it could be a small one or a large one. Get a map of your city and place it on the table. Look at all the street names and numbers, all the intersections and thoroughfares, and consider all the people who live in your city. Now take a tiny step back and think how your business would grow if you had ten salespeople or ten locations spread throughout the city. Those ten salespeople or ten outlets would raise the potential for higher revenue by at least 1000 percent.

As you read this, you're probably thinking, "But I have a small business. I run my business all by myself from my bedroom. I don't have the money to hire ten salespeople or open ten outlets." This is where I smile and say, "Think again." You do have the resources to put at least ten centers of influence out into your city—by using a referral marketing program.

HOT TIP *People buy with their emotions, so design your direct mail piece to touch people emotionally. It should touch the recipient's heart, soul, and senses.*

Step 2: How to Grow Green

My wife and I have always said that our businesses are like our children. This analogy is true, but here I would like to use a different analogy—gardening. As you plan to start a referral marketing program, consider that you are planting a garden. It will take time, effort, and commitment to begin, but the rewards will far outweigh the work.

It is difficult for you as a business owner to stay in touch with all the areas where you have potential customers. If your business is in a large metropolitan area, it is impossible. However, there is a simple and effective way to stay plugged into every aspect of your marketing area—through individuals and organizations. By doing this, you are using the friend-of-a-friend approach; your referral sources lay the groundwork for you, introducing their friends, associates, and acquaintances to the products or services your business offers.

In the referral marketing program, there are two areas to work. You can think of them as two types of ground. The first is already prepared, with the soil turned and seeds planted. The second is untilled ground. It is fertile, but the potential lies beneath the surface, waiting for someone to take it from possibility to profit through work, water, and sunshine.

> **HOT TIP:** *Show your referral sources your appreciation by giving them a gift certificate to a restaurant, movie tickets, or a free gift.*

Prepared referrals are those people, companies, and organizations that know you and your business. Prepared referral sources include:

- Family, friends, and acquaintances
- Current or previous customers
- Companies your business works with, such as suppliers and contractors
- Organizations that your business either belongs to or supports through donations of time or money

Unprepared referral sources can be any person or group. Some examples of unprepared referral sources are:

- Companies associated with your industry
- City, state, county, and federal organizations that are connected to your industry
- Your competition

As you continue reading, keep in mind these two separate areas where you can generate a limitless flow of new customers. Referrals have proved to be the best way to get new customers.

Step 3: Get Referrals from People Who Know You and Your Business

Current customers that come to your business are a foundation on which you can begin. The first thing to consider is how much you know about your current customers. Do you have a list of their names, addresses, and phone numbers? If not, start your marketing program by gathering this information on your base of current customers.

Referrals

There are several ways to gather customer information:

- Hold a drawing in your store for a medium-priced item that you stock.
- Give a 10 percent discount to everyone who fills out a survey form.
- Ask for the customer's name, address, and phone number when he or she checks out.
- Keep a record of all previous and current customers' contact information from invoices.
- Set up a Web site with a discussion group covering the topic of your product, service, or industry and invite your customers to register (free of charge) to become a member of this discussion group.

Once you have information about your customers, such as their names, addresses, and telephone numbers, it's time to move on to the next step. There are several ways to make contact with your customers and discuss a referral program with them.

Establishing Referral Sources Using the Phone. Mary Doughty owned a sewing and monogramming service called A Stitchery. Mary had owned the business for nearly twenty years. She used it to supplement the family income. When Mary retired, she turned the business over to her daughter, Gina.

Gina had lots of energy and didn't want A Stitchery to just provide supplemental income. As a single mother, Gina needed the business to bring in not only more money but also more profit, and so she wanted to grow the business. However, she had no money for marketing or advertising. This is when Gina and A Stitchery came to my attention.

Together, we formulated a referral marketing plan that would cost Gina next to nothing. We created a list of her current customers through invoices and claim tickets. Almost all the customers had given Mary their telephone numbers. Gina began by calling previous and current customers. She used the customer satisfaction follow-up approach, which is shown in Sample 2.1.

Sample 2.1 **Script for Approaching Current Customers for Referrals.**

> Hello, is James there? Hi, James, my name is Gina Doughty, and I'm the owner of A Stitchery. I have here in our records that you had 15 shirts monogrammed for Tripp's Automotive a couple of months ago. The reason I'm calling is to ask about the service here at A Stitchery and the quality of the work you had done. Were you satisfied?
>
> Great; it's always nice to hear that you got more than you expected. We want all of our customers to know how important they are to us. That's why I'm calling to let you know that we are giving a 25 percent discount on all monograms between now and the end of the month. Yes, you're right, that is quite a deal, but it gets even better. For every referral that becomes a customer, you will receive an additional 10 percent off your next order. Who else do you know that could use our services and might want to take advantage of our special? Thank you, yes, I will contact them. If they come in before the end of the month and take advantage of our special discount, I'll even throw in an extra shirt and monogram for each 10 that they order. Of course, the same discount and special offer are extended to you as well. After finding out what a customer did or did not like about her or his experience at A Stitchery, Gina asked if the customer knew of any other business owners who might need monogramming, or other mothers who needed costumes sewn for their children's school plays. After spending two days with this referral program, Gina had over 50 new customers. The program worked so well that Gina didn't stop there. As new customers came in, she talked to them about others who might need her service. Eventually, like a snowball rolling downhill, the momentum gathered and Gina had to hire her mother back just to keep up with all the business.

Using this marketing program, it is simple to set up existing customers as centers of influence. The last time I spoke to Gina and Mary, they had just landed an order from Palace Pontiac for more than 150 monogrammed shirts. Paul Rafke, who owns SafeSeal Oil Disposal, referred the owner of Palace Pontiac, Lance Owen, to Gina. Paul had used A Stitchery for monogrammed employee shirts. Gina got several other referrals from Paul. As Gina found out, the best way to get referrals is from the customers who visit your store.

Establishing Referral Sources from Customers as They Come to Your Business. Dennis Harton owned the Phoenix Dollar Theater. In the hectic rush of everyday operations, it had been nearly three months since Dennis had taken the time to sit down and take stock of where his business was heading. Of course, there were the regulars. In fact, if it hadn't been for them, Dennis and his employees would have been out of work completely. Dennis knew that there were many people in town who came to the theater only occasionally and many more who never came at all.

Dennis is a friend of mine. I watched him buy the Dollar Theater and try to keep it running for over two years. As we played basketball one Friday evening, Dennis confided that he needed to get more customers. He beat me that night twenty to sixteen, and as we walked back to the car I asked him if I could make a few suggestions to help him get more customers.

A few hours later, sitting at my dining room table, Dennis came up with several plans to raise his business from a level where he was barely making ends meet to having enough profits that he could start a savings plan and even reinvest some money in the business.

The plan we liked best was the Double Date Special. The concept was that the more people that came to the show, the more Dennis could make on concession sales. Many theaters make no profit from ticket sales, since the large majority of that revenue goes to the companies that make and distribute the films. A theater's profit comes from concession sales—soda, popcorn, hot dogs, and candy.

Considering that 96 percent of the Phoenix Dollar Theater's customers were couples or groups of two or more, we couldn't wait to put the plan into action. Dennis had several hundred flyers made up that read: Double Date-Double Movie at the Phoenix Dollar Theater. Any couple with this flyer and another couple got tickets for two movies for $2 per couple, meaning that four people could see two movies for $4. Not only did this encourage double dating, or four customers, it also encouraged both couples to stay in the theater longer, thus increasing the concession sales.

Establishing Referral Sources Using the Mail. Laurie Ferguson was first and foremost a mother, although not that many years ago she had been a gymnast. Laurie's current passion was passing on the gift of grace, strength, control, and movement to girls under ten. It wasn't just a job for Laurie, and it wasn't just a business. It was her mission in life, one that she felt could be even better if only there was a little more money.

My daughter was one of the girls she taught. One day, as I watched my daughter warm up with the other girls, Laurie struck up a conversation with me about marketing. I told Laurie that there were many ways she could get more business. We went back to her office and brainstormed. Laurie had a file on each student, with the parents' names and address in it. As soon as I looked over those files, I knew that Laurie could have as many new students as she wanted. We worked up a marketing program targeting the customers Laurie currently had. We drafted the letter and form shown in Samples 2.2 and 2.3, and she sent these out to her current customers.

Getting Referrals from Centers of Influence. You may have heard the sales term *center of influence*, but few business owners understand what this term means or how they can benefit from it. Simply put, a center of influence is someone in your area of business (in your city, industry, line, or scope of business) who knows many people and has established contacts. A center of influence could be someone you know or should get to know. It is a person who receives a great deal of respect and will frequently be a community leader or business leader who oversees many people.

I'm sure that once you take time to think it over, you will find that you already know a few people who fit this description. Even if you don't know them personally, you know of them—who they are, what they stand for, and what type of business they own. Research these people and find out all you can about them. Then find a way to either introduce yourself or be introduced by someone else. Personally invite them to your business. Have a special day honoring them. In return, they will tell people they know about you and your business and the special way you treated them.

If one of these people is trying to change a law and you believe in what the person is doing, you could help by having a petition drive at your store or place of business. Community leaders, politicians, and even celebrities are more accessible than you may realize, and you can use this to your advantage. Use your imagination to find ways to get to know these influential people. Turn centers of influence into loyal customers and they will be a valuable asset to your business.

One of the most encouraging aspects of working with centers of influence is that the people involved generally are looking for situations where everyone can gain from the association. Take, for example, Mark Reeves, principal of Grant Elementary School, and Leslie Jacobs, the owner of Pizza Fun Palace.

Sample 2.2 **A Letter to Motivate Referrals.**

Ferguson Gymnastics
472 S. Cooper
Euless, TX 76052

Dear Jamie Luxton,

   Please let me take this opportunity to tell you how much I have enjoyed having your daughter, Brittany, in my gymnastics program. As you know, my teaching philosophy revolves around group lessons, group interaction, and group progress. I feel that in a group, the girls can learn not only gymnastics but also group working and cooperation skills.

   As Ferguson Gymnastics grows, we all benefit. Because I realize that you take the instruction of your child seriously, and because I know from experience how expensive raising a child can be, I'd like to offer you a special discount.

   Enclosed you will find a form for 25 percent off on a three-month tuition program. Additionally, at the bottom of the form is a place for you to list other parents who might be interested in either getting more information on Ferguson Gymnastics or bringing their girls in for professional instruction. If two students referred by you sign up for the three-month tuition program, this will entitle you to a month's extension of your child's current program for free.

   I thank you for your continued support and encouragement as we aspire to raise physically fit and mentally strong young women.

Sincerely,

Laurie Ferguson
Owner and Instructor

Sample 2.3 **Name Gathering Referral Form.**

FERGUSON GYMNASTICS
25% OFF A THREE-MONTH INSTRUCTION PROGRAM

To redeem this discount coupon, please fill out the form below and return this to us on your next visit to Ferguson Gymnastics.

Student's Name _____

Parent's Name _____

Address _____ City _____ Zip Code _____

Class student is currently attending _____

If you know of anyone who would like more information about Ferguson Gymnastics, list their information below:

Name _____ Phone _____

Address _____ City_____ Zip Code _____

Name _____ Phone _____

Address _____ City_____ Zip Code _____

Name _____ Phone _____

Address _____ City_____ Zip Code _____

THANK YOU!

Leslie found that her business had many things in common with Mark's initiatives in the school, such as building community and family bonds. Together, they established a special Grant Elementary Night at Pizza Fun Palace. From the school's perspective, this was a great way to get families to know one another, to socialize in an informal setting. These closer bonds helped to build the community cooperation the school needed. On the second Tuesday of every month, Pizza Fun Palace offered a special where students and their parents received free drinks with the purchase of a pizza. Every student also received two tokens for the price of one to play the video games. The principal had invitations made up, and each student was given one to take home.

Leslie Jacobs knew that Tuesday was the slowest night at Pizza Fun Palace, which was why she chose it for Grant Elementary Night. After a few months, she realized that Grant Elementary Night was not going to be a slow Tuesday by any means. She was thrilled by the success of her alliance with Mark Reeves. Many customers who came into Pizza Fun Palace because of the special school night became loyal customers. Leslie was so pleased that she decided to try to get three other school principals as centers of influence. If she succeeded, she would have four schools, each enjoying the Pizza Fun Palace one Tuesday night a month.

Getting Referrals from Birddogs. *Birddog* may seem like a strange term. However, birddogs can be great for business if you use this resource correctly.

A birddog is someone whom you recruit to tell others about your business. In most cases, it will be a current customer who is satisfied with your service or product. Ask current customers to refer people to you, and offer to give them something in return. You could offer them an incentive like a certificate to their favorite restaurant, theater tickets, a weekend getaway, or cash.

> **HOT TIP** *You can recruit unemployed and disadvantaged people to be birddogs and bring in business.*

For example, we set up a unique birddog program for the Country Cupboard Restaurant in Des Moines. The owner, Sara Barber, recruited homeless people and people on welfare from the area around her business to hand out coupons. In exchange for their work, they received a free meal and a small percentage of the profit from meals purchased with the coupons. Sara stamped each coupon with the name of the volunteer so she could track the results and knew who was working and who wasn't. If one of the volunteers didn't have a coupon with his or her name stamped on it redeemed for a few days, Sara wouldn't ask that person to volunteer any more.

Each day between the hours of two and four in the afternoon, the volunteers (birddogs) had a hot meal at the Country Cupboard Restaurant instead of the soup kitchen. This situation benefited everyone involved. Sara got many coupons passed out without paying big salaries, since she paid the volunteers on the basis of the coupons redeemed. The disadvantaged got an opportunity to work and a nutritious meal in a nice restaurant, which boosted their self-esteem and gave them a reason to be proud.

Developing Strategic Referral Alliances

Step 4: Get Referrals from People Who Don't Know You and Your Business

Nations see the mutual benefit of forging alliances of all sorts—social, political, and economic. In the same way, business owners should see how building referral alliances can bring rewards to them. One way to gain credibility is to align with worthwhile organizations such as the local chamber of commerce or community charities.

The Chamber of Commerce. Joining the chamber of commerce will expand your contacts and increase your range of influence. The chamber of commerce usually holds monthly meetings that include round-table discussions. These meetings are prime opportunities to introduce the product or service offered by your business to other members. The average annual cost of membership ranges from $300 to $1200. In my experience, the return justifies the investment.

> **HOT TIP**
> *When a referral makes a purchase from you, give that person something extra, such as a free gift or a discount on the purchase.*

Complementary Business Alliances. These are referrals that come from complementary businesses. To bring your business to the attention of new customers, find a business owner who sells a product or service that is complementary to yours.

If, for example, I owned an insurance agency and wanted to expand my referral base, I would locate realtors, apartment management companies, auto dealerships, auto repair shops, and clinics and strike up alliances with the owners.

I would make the owners this offer: I will refer to you all my customers who are looking to buy a house, rent an apartment, buy a car, or have a car repaired, or who need competent medical care. You refer to me all your customers who are looking for homeowner's insurance, renter's insurance, auto insurance, and medical insurance. We could even offer each other's referrals special discounts. The exchange of customer names benefits both parties.

By establishing an alliance with a business that is already in contact with customers who need your product or service, you have the advantage of an introduction from someone customers know and trust, and it becomes simpler to approach them.

Start off by studying and anticipating what businesses your customer might visit before and after yours. Then establish a relationship with those businesses. As an example, the point of customer contact for an insurance agency might look like this:

> Customer buys a house—before my point of customer contact.
>
> Customer rents an apartment—before my point of customer contact.
>
> Customer buys an automobile—before my point of customer contact.
>
> **Customer buys insurance—my point of customer contact.**
>
> Customer moves to a new area—after my point of customer contact.
>
> Customer wrecks the car—after my point of customer contact.
>
> Customer goes to an auto repair shop—after my point of customer contact.

Looking at this list, any place before or after my point of customer contact is a resource I can contact in order to build a relationship for exchanging referrals. Below are further examples of before and after sales point alliances:

- A law firm exchanging with an accountant firm.
- A commercial real estate brokerage exchanging with an office furniture supplier.
- A graphic designer exchanging with a printer.
- An apartment leasing company exchanging with an insurance agency.

Chart out the point of customer contact for your business and pin down areas before or after this point that are potential sharing ground for you and other business owners.

Not all business owners will see the mutual benefit of referrals. Don't get discouraged if the first few businesses you contact aren't interested. Use your sales ability and keep asking for a mutual exchange. You will eventually find other business owners who are smart enough to see the mutual benefits and take you up on your offer.

HOT TIP: *One of the best sources of referrals is your competition.*

Alliances with Your Competition. This technique works well if you own a small sales-oriented business or if your business uses several sales representatives. For example, using a home improvement company, I will show you how this technique can increase your sales by 50 percent or more.

It was February, and like every year around this time, the Spring Home and Garden Show was set to begin. Plans for our booth were basic, so I didn't feel the need to set up two or three days in advance. The show was scheduled to kick off at noon, and I arrived at 9:00 A.M. to set up the display table. Amid the normal buzz of excitement and noise, of brochures and window and siding samples finding a three-day home on brightly decorated tables, I walked the aisle to find my little 10 x 10 plot.

I set down the window sample and the box of drawing registration forms and looked around to check out the other companies around me. What I saw came as a shock—my company, American Home Designs, was not the only siding and window company in this aisle. In fact, there were so many companies similar to mine that the aisle could have been called Siding and Window Row. Directly south was a competitor; another competitor was two booths north; and there was one more diagonal from my booth. There were at least six or seven siding and window companies in our aisle.

At first, this crowding together of competitors felt uncomfortable. They looked my way and I looked back, each of us silently laying out territorial rivalry with body language. Here within a 50-foot radius were a number of companies that were getting ready to knock one another out of a sale in order to capture customers for themselves. I have done the same thing, though I never enjoy the process. This type of competition always seems like a waste of time to me. The practice of battling back and forth, cutting prices to get the sale, ends up with nobody making much money. I've always believed there was a better way to handle competition, and I still do.

At the Home and Garden Show, I talked with a couple of competitors. I was surprised to find that these people were actually nice. If we hadn't been competitors, we might actually be friends.

This experience got me thinking. Instead of viewing each other as competitors, we might consider ourselves allies, and in the process increase sales and profits for everyone involved. Our businesses have a few things in common: We all want to make more money, we want to increase our sales, we want to do quality work for the customer, and unfortunately, none of us sells 100 percent of the customers we meet.

There are various reasons why we don't close a sale. It could be a personality conflict, lack of interest, failure to hit a particular hot button, or the inability to get financing, or the potential customers might have had a big fight right before the appointment and so would not be buying anything from anyone that night.

The reason doesn't matter; the result is still the same: We walk away without the business, and no one makes any money. Keeping this result in mind, I asked myself how we could turn the situation around. Is there a way to make money from every potential customer?

This is the solution I proposed: If you make a valiant effort and don't close a sale, turn over the potential customer to your competitor and give him or her a shot at it. Talk up that firm to the customer. By the same token, if your competitor has potential customers who don't buy, he or she gives you a shot at them. Your competitors can be your best allies.

Take a minute and think about this arrangement. Exchanging potential customers with your allies gives you both the opportunity to increase profits. If you each sell 50 percent of your appointments, why let the other 50 percent go to waste? For example, if you strike up this sort of alliance with only one competitor and you each sell half of the exchanged leads, business will increase by 25 percent, with no increase in marketing expenses. If you make this arrangement with two competitors, your sales could increase by 50 percent. Are you aware of any other technique that can increase sales by up to 50 percent with zero expense?

Not only will this arrangement give you increased sales, but it can also safeguard your sales from being undercut. If you run across a customer sold by your competitor, don't try to knock that competitor out of the sale, let him or her keep the profit. In turn, your competitor should reciprocate. This way, everyone gains.

This idea can and does increase profits. My business increased by over 50 percent when I aligned with two former competitors. In return, my competitor-allies increased their sales by selling to some of the potential customers I was unable to close.

This marketing approach may not work for everyone, but I have seen it work often enough to have no reservations about recommending it. If your business is sales-oriented, such as a car dealership, an insurance agency, or a mortgage brokerage business, this program would work well for you. There are ten mortgage companies in Oklahoma City that I introduced to one another that are now doing a substantially increased business by sharing potential customers. If your business is not a sales-oriented business, this may not work as well as some of the other programs in this book—but then again it might. You will never know until you try it. Look at car dealers. Many years ago, dealerships specialized in one make of car. Today, a single dealership may sell Ford, Chrysler, Lexus, Toyota, and Honda all under one roof.

Let the Garden of Customers Grow

I want to emphasize the importance of cultivating your own referral field. Prospecting for customers through referrals can be compared to the early gold miners' endeavors. These brave men and women spent their lives setting up their claims, establishing their rights, panning for eighteen hours a day, usually with little to show for their efforts. They did not give up, however; they persevered. Eventually, many of them became wealthy beyond their wildest dreams. They stayed with the process of prospecting until it paid off. They laid the groundwork, which eventually proved worth their time and energy. Sheer tenacity may very well be the one thing that all successful people share in common. It is the same with gardening and with cultivating a referral field. It is vital that a business owner understand how to nurture referral sources and believe that these efforts will pay off in the end.

Some business people develop a good list of referrals but then make the mistake of being so aggressive in their presentations that the prospects are turned off. This, of course, leads to only one thing—dried up referral sources. There is a balancing act between making immediate sales and building goodwill that the business owner must be proficient at maintaining. Keep long-term benefits in mind and understand that one sale is not worth losing years of referrals. Never forget that even if someone to whom you make a presentation today does not buy from you, if he or she likes what you have to say, that person may tell others about you. Always look at every new prospect not just as a potential sale, but as a potential salesperson for you, telling his or her friends about you.

Step 5: Cultivate the Garden of Prospects

So far in this chapter, I have discussed techniques for cultivating centers of influence and strategic alliances. By following these techniques in locating, establishing, and maintaining these alliances and referral partners, you will dramatically increase your ability to generate customers. The point to always remember is that these alliances do not happen automatically. They are created and maintained by your continued energy and attention. Following is a list of reminders and tips when using the technique of developing business alliances and referral sources:

- Establish mutual trust with all referral sources.
- Make a plan for locating sources, including the best way to reward them.
- Look for ways to make your potential customers feel special.

- Be willing to give first without expecting anything in return.
- Allow time for these relationships to mature.
- Maintain your status of being reliable and trustworthy with the referred prospect.
- Be flexible with referral sources. If you plan to give a source $50 for a referral and the source wants dinner at the city's best restaurant instead, do it. Sources will remember how you went out of your way to give them what they wanted. More important, they will spread the word about your product or service.

Always remember how important it is to treat the alliance and the referral with respect. Referral sources are putting their reputation on the line every time they give you a referral. They are trusting you enough to let you be involved in a situation that could affect their career, reputation, and livelihood. This is a great responsibility.

Step 6: Approaching Referrals

Your referral source has paid off. You've gotten it—your first referral! After the excitement wears off, you may begin to wonder how to approach this precious treasure. What do you say? Here are some tips and approaches:

- View the potential customer as a relationship that will take time to build. In other words, don't be overly anxious to jump in and force a sale.
- If at all possible, have the referral source call the prospect and tell him or her to expect a call from you inviting the prospect to your business or setting up a time when you can show what you have to offer.
- Write a personal note to the referral within twenty-four hours. It doesn't need to be long, just a brief note expressing that you are looking forward to having the referral come to your place of business. If the referral is extraordinarily large,

meaning that a large profit hangs in the balance and you want to make a good impression, send a gift basket. This note or other communication is also a way to give your referral an in-hand reminder of the commitment to visit your business.

- Write a note of thanks to the referral source within a few days of the meeting. If the source is expecting some form of compensation for the referral, enclose it with this note and make sure it is received.

- After the sale is made, send your new customer a thank you note for the business. This is an excellent opportunity to start cultivating this new customer as a referral source. Depending on what type of service or product you are selling, at this point you might want to send the new customer a gift certificate to a quality restaurant, a gift basket, or tickets to a show, ball game, or concert.

- Another way to make the new customer feel appreciated and important is to give a discounted rate on the product the customer is buying or to throw in something extra, often called an "added value."

Step 7: Nurture the Garden

Keep your promises. Don't disappoint the customer or the referral source. Give both of these valuable resources all you can. Give them more than they expect. In this way, you can continue to reap even more new prospects from these two fields.

It has been my experience that too many business people approach referrals in a cold and defensive manner. I have tried to find the source of this type of behavior for a long time. The only reason I've found is the misconception that business people must always be serious, cold, composed, and impersonal when dealing with customers. Please don't fall into this trap. More than members of most professions, business owners should be warm, caring, and personable. Be creative; don't be afraid to make every contact count whether a sale comes from it or not. Make each contact a meaningful experience for yourself and the other person.

Try to find out as much about the prospect as you can before you talk to her or him. If possible, cover the prospect's likes, dislikes, hobbies, and favorite spots to visit around town, and whether the prospect is married and/or has children. This knowledge will give you insight into the person: how he or she thinks and what hot buttons to emphasize. What's more, it will give you a topic to discuss. To get this type of information on the prospective customer, talk with your referral source.

Do not call up a referral and say something like, "Mr. Abenville, I was given your name by Jane Clark. Do you want siding for your house?" This is not a successful approach, and the number of referrals turned into appointments will be very low. Instead, try the approach in Sample 2.4.

Sample 2.4 Script for Approaching Referrals.

> *Henry, hello. My name is Pat, and I am with Acme Siding Company. I helped Jane Clark get siding, and Jane thought we might be able to help you the same way we helped her. Jane also said you are a baseball fan, and I've got two extra tickets to Saturday's game that I thought you might like to have. I can't go to the game, and I hate to see the tickets not be used. I would like to find a convenient time to drop off the tickets for you and explain our program to see if we can help you the way that we helped Jane.*

In this script there are several elements to consider:

- Using first names and repeating Jane's name several times will remind the referral that you are a friend of a friend and not a sales monster.

- Repeating that you want to help the referral the same way you helped his or her friend suggests that the prospect needs help and that you can provide it, because you have an established track record with someone the prospect knows.

- Offering the referral something he or she wants (ball game tickets) gives the referral a reason to allow you the opportunity for a presentation. It will give the referral something tangible in return.

Step 8: Informed Prospecting

Experienced business owners have a list of prior customers to use as referral sources. As a new business owner, you won't have such a list, and you may choose not to focus on friends and relatives as potential customers. However, when you use informed prospecting, you can turn every person into a referral. This is a technique I developed that has proved effective in actual business situations. This technique can be customized to fit almost any type of business. It works best if your business is sales-oriented, such as a siding and replacement window company. It also works if you have a retail business, such as a gift shop or pizza place, or a service, such as an accounting firm.

Informed prospecting works exactly as the name implies: You have an advantage because you are armed with adequate information before you approach the customer. For example, when I had time between appointments for my home improvement company, instead of sitting in a restaurant, I was productive. I drove around various neighborhoods and wrote down addresses of homes that needed siding and replacement windows. Next, I went to the local public library and used the city directory to find out who lived in each house, if the person was a homeowner, how long the person had lived there, the spouse's name, and where the person was employed. Once I had all this information, a transformation took place. I now had much more than an address on a piece of paper. I now had a potential customer who I knew needed siding and windows.

If you are a car salesperson, the same approach would work for you, except that you would pick out the houses with older cars. If you own a restaurant or retail store, every house has potential customers. You can gather information about everyone in your business area. It is much more effective to approach a customer whom you have information on than to simply knock on doors asking for the adult or owner of the home. This approach can be geared toward any company's potential customers. You can learn more about using the city directory in Chapter 9, Third-Party Endorsements.

BUSINESS MYTH:	MONEY TREE REALITY:
A referral is someone who was sent to your business by a previous customer or someone that you know.	With informed prospecting, everyone becomes a referral.

Carrying out these techniques takes time and effort. However, it is better to make good use of your time in this way than to waste it waiting for the next appointment. This technique also saves you time in the long run because you are talking only to potential customers who have a need for what you have to offer and were referred to your business (by you, of course).

There are two ways to approach this type of referral—by telephone or in person. I prefer to do it in person, because for me this seems the most effective method. I write all the potential customers' information down on 3 x 5 cards and then go knocking on doors. No one likes to cold call, but this approach is not cold calling, because you know who is on the other side of the door. It is not much different from knocking on a friend's door. I don't get in every house when I use this approach, but I have never had a door slammed in my face either. Even if your business is retail-oriented, you can be successful by personally asking potential customers to do business with you. In some ways, these potential customers are more accessible than if they were referred to you by a previous customer. I think the reason for this is that people are aware that you've taken the time to do your homework and collect all this vital information about them.

The basic scripts shown in Samples 2.5 and 2.6 can be revised for almost any business. If you approach people at the door, you will most likely have more luck than if you use this approach over the telephone. You are competing against many telemarketers, but very few people knock on doors to personally invite someone to do business with them.

Sample 2.5 Script for Informed Prospecting (in Person), Sales-Oriented Business.

> *Is Henry around? Hello, Henry, my name is Patrick Bishop, with American Home Designs. You have been referred to us as someone who would be interested in allowing us to use your home as a show home to display our unique siding and energy-efficient, double-pane, tilt-in windows. If yours is a show home, we ask you to do three things for us: allow us to put a sign in your yard for thirty to sixty days; write us a letter after your siding is installed, telling us what you think of our products and service; and let us take before and after pictures of your home. If you do these things for us, we will give you a substantial discount on the siding and windows.*
>
> *According to what we've been told, you have owned this house for eight years. Is that correct? And do you still work at Jackson Automotive? Great.*

Referrals

> *I can take a few minutes now to explain our show home program to you, or I can stop back tomorrow evening between 5:00 and 5:30 P.M. Which is more convenient for you? Great! I'll see you tomorrow evening.*

One bit of advice: When making the initial contact at the home or by telephone, ask for the prospect by first name only. Do not use the prospect's last name. Using the first name makes it sound as if you are already the prospect's friend. Believe me, it works! This approach can be used to sell anything to anybody. Getting background information on the prospect will make the prospect feel that he or she must have been referred to you. Otherwise, how could you know so much personal information?

Sample 2.6 Script for Informed Prospecting (Other Businesses).

> *Is Henry around? Henry, my name is Patrick Bishop and I'm with Two Brothers' Pizza & More Restaurant. You have been personally selected to try our new homemade onion rings, absolutely free with any pizza purchase.*
>
> *Furthermore, if you stop in this week, you'll get a 25 percent discount off your pizza and you will also be entered in a drawing to receive an entire month of pizzas free. What day do you think you will be able to stop in? Great. As I said, my name is Patrick Bishop and we are located at 123 Main. Just ask for me when you stop in.*

If you do use the in-person approach and no one is home, your results will be improved if you leave a flyer on the door. If the flyer is designed to get attention and is easy to understand, the prospect will read it. Also, be sure to write a short personal note to the prospective customer so that he or she will know you stopped by to personally visit. Samples 2.7 and 2.8 show flyers that have been used with great success.

Step 9: Uninformed Prospecting

Some business owners sell their products or services to other businesses, but don't have the time to do the research needed for informed prospecting. Can you still use this technique to approach potential customers? Yes, you can.

It is wiser to take the time to find background information on your potential customers. However, if you sell to other businesses, you can go to the county clerk's office and ask for a copy of the fictitious name certificate of a

Sample 2.7

WANTED

TWO SHOW HOMES

TO DISPLAY OUR UNIQUE NEW SIDING, TILT-IN WINDOWS, OR ROOFING

As a show home, you will:

- Receive free merchandise.
- Add long-lasting beauty and security to your home.
- Increase the value of your home.
- Be the talk of the neighborhood.
- Get a free security system.*
- Be guaranteed savings of at least 30% on utility bills.
- Receive a monthly referral income.

We also have refinancing and consolidation loans available. In most cases we can actually reduce your current monthly payments. We are looking for **TWO HOMES** in this area. Don't hesitate, call American Home Designs **NOW**!

*Does not include monitoring.

Patrick Bishop xxx-xxx-xxxx or 1-888-xxx-xxxx

WANTED

Sample 2.8

YOU

HAVE BEEN PERSONALLY SELECTED TO RECEIVE FREE ONION RINGS WITH ANY PIZZA PURCHASE. YOU WILL ALSO RECEIVE A 25% PIZZA DISCOUNT.

FREE PIZZA FOR ONE MONTH!!!

At the Pizza Fun Palace located at 123 Main Street

PIZZA FUN PALACE INVITES YOU TO REGISTER FOR A PIZZA A DAY

The holder of this coupon is entitled to 25% off the purchase of one pizza (size medium or larger) and a complimentary order of onion rings with the order of a medium or larger size pizza.

Name _____

Address _____ City _____ Zip _____

Phone Number _____ Coupon expires on _____

This coupon is redeemable any time before the expiration date; it may not be used in conjunction with any other special offers or discounts.

particular business, or you can get a list of fictitious name certificates of all the businesses in your area. (There is detailed information about fictitious name certificates in Chapter 3, Direct Mail.) Doing this gives you information about who owns the business and when it was established. If you choose not to get this information, you can still use this technique, and it will still be effective. The only difference is how you approach the potential customer.

When you walk into a business and ask, "Is the manager in?" or "Is the owner in?" right away the employees will assume you are there to sell something. If you are a business owner in a retail space, then you know that soliciting happens in your area just as much as it does in residential areas. However, if you walk into a business with a spring in your step, with confidence and purpose, and ask, "Is the boss around?" the employees will normally assume you are one of the owner's friends. The reason for this assumption is that few salespeople approach potential customers this way, but friends do. Then the employees will usually yell back at the boss that you are there to see her, and when they do, you will know the owner's name. Sample script 2.9 illustrates this approach, and Sample 2.10 shows follow-up conversation.

Sample 2.9 **Approach for Uninformed Prospecting.**

> "Is the boss around?"
> "Yes."
> "Great, will you tell him Pat is here to see him?"
> "Charles, Pat is here to see you."

Sample 2.10 **Script for Uninformed Prospecting.**

> Charles, I am Pat Bishop with E-Z Printing. Your business was personally selected for me to stop by to give you a certificate for free business cards and explain why we are one of the top printers in town.
>
> We specialize in printing for restaurants such as yours. Let me take five minutes to explain why many other restaurants (or whatever business you are visiting) in town choose E-Z Printing for their printing needs. And then I will also get the information from you that I need to print up your free business cards. (This is the enticement for the prospect to give you five minutes; if the prospect doesn't immediately have the time, set up an appointment to stop back later.)

From here, explain your product or service. These scripts can be adapted for almost any business, and they do work. I have used these techniques and scripts for many different businesses. This approach makes it sound as though the potential customer has been referred to you, but prospects almost never ask who referred them.

Not everyone you approach will have the time to talk to you or be interested in what you have to offer them. You can either spend time trying to convince the prospect to set up an appointment with you or you can spend that time on the next prospect. If you are not highly experienced in sales, I recommend you go on to the next prospect. However, keep the person's information in your Rolodex and contact him or her about a month later. The combination of patience and persistence could win over this person in time.

> **HOT TIP**
> *After the referral visits your business, send a thank you card to the referral and to the person who referred him or her.*

Step 10: Continued Cultivation

If you follow the methods outlined in this chapter, you will see that referrals really are the greatest source for getting new customers. Each of the referral programs explained is rewarding and simple to implement. Once you've found out how these techniques work for your business, continue cultivating the field for more referrals. In fact, some business owners like this technique so much that they train their employees to set up referral sources and increase their business in this way.

I hope you have found many ideas in this chapter that you can put to use for increasing your profits. Try one or try them all, but keep two things in mind:

- Referral sources are fields to be cultivated.

- Without attention and nurturing, referral sources will dry up and cease to produce quality customers.

All the ideas and programs I've explained in this chapter are only the beginning. Trust your insight and your ability to create unique customer-generating programs that will work for your service, your product, and your business.

CHAPTER 3

Direct Mail
Getting the Postal Service to Deliver Cash and Customers to Your Business

Last night I watched the movie *The Postman* with Kevin Costner. As I watched all the hardships this fictional character underwent, I began to remember how much mail used to mean to me. As a child, it was an inexpensive way to keep in touch with relatives who lived out of state. As a teenager in the early 1970s, mail was my connection to a world far beyond the small and culturally backward state of Oklahoma.

Mail was always friendly, always fun, always something to anticipate—that is, until I got a little older. Once I reached my early twenties, I learned that the mail also brings bills and sometimes bad news. Like clockwork, the mail also brings junk.

Junk mail comes in many forms. Like many other junk mail novices, I fell for my share of scams: the lottery scam, the long-distance service check scam, the "you've won one of these prizes" scam. If there was a list titled Pure Sucker, I was surely on it.

BUSINESS MYTH:	MONEY TREE REALITY:
If a direct mail campaign produces a response rate of 2 percent, it is considered successful.	A direct mail campaign can produce a response rate of over 100 percent.

The thrust of this chapter is to show you the difference between junk mail and direct mail. It all begins with how the consumer perceives the two terms. You, as a business owner, can research, plan, prepare, and execute your direct mail programs in a way that makes them welcome to and even anticipated by consumers, instead of being dreaded and finding a final resting place in the circular file.

Business Owners' Perceptions of Direct Mail

Business owners know that most businesses use direct mail. If this marketing approach is so prevalent, they assume, it must be both successful and easy to use. Of course, direct mail campaigns are not automatically either successful or easy to use.

Direct mail is probably the most misunderstood marketing program available. Businesses of every size use direct mail. In fact, so many businesses use direct mail that many consumers ignore the medium altogether. The reason for this consumer attitude is not the large amount of mail competing for the public's attention but the fact that most business owners have no idea of the power they are wielding with this marketing medium. They abuse it or ignorantly misuse it. They automatically assume all that is required is a message typed on a couple of sheets of paper, an envelope, and a stamp. Like magic, the responses or orders will miraculously appear.

The truth is, when used correctly, direct mail is the most effective marketing tool any business can use. Most businesses do not understand how direct mail can be a welcome connection between them and new customers, as well as a bridge to build loyalty and trust with their current customers.

Although businesses spend a larger percentage of their marketing budgets on television and print advertising, these two mediums are passive, whereas direct mail is proactive. It is this proactivity that allows business owners to use direct mail as the ultimate tool for:

- Initiating and tracking consumers' purchasing habits and activities
- Building and nurturing a relationship with customers
- Encouraging high volume and repeat sales

Direct Mail

Among the other advantages of direct mail are that:

- Using direct mail can keep you connected to existing customers.

- A direct mail marketing campaign can help you stop thinking in terms of making a sale and start thinking in terms of building a relationship. Instead of share of market, strive for share of loyal customers.

- Direct mail has a wide reach and can carry the message about your product or service nationally or internationally.

- Brand awareness can be created, built, and maintained through the use of direct mail.

- Campaigns can be directed at consumers, other businesses, or both.

- Direct mail offers cost-efficient testing, flexibility, and concrete cost-per-order and cost-per-inquiry analysis and tracking.

- For a business with a limited marketing budget, direct mail is ideal because it is easily focused for specialized efforts.

- Direct mail can increase the effectiveness of television and print campaigns.

- Samples of a product can be introduced to the public through direct mail.

- There are no limits to a direct mail campaign except for imagination and available funds.

- Direct mail can provide an individualized product or service presentation, acknowledging the consumer's unique status and needs.

- By using an ongoing direct mail campaign, any business can develop a lifetime relationship with its customers.

Consumers' Perceptions of Direct Mail

As has already been stated above, consumers divide direct mail into two categories:

1. Junk mail—a waste of their time
2. Informing mail—mail that gives them information and that they appreciate receiving

Junk Mail

Mail is a marketing technique that is most often used to reach directly into the potential customer's home. Because of the personal nature of this medium, consumers often feel that junk mail invades their privacy. They resent the high volume of unsolicited mail they receive and feel powerless to stop the continuous flow. I've heard a friend say, "I'm tired of all those bloodsuckers trying to get my money." This is a perfect example of the general public's perception of unsolicited mail.

When consumers receive informing mail that they feel is important, the situation changes entirely, and their reaction is entirely different. As a business owner, it is your objective and challenge to design your direct mail program so that the consumer considers it to be informing mail and not junk mail.

Informing Mail

What is it about informing mail that makes it important to the consumer? Where is the line that distinguishes junk mail from informing mail? To answer these questions, let's look at the stages a consumer goes through when he or she receives informing mail, followed by questions you should ask yourself when designing a piece or campaign.

1. Read the direct mail piece and evolve and recognize a need. Does the direct mail piece offer the consumer a product or service that is needed?

2. Do research on the company and any competitors. What is it about the direct mail piece that gives the consumer the

impression that this company will give him or her more of the product, better quality, or both?

3. Purchase. What does the consumer expect to get with the purchase? Is the consumer enthusiastic, anticipating the best?

4. Post-purchase. Is the consumer confident in the decision? Does the consumer understand how the transaction works? Does the consumer know how to reach the company if he or she has a change of mind or if there are any problems?

There are ways to deal with each of these four stages of consumer processing to optimize the delivery of your message. First things first, however: You must know that consumer before you start creating a direct mail program that will work for your business.

Preparation Is Vital

"If I had six hours to cut down a tree, I would spend five hours sharpening my ax," Abraham Lincoln once said. Obviously, Lincoln's point was that preparation is often the key to any challenge. Direct mail is no different. In order for your direct mail campaign to be successful, it will require research, planning, and preliminary work before you ever go to the post office.

The first step is to discover and pinpoint your ideal target market. Contrary to what most business owners have heard or believe, it is not cost-effective or smart to target a direct mail campaign at names picked randomly from the telephone book. While this approach may seem like a viable strategy, it will lead to a response rate of only 1 to 2 percent, in optimum circumstances. It is important that you focus your attention on your ideal target (or niche) market. Sample 3.1 offers eight primary questions that will help you profile and get in-depth knowledge about your target customers.

Even if your business is one with wide appeal, such as a restaurant or an automobile dealership, it is imperative that you focus each direct mail campaign on a particular target market. If your business sells to other businesses, you can follow the same customer profile, but answer the questions with the ideal target business in mind. Sample 3.2 shows how this can be done with a pest control service.

Sample 3.1 **Reproducible Customer Profile Form.**

CUSTOMER PROFILE

1. What are my customers' interests or hobbies?
   _____

2. What sets my customers apart from other people?
   _____
   _____

3. What is the general income bracket of my customers?
   _____

4. Does the employment status of my customers affect my ability to sell to them?
   _____

5. What type of magazines or local papers do my customers read?
   _____

6. What percentage of my customers are homeowners and renters?
   _____

7. In what general area do my customers live?
   _____

8. What can I offer that will cut through the solicitations my customers receive and make them take notice of my business?
   _____
   _____
   _____
   _____

Sample 3.2 **Model Customer Profile.**

CUSTOMER PROFILE

1. What are my customers' interests or hobbies?

   Family-oriented activities.

2. What sets my customers apart from other people?

   They do not like the intrusion of pests and are too busy to take care of the problem themselves.

3. What is the general income bracket of my customers?

   $15,000-$50,000 plus.

4. Does the employment status of my customers affect my ability to sell to them?

   Yes. If they are not employed, they can't pay for my service.

5. What type of magazines or local papers do my customers read?

   TV Guide, local Sunday paper, classified section of local paper.

6. What percentage of my customers are homeowners and renters?

   Normally, they are homeowners, but they can be renters too.

7. In what general area do my customers live?

   Within a 10-mile radius of my business, within the city limits.

8. What can I offer that will cut through the solicitations my customers receive and make them take notice of my business?

   A pest control guarantee—if any pests are seen within 30 days of treatment, a second treatment is free; or a flat rate of $150.00 for six months of regularly scheduled monthly treatments. Coupons for 10 percent off an initial treatment.

Take the information you've compiled from the customer profile to set boundaries within which your target market is found. Next, let's explore the many ways to find lists of people who fall within your target market.

> **HOT TIP:** *A list of magazine subscribers is usually the best list to rent to focus on a particular target market. Today, there are magazines for almost any niche group. A quick way to research magazines is an online resource called The Electronic Newsstand (www.enews.com).*

How to Develop Lists of Potential Customers

Once you have determined your target market, you need to compile a mailing list. This can be done in two ways—by contacting a list broker or by making a list yourself from various public and private sources.

Using a List Broker

Contact a list broker and tell the broker what type of mailing list you are interested in obtaining. Many companies sell or rent mailing lists. Your local yellow pages directory also has information on list brokers. Mailing lists are available for nearly any subject or target market. They are categorized according to specific criteria, such as occupation, age, income, hobbies, geographical area, and nationality.

Mailing List Companies

A Caldwell List 1 (800) 241-7425	**Dun & Bradstreet** 1 (800) 624-5669
AAA Direct 1 (800) 999-9151	**Dunhill Hugo** 1 (800) 611-0544
American Business Lists, Inc. 1 (402) 331-7169	**Int. Business List** 1 (800) 535-0350
Compilers Plus 1 (800) 431-2914	**Marketry Inc.** 1 (800) 346-2013
Data Base 1 (800) 545-7965	**Metromail** 1 (800) 316-2637

Most list brokers require you to rent a minimum of 5000 names at a cost of $70 to $100 per 1000 names. They offer preprinted labels, which is convenient and saves time. Believe me when I say that you can rent a list for almost any category. The only list I have been unable to find was of MCI long-distance customers. However, the list broker suggested another list that proved to be very profitable.

> **COOL RESOURCE:** *For low-cost printing on postcards, contact Henry Birtle & Sons, 1143 East Colorado Street, Glendale, CA 91205, 1 (818) 241-1598.*

Here are some tips for renting mailing lists and dealing with list brokers:

1. Request the most current mailing list.
2. Request a list that gives the name, address, telephone number, and economic and purchasing statistics. You will need the telephone numbers if you decide to do follow-up calls.
3. If you receive a list on peel-off labels without a hard copy, make a copy before peeling off the labels.
4. Test potential markets before each full direct mail campaign.
5. If there is no list available for the category you want, ask the list broker for suggestions.

If you are considering renting a list of magazine subscribers, first try contacting the magazine directly. Often you can save time and money by dealing directly with the publisher or magazine fulfillment service. You can find this information in the masthead of any reputable magazine.

List brokers maintain lists for long periods. If you do not specifically request an up-to-date list, you may get a high percentage of old addresses. That means mail will be returned, which is a waste of resources and time. When you receive the list, make a copy before peeling off the labels. If you have been supplied a copy of the list, put it in a safe place. You will need a hard copy of the list later to make follow-up calls. Keep in mind that a majority of list companies will rent the mailing list for one-time use only. Ask them before you rent it if they will allow you to send out multiple mailings to the list. Keep researching until you find a list broker who will allow you to use the mailing list for more than one mailing.

HOT TIP *Try to get more for your money: Tell the list broker that you will rent the list if the broker will give you an additional 1000 to 2000 names free. It never hurts to ask, and the worst the broker can do is say no.*

Creating a List Yourself

If your marketing budget is small, with a little legwork you can get a free or low-cost mailing list. In the majority of cities, the city directory is available at the public library. The city directory gives the following information:

- Residential status—renter or homeowner
- How long the person has been a homeowner or renter
- The economic trend in the general area
- Employment status and employer's name
- Address and telephone number

With the answers to the questions on the customer profile, you should be able to analyze the information in the city directory and use it to compile your own list of consumers in your target market. Locate streets in areas where your customers would be most likely to live. Write down the names, addresses, and telephone numbers of the people who live on those streets. In this way, you're creating a mailing list that costs you nothing. Two directory companies of note are:

R.L. Polk
1 (800) 635-5522

Criss Cross Directories
1 (800) 839-9975

HOT TIP *If you use the city directory frequently, it is a good idea to lease it. This gives you easy access and saves time. Most city directories are also available on CD-ROM disks.*

Direct Mail

Newspapers. You can also find a wealth of information in various newspapers. You may not realize how much information on potential customers you pass over every day. Newspapers supply information such as:

- Births
- Engagements
- Weddings/marriages
- Divorces
- Bankruptcies
- Mortgage applications
- Business start-ups
- Business failures
- Businesses incorporating

If you want an extensive list, all of this information is at your county clerk's office at the county courthouse. The potential information you can get from this source is limitless as long as you are willing to put forth the effort to find it. If your direct mail program is business-to-business, you can get a list of fictitious or assumed name certificates from the county clerk's office. A fictitious name certificate tells you the name and address of a business, the name of the owner, and when the business was started. This way, you can send your direct mail personally to the owner instead of just blindly sending it to a business.

If you have been in business for a time, you can also compile a mailing list from information you have on current customers.

Tips for Using Incentives

Once you have determined your target market and compiled a mailing list, the next step is to decide on an incentive. Consumers will respond differently to different incentives, so decide on one that will entice potential customers to respond either by mail, by telephone, or by visiting your business.

Giving consumers a reason to open and read your direct mail offer is imperative. No direct mail piece will be effective if it is not opened and read. Incentives are the key to getting a consumer's attention. What can you offer that will generate excitement and enthusiasm? You are the only person who can answer that question. It could be a discount, a free gift, or a special bonus if the consumer replies by a certain date.

Again, knowing your target market will help you determine what type of incentive will work best for your business. Obviously, a pest control company would not use the same incentive as a beauty salon. Knowing what the consumers in your target market want and need should help you find an effective enticement.

Some types of incentives are:

- Coupons or vouchers

- Two-for-one specials

- A free item associated with the product or service being offered

- Product samples

- Notification of sales before the information is released to the general public

These are only a few general types of incentive devices. They can be customized to fit your business, your marketing budget, and your target market. The purpose of an incentive is to generate excitement and enthusiasm. Even if the goal of your direct mail program is only to distribute information, as is the case with many nonprofit organizations, giving the consumer an incentive to request information will produce better results. You could offer additional information to those who respond by a certain date, or offer those who respond quickly a trial subscription to your newsletter.

One technique proven to raise a consumer's curiosity is to put a bulky item in the envelope, such as a pen or product sample. The consumer will want to know what's inside, and once the envelope is opened, there is a greater chance that the consumer will read the direct mail letter.

HOT TIP: *Send your direct mail message in a Western Union telegram. It is rare to get a telegram; therefore, it will get the interest of the recipient.*

Creating Direct Mail Pieces

Direct mail programs are like cars, clothes, or food. Not everyone will like or respond to the same thing. You need to know your target market and what type of direct mail pieces will catch their attention. If your target market is made up of physicians, your approach will be totally different from the one you would use if your target market were made up of mechanics. General aspects to consider are education and economic level, location in relation to your retail business, regional or local attitudes toward your industry, and the desire and needs your product or service would fulfill.

Take an objective look at the direct mail pieces you receive every day. What motivates you to open some and not others? Why do you throw some direct mail in the trash without even opening it? In creating a successful direct mail program, knowing what doesn't appeal to a consumer is as important as knowing what does.

Your Options

Direct mail can and does take many forms. From postcards, to letters, to full-size posters, direct mail can take on any form appropriate for your budget and message. A study done by Chilton Research Service shows us the following trends:

Type of Direct Mail	Open Rate	Reading Rate
Postcard	N/A	76.1%
Letter size	45.2%	74.3%
Over letter size	44.4%	71.8%
Newspaper/magazine	33.8%	70.5%
Flyer	N/A	67.6%
Catalog	N/A	67.1%

Companies that specialize in using direct mail to market a product or service frequently use more than one type of mailer. Consequently, the above figures total more than 100 percent and show what types of direct mail are used the most and which type of mailer gets the highest percentage of readers' attention. Postcards get read the most because the message is right there in plain sight. They're short, so they don't take a long time to read. And usually, the message is simple to understand.

These are some of the forms of direct mail available to you. Statistics also show that consumers are more likely to read direct mail from a company they recognize than from one they do not. This is one reason sequential mailings are preferred by companies that make direct mail a high-priority marketing technique, because when you send out direct mail to someone several times, the person will eventually come to recognize your company as familiar.

> **HOT TIP**: *You can send your direct mail message in a bottle. Call 1 (815) 877-4069 to order message bottles.*

Postcards

Postcards are best suited for giving consumers a simple message. If you're having a sale related to an upcoming holiday, use postcards. Picture postcards frequently produce the best response for discounts and coupons, too. For example, you could send a picture postcard of Las Vegas with the message, "You Don't Have to Go to Vegas to Win Big. You have already won a 25 percent discount on your next purchase at A Gift Exchange." Or you could send a picture postcard of Italy with the slogan "You Don't Have to Go to Italy for Great Italian Food. Bring this card in to A Little Bit of Italy restaurant and get a 25 percent discount and homemade Italian food."

I worked with one grocery store that bought a list of driver's licenses from the department of transportation. The store sent out birthday cards each month that said simply "Happy Birthday. We would like to help you celebrate your birthday by giving you a free birthday cake with a $50 grocery purchase. Please bring in this card to get your free cake." The store got a monthly average response rate of 37 percent.

Direct Mail

The Envelope

If your direct mail program uses a letter format, the envelope is the first component of your direct mail package the consumer sees and evaluates. It is often at this point that the decision is made to open and read it or throw it away. The envelope may seem to be only a means of getting the information inside to the consumer, but it is more than that: It is the outer covering of your message, and it can make your direct mail campaign more effective or it can be a detriment.

Some possibilities for the envelope that you should consider are:

- Addressing the envelope by hand.

- Putting your return address on the envelope without the name of your business.

- Using humorous stickers to decorate the envelope and make it fun and inviting.

- Hand-writing a personal note on the envelope—for example, "John, I know you'll want to take a look at this."

- Addressing the envelope using a person's name. Avoid the use of Occupant or Resident.

- For business-to-business direct mail, addressing the envelope with the owner's name and the name of the business. Avoid addressing the envelope to Manager or Owner.

- For typed addresses, printing them directly on the envelope. Avoid the use of labels.

> **HOT TIP** *Personalize your envelopes—never address them to "Occupant" or "Resident."*

The envelope or mailing package should be memorable and stand out from the normal stack of direct mail. Often, when selling to executives of large corporations, you may have difficulty getting past the secretary. Send the CEO a package that is unlikely to be opened by anyone else. Send a gift basket in a large box and then in a few days call the executive back. I guarantee the executive will know who you are after receiving a nice gift.

Another way to make your direct mail package stand out is by sending it in a long tube, the type normally used to mail posters. You may get a lot of mail every day, but how many gift boxes or tubes do you receive? If you use an approach like this, your message and offer will stand out. Granted, if you are sending out a thousand pieces of direct mail, these alternatives may not be cost-effective, but if the profit per offer is high, this could be an alternative that you should test on your target market with a few preselected people.

HOT TIP *You can use direct mail envelopes that look like express mail envelopes. This will convey a sense of urgency to the consumer. Golden State Envelopes offers these envelopes. It can be reached at 1 (818) 865-7940.*

The Letter

In my more than twenty years of experience in using direct mail programs, I have used various letters and techniques and I have always found a short letter to be more effective. (I am calling this material the letter, but in different situations it could take any of a number of forms.) This is the main component of your direct mail package, what we might call the heart of your message. It is the portion of your direct mail package that will:

1. Introduce your business to the consumer.
2. Deliver the product or service information.
3. List the features, advantages, and benefits of your product or service.
4. Detail any special discounts or promotions available to the consumer.
5. Explain what action the consumer must take to get the incentive.

It is important to create the letter in a way that is consistent with your target market. Once you have the consumer's attention and he or she has opened the envelope, the letter must spark customers' curiosity or intrigue them with a dynamite offer. One of the worst things you can do at this point is have a boring message. Your letter should be short and to the point.

The Four Motivators That Guarantee Success in Direct Mail

Some business owners spend a great deal of money on postage and supplies to send out direct mail but do not spend any time or effort designing the direct mail piece. There are four techniques that can make any direct mail program successful. If you fail to use any of these techniques, your direct mail will not be as successful as it could be. The four motivators are:

1. Fear
2. Guilt
3. Greed
4. Exclusivity

You do not need to use all four of these techniques in your direct mail piece, but you must use at least one if you want to produce results.

Fear is a great motivator. If your letter touches on a person's fear, it will move the person to act. Everyone is afraid of something. Fear of crime, fear of being different, fear of loss—these are just a few examples of fears that can be used in creating direct mail pieces.

An insurance agency might start out a direct mail letter, "If the survival of your family is important to you,..." A security company might start out its letter with "Anytown has the third highest crime rate per capita in the nation." By starting out the letter this way, you are grabbing people emotionally by immediately pushing their fear button. Fear is the number one motivator. If it is at all possible to include this technique in your direct mail piece, be sure to do it. Every direct mail piece can touch upon a person's fear of loss if you simply end the letter with something like "Don't miss out on our special. Respond now!"

Guilt is the second technique that is easy to incorporate into your direct mail piece. For example, suppose I were to say, "It really hurts me to lose a customer, especially one I value as much as you." You wouldn't want me to be hurt, would you?

Greed reaches people in their pocketbook. This is the reason why so many businesses have perpetual sales. For example, the line "This extra-special discount is only for a few select individuals" lets you know that you are getting in on something that will save you money, and who doesn't want to save money?

Exclusivity should be a part of every direct mail piece. Everyone wants to feel special, part of a select group, specifically chosen to receive your offer. To use exclusivity in your direct mail campaign, you should address the envelope and letter personally to the recipient. If you send a letter to Occupant and then say that the person was specially selected, it isn't believable.

It is easy to use exclusivity in a direct mail piece. For example, a car dealer might have a direct mail piece that says, "Quite frankly, a Lamborghini sports car isn't for everyone," or a restaurant might say, "You have been selected to receive a free dinner with the purchase of another dinner."

If you use one or more of these four motivators in your direct mail piece, your draw rate will go up. Beginning the letter with the right focus will help to keep it out of the trash can.

Most potential customers will read only the first three or four lines and the postscript. If you can hold their interest this far, they will then look for the price or a way to contact you. In my experience, many direct mail letters contain too much information. There is such a thing as information overload. If consumers are given too much information, they tend to feel overwhelmed and will react by simply throwing the direct mail piece away. Consumers are busy, but they will read your message if it doesn't take up too much time or mental energy. Do not be fooled into thinking more is better. In this case, a short letter is more effective than a long one.

HOT TIP

People buy with their emotions, so design your direct mail piece to touch people emotionally. It should touch the recipient's heart, soul, and senses.

Direct Mail

> **COOL RESOURCE:** *To expose your product to the catalog industry, send a news release and product sample to* **Direct Marketing Magazine, 24 Seventh Street, Garden City, NY 11535.**

We learned earlier in this chapter that a consumer's response when receiving direct mail falls into four stages:

- Read the direct mail piece, then evolve and recognize a need.
- Research the company and any competitors.
- Purchase.
- Post-purchase.

Be Irresistible

The average consumer has a very short attention span when it comes to direct mail. The main component of your direct mail package must pique the consumer's interest. In order to accomplish this, you can use certain proven hot words in your main message. Statistics show that some words will grab a person's attention while other words don't. In order to be a successful direct mailer, you must tap into a consumer's emotions in as few words as possible. In order to increase the response rate of your direct mail program, the main component should include the following words or combinations of words:

Free	Hot	Only you	Secret
Bonus	Save	There's more	Never before
Sweepstakes	New	Stop	Act now
Unique	Revolutionary	Naked	Giveaway
Special	Wanted	Better than	Bonus
How to	Preapproved	Rich	Don't hesitate
Limited time offer	Guaranteed	Giant	Don't lose out

There are three words that, when used together, carry a magic all their own: credit cards accepted.

> **HOT TIP:** *Send out a direct mail piece that gets the recipient involved and asks him or her to do something that requires action.*

When designing the main component of your direct mail package, keep in mind that you need to motivate the consumer to take action. You must touch him or her emotionally. As we said earlier, one of the greatest sales tools is the fear of loss. Give the consumer a deadline for responding to your direct mail offer. It should be within a week of receiving the offer. If a response deadline is any longer than this, the consumer will set the offer aside and forget to follow up.

Information in direct mail is a sales tool. Treat it as such by double-checking that the basic information about your business is on the main components of your direct mail package. You would be surprised how many pieces of direct mail I've received that contained no contact information whatsoever. Nothing is more discouraging to a consumer than to get a direct mail offer, want the product, and not be able to contact the company.

When you are writing the direct mail letter, read it over many times to check for typographical or grammatical errors. This type of simple mistake could cost you thousands of dollars in prospective sales. Also watch the transitions from one paragraph to the next—each paragraph should end in a way that intrigues the reader enough to continue.

> **HOT TIP:** *When you send out monthly statements to your customers, always include a flyer with a special offer for them to make a purchase.*

Involvement Devices

An involvement device is a component of your direct mail package that asks the consumer to do something. Some examples of involvement devices are scratch-off cards, peel-and-stick labels, preaddressed response cards or envelopes, and surveys.

Involvement devices are used specifically to engage consumers in an activity that empowers them. Choice and action are highly effective consumer empowerment tools. If you have any doubt that consumers are begging to feel empowered, ask a random group of people which they prefer, a direct mail letter with a sales message or a direct mail letter with a scratch-off circle that will reveal the percentage discount they will receive. Hands down, consumers prefer the empowering feeling of action to the passivity required by only reading.

Once you've decided on a direct mail incentive, incorporate it into the involvement device. Give your customers a chance to act, an opportunity to make a choice, and you will reap large rewards from your direct mail program.

> *The best way to have an idea*
> *is to have lots of ideas.*
> *—Linus Pauling*

Increase Your Draw Rate with Personal Packages

The advantages of using a package form of direct mail are obvious. Who doesn't like to get a package? Packages speak of gifts and fun; they say the recipient is special. If you can justify the expense with a high cost-to-sale amount, packages are an excellent medium to introduce a new product or send a sample.

As an example, if you are a consultant or a wholesaler, you might send a small piggybank with your brochure stuffed inside and include a hammer with a note that says, "Inside is the secret to making more money in the new year."

Direct Mail Opportunities

There are many opportunities sending direct mail. You can include a flyer or promotional brochure with your customer's monthly statement. If a customer requests information on one product, send information on all related products or services. You never know where your next customer will hear about your product or service, so make it a habit to include information with all mail that leaves your office.

Retail businesses can generate store traffic by including coupons and promotional flyers in their direct mail programs. As an example, you might want to have a senior citizens' day and send out direct mail offering a discount to senior citizens. You might want to have a businessperson's lunch special and send out direct mail to attorneys, accountants, and business owners.

If your business markets to businesses, use the approach and follow the techniques outlined in this chapter, but substitute businesses for consumers.

Presorted Standard Mail (a.k.a. Bulk Mail)

The term *bulk mail* has grown old. Even the post office doesn't use it anymore. The current term is *presorted standard mail*, or *PSM, (A)*. This postal designation means any mailing of at least 200 addressed pieces (or 50 pounds) of mail sorted and prepared according to postal standards.

Presorted standard mail (A) is a work-sharing program. By this I mean that you and the Postal Service share the work of processing the mail. When you do some of the preparation and sorting, it saves the Postal Service time and money. The savings are passed on to you in the form of postage discounts.

> **COOL RESOURCE:** *There are several ways to contact the U.S. Postal Service. There is the Rapid Information Bulletin Board System (RIBBS), located at www.usps.com. You can also contact the National Customer Support Center at 1 (800) 238-3150 for postal products and services. Another way to get help and advice for your direct mail program from a local source is to contact the Postal Business Center in your area. Look for contact information in the government section of your telephone directory.*

Presorted standard mail (A) usually consists of sales flyers, form letters, or other printed pieces that are generally identical in content. Each piece must weigh less than a pound.

Direct Mail

Because PSM (A) is geared toward business promotional mail, these rates do not apply to correspondence such as personal letters and these other types of mail:

- Bills or invoices
- Statements of account
- Contracts
- Handwritten or typewritten matter
- Valuables
- Currency

PSM (A) can be forwarded to customers who move. You can also choose to have address corrections sent to you so that you can stay in touch with your customers.

PSM (A) is also a cost-efficient way to communicate with customers particularly suited for direct mail programs. The mailing options for PSM (A) are pre-canceled stamps or a permit imprint.

You will need computer software that is compatible with your direct mail program. Avery has a software program that will automatically put the bar code on your envelopes.

Using Presorted Standard Mail (A) can save your company money. Specific and detailed instructions about the requirements and restrictions for this program are available in U.S. Postal Service publication 49, *Preparing Standard Mail (A)*. When obtaining this publication, be sure to get the most current version.

An alternative to doing all the presorting yourself is to use a presort service bureau. Look in your local telephone directory under Mailing Service for these companies. Depending on the volume and cost of your direct mail program, a presort service bureau (mailing service) can save you time and money by doing the presorting and required verifications for you.

Direct Mail Trade Associations

Alliance of Independent Store Owners and Professionals
3725 Multifoods Tower
Minneapolis, MN 55402-3719
1 (612) 340-9350

National Mail Order Association
2807 Polk Street NE
Minneapolis, MN 55418-2954
1 (612) 788-1673

Advertising Mail Marketing Association
133 F Street NW, Suite 710
Washington, DC 20004-1146
1 (202) 347-0055

Direct Marketing Association
1120 Avenue of the Americas
New York, NY 10036-6700
1 (212) 768-7277

Mail Advertising Service Association International
1421 Prince Street, Suite 100
Alexandria, VA 22314-2806
1 (703) 836-9200

Authorized Lessors

Ascom Hasler Mailing Systems Inc.
19 Forest Parkway
Shelton, CT 06484-0903

Francotyp-Postalia, Inc.
1980 University Lane
Lisle, IL 60532-2152

Neopost
30955 Huntwood Avenue
Hayward, CA 94544-7005

Pitney Bowes, Inc.
1 Elmcroft Road
Stamford, CT 06926-0700

Testing Your Direct Mail Program

You have compiled a mailing list, created an incentive, and designed your direct mail package. Now it's time for action. But don't jump too fast. It is vital that you test your direct mail program prior to a full-fledged mailing. The ideal situation is to develop three or four envelopes and direct mail pieces and send each one to 200 to 1000 names from your mailing list, depending on your budget. In order to track the results, place a simple code on the part of the direct mail package that will be returned to you. If the letter asks the consumer to call, then assign to each letter a different name for the consumer to ask for when calling back. If the letter asks them to respond by mail, use a numerical code on it that will tell you which offer has brought a response.

Also keep track of any mail that is returned and remove these names from your list. This will save you money on the second or third mailing from this list. There are two types of tests that you must do before you put your direct mail program into full swing, list testing and offer testing.

List Testing

While most list brokers will go out of their way to supply you with a profitable list, since this is how they ensure that you will become a regular customer, there are times when a certain list may not pull an acceptable draw rate. In order to determine what is acceptable, consider the following possibilities:

- The cost per direct mail piece, including postage, materials, printing, and design

- The amount of markup for your product

- The minimum required draw rate for profit

Offer Testing

Testing the incentive offer and the product price is vital to making the highest profit from your direct mail campaign. There is what is known as a price breaking point for every product or service. A price breaking point is the highest dollar amount that a consumer commonly considers reasonable to pay for your product or service.

For example, in the publishing industry, $20 is a common price breaking point for a book. Consumers look at a book that is under $20 differently from the way they look at a book that is over $20. The publishers of most fiction books will price their product under $20, whereas the publishers of books on alternative medicine will usually price the product over $20. A consumer anticipates paying more for a book that gives medical advice than for a fiction book. In the same way, if the book on alternative medicine were priced under $20, sales in most cases would probably be less than if it were priced over $20. This is due completely to consumer expectation and the commonly recognized price breaking point for this product.

Your product has a price breaking point as well. One way to gauge this breaking point is to send out at least three different direct mail letters with three different prices. By tracking the results of the testing, you will be able to find the price breaking point of your product or service.

HOT TIP: *The direct mail piece should sell a solution to a problem, not a product or service.*

Direct mail can be successful in generating profit and bringing in new customers. Let me tell you a story to illustrate this point. Roger DeValle ran a small mortgage brokerage in Dallas, Texas. His business was profitable, but the profits had leveled off and the number of new clients seemed to decrease more each quarter. He was looking for a way to increase his business and make potential clients aware of his services. Most of his marketing consisted of advertisements in the local newspaper under the financial services category.

When I began working with Roger, he was closing about four or five loans per month. He handled both new purchases and refinancing of existing mortgages. He worked with customers with bad credit and good credit. He really enjoyed doing refinancing the most because he could consolidate a customer's bills, lower the interest rate, and lower the customer's payments considerably.

Our first step was to decide on a good mailing list source. We decided we needed a list of people who had taken out mortgages at least three years previously. Next, we went to the county clerk's office to get a list of consumers who had done so.

> *The best time to plant a tree was twenty years ago. The second best time is today.*
> *—Chinese Proverb*

Roger and I picked an incentive that would interest a wide range of potential customers—a $50 gift certificate to Top of the Tower Restaurant, one of the most upscale establishments in the city. This incentive may sound expensive, but it wasn't. We contacted the restaurant owner and arranged to buy each $50 gift certificate for only $25. The restaurant owner agreed to this price because we brought in volume—40 gift certificates for $1000—and paid up front. The cost of the direct mail campaign and the cost of the incentives were worthwhile to Roger because he would net at least $2000 on each customer. Your circumstances and business may be different, and using a $50 gift certificate as an incentive may not be realistic for you. However, you can still come up with an incentive that will work and entice customers into your business.

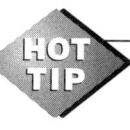

HOT TIP *One of the best places to get a mailing list is the county courthouse. You can get lists of people getting married, getting divorced, buying a house, having a baby, starting a business, and more.*

Sequential and Nonsequential Mailings

The next decision to make is whether to use a sequential or a nonsequential direct mail program. With a nonsequential program, you will send out a direct mail piece to people on your mailing list only once. With a sequential program, you will send direct mail to people on your mailing list more than once. A sequential program can have two, three, or even as many as ten steps.

Nonsequential Direct Mail Programs

This type of program involves only one step and is the simplest form of direct mail. The majority of businesses, including most of your competitors, use this program because it is the easiest to implement and the least expensive. The downside is that this type of program also yields the lowest draw rate.

Basically, with a nonsequential program, you send the direct mail pieces to potential customers on your mailing list and then wait for them to respond. For some businesses, this program has many drawbacks: Consumers may not be familiar with the company and so may not open the direct mail piece or may open it and then forget to respond. Often it takes more than one exposure to get a response. Consequently, if a nonsequential program is used, the business loses potential customers and therefore profits.

If you use a nonsequential program, it is imperative that you add the element of urgency to your incentive offer. Placing an expiration date on the offer can motivate consumers to act quickly. You can also use a consumer survey as one form of nonsequential direct mail.

Sequential Direct Mail Programs

Two-Step Program. A sequential direct mail program will increase your draw rate over what you will experience with the one-step program. The key to a sequential program is sending another direct mail piece to the same mailing list about thirty days later. As incredible as it may sound, you will get the same or a higher draw rate from the second mailing. It is imperative that you send out a different flyer, letter, or brochure with a slightly different offer for each mailing.

For example, suppose your business offers a mail-order real estate course for $195. The first direct mail letter would have a price of $195. When you send out the second direct mail letter, give the consumer the option of making six monthly payments of $45, for a total of $270. With this second offer, your total profit will be higher. You won't get all the money up front, but people who are not familiar with your business will be more likely to trust you with $45 initially than with $195. Furthermore, having monthly payments can help your cash flow. I owned a business for several years where I received monthly payments, and knowing that I would get payments of more than $2000 in the mail every day gave me some security.

> **HOT TIP:** *Send your direct mail package to the same mailing list several times, but vary the letter and offer with each sequential contact.*

If yours is a home-based business that sells merchandise from a catalog, ask for a down payment that is large enough to cover your cost and shipping, plus 10 percent. Suppose your product retails for $35, with a wholesale price of $12. You could offer the product for a down payment of $16 and finance the balance with monthly payments. A certain percentage of your customers won't pay what they owe, but this percentage will be smaller than you think, and the customers who do pay will offset your losses from the ones who don't pay. With this formula, you won't lose any money even if customers don't pay.

An alternative way of doing a sequential mailing is to approach potential customers from your mailing list by telephone to briefly explain your offer and ask their permission to send out more information, or to run an ad asking potential customers to call you for more information. This approach may take extra time and effort, but the compensation is that now you are sending direct mail to customers who are potentially interested in your product. The potential customer is anticipating the offer, so your direct mail package isn't considered unwanted junk mail.

Three-Step Program. Although the three-step program takes the most time and effort, it also yields the highest draw rate. This program is similar to the two-step program, but as the name implies, you take it one step further. With this program, you send out direct mail to the names on your mailing list every three or four weeks. Vary the offer and the price of your product or service with each mailing. Repetition is the name of the game with direct mail. Potential customers who don't respond to your first or second mailing may respond to your third or fourth. In fact, I have seen some businesses do repetitive mailings to the same mailing list eight or nine times. These business owners received the same draw rate on the ninth mailing as they did on the first.

Consider this: If you get a 3 percent draw rate on each mailing, and you send out varied offers nine times, you're actually getting a 27 percent draw rate from the original list.

The most important aspect of this program is using the telephone. It's common for business owners to feel uneasy about using the telephone to initiate contact with potential customers. I always tell them that just as with learning anything else, it takes practice to get good and to feel comfortable. Every business owner would love to send out direct mail and wait for the business to come rolling in. When you're self-employed, however, real success comes from interacting with your potential customers.

In the three-step program, after you send out the direct mail piece, you call the people on your list and personally invite them to do business with you. To illustrate how the three-step program works, I'll again use Roger DeValle's mortgage brokerage business as an example.

After compiling his mailing list and buying the restaurant gift certificates, Roger and I decided to give a twist to the program that would add fun and excitement for his potential customers. Roger bought a treasure chest and a lock and several extra keys. Now he was ready to put his plan into action.

The plan was to offer potential customers the opportunity to win $1000. He began by calling people on his mailing list to introduce his company and ask their permission to send out a key that could win them $1000 if it unlocked the treasure chest. The script in Sample 3.3 illustrates how this is done.

Sample 3.3 Script for Three-Step Incentive.

> Is Dave in? Hello, Dave, this is Roger with DeValle Mortgage Brokerage. The reason I'm calling is to tell you a little about my company and notify you of a promotion you've been chosen to participate in that could put $1000 in your hands.
>
> With interest rates currently at or near an all-time low, we can save you thousands of dollars on your current mortgage and even provide you with extra cash for home improvements or money to consolidate your bills into one payment.
>
> You have also been selected to receive a $50 gift certificate to the Top of the Tower Restaurant, and you have the possibility of winning $1000.

Direct Mail

> *This is for giving us the opportunity to show you how much money we can help you save. We want to send you a key and then you can bring it in to see if it's the lucky key. Is your address still 123 Main Street? Great. I'll send the key out to you today.*

When you use this approach, you will not get many objections because you are not pressuring the person into buying something. You are asking for permission to send something of value, something the person may want or need.

If, however, you get an objection from a potential customer when using this technique or any other technique in this book, it is very easy to handle and overcome it.

When you are trying to make a sale to a potential customer, keep in mind that as you are trying to close the sale, set up an appointment, or get permission to send something, it is similar to a boxing match. The prospect puts her defenses up as protection against everything you are throwing at her. The objective is to get the person to drop the defensiveness. For example, the main objection you will hear in sales is, "I want to think about it." This is not really an objection, but a defensive mask your customer is putting on. You respond by asking questions to find out what the real objection is.

Using this objection as our example, the quickest way to get the person to drop his or her defenses is to ask, "Is thirty days long enough to think about it?" Right away, the prospect will cease being so defensive. He will feel safer because he thinks you're going to call back in thirty days. Once the defenses are down, you close the sale or make the appointment. Perhaps you tell the person she can postdate the check for thirty days or get a thirty-day guarantee, or as in the case of our phone script, you can tell the person you'll send the item in thirty days. This technique will help you handle almost any objection.

It helps to empathize with your customers. A great technique in handling any objection with empathy is the 3F technique: Feel, Felt, and Found. Let's say a potential customer gives you the objection: "I can't afford it." You respond, "Well, Mr. Jones, I understand how you feel. I once felt the same way, but you know what I found? I found that in the long run, this product will actually save you money. Let me show you how." In this way, you are demonstrating empathy and getting rid of the objection at the same time.

Sample 3.4

Here Is Your Key to $1000

You have already won a $50 gift certificate to Top of the Tower Restaurant.

Call Roger at 555-9087 to claim the gift certificate and see if you have the lucky key that opens the treasure chest containing $1000.

We would also like to take about 15 minutes to show you how we can probably give you a lower interest rate and save you thousands of dollars on your mortgage.

> **COOL RESOURCE:** To find a catalog to promote your product, order **The National Directory of Catalogs** from Oxbridge Communications, 150 Fifth Ave., New York, NY 10011, 1(800) 955-0231; or **Catalogs Worldwide** from Interstate Publications, P.O. Drawer 19689, Houston, TX 77224; or Klein Publications, P.O. Box 6578, Del Ray Beach, FL 33482, 1 (407) 496-3316.

Now the potential customer expects your direct mail package, and what you are sending is no longer considered junk mail. The letter Roger sent out looked like the one in Sample 3.4.

With this basic letter, Roger received quite a few calls. If the people didn't call Roger, he called them. The three-step program worked so well for Roger that people literally waited in line to talk to him. He used the script in Sample 3.5 for calling people from his list.

Sample 3.5 Three-Step Telephone Script—Callbacks.

> " Is Dave in? Hello, Dave, this is Roger with Devalle Mortgage Brokerage. I talked to you a few days ago about our promotion. At the time, you requested a key that could open the treasure chest to win $1000. Did you receive your key? Great!
>
> I would like to set up a time that is convenient for you to stop in and pick up your free $50 gift certificate to Top of the Tower Restaurant and to take a shot at that $1000. Is tomorrow at 10:00 A.M. okay, or would Wednesday at 7:00 P.M. be better? "

If the person says that he or she is not interested, do not take it personally; simply go to the next person.

You can adapt the three-step program to nearly any type of business. For example, if you own a retail store, you could send out a key with a letter that says, "This is the key to your savings." Then have three treasure chests, one for a 10 percent discount, one for a 25 percent discount, and one for a 40 percent discount. The customer receives the discount on the purchase that corresponds to the treasure chest his or her key opens.

There are as many variations to your direct mail letter and your offer as there are businesses. This is the time to be creative and think about what your customers would find fun and intriguing.

How to Measure Success

Most direct mail experts say that if your direct mail program gets a 1 to 2 percent draw rate, it is successful. While I do not dispute that a program pulling 1 to 2 percent can be profitable, I disagree with the idea that such a rate is normal or successful. Depending on your experience with using a direct mail campaign, I would anticipate a much larger draw rate. I know from experience that a moderately successful direct mail program can pull a 10 to 25 percent draw rate. You can achieve this draw rate for your business if you follow the steps outlined in this chapter.

Although initiating a direct mail campaign involves more than printing your message, stuffing envelopes, and licking stamps, the rewards in revenue and new customers are well worth the effort. If your current direct mail program pulls a 1 to 2 percent draw rate, consider the increase in revenue if you raised it to 7 or 8 percent. This type of increase is within your reach. In fact, this section will show you how you can raise your draw rate to 100 percent, send out direct mail for free, or even get paid by other companies to do it.

Send Out 10,000 or More Direct Mail Pieces for Free

Roger was successful with this direct mail program, but he decided he wanted to blanket the area with 10,000 mailers without spending the $4000 it would take for the printing and postage to do a campaign of that size.

Using the financial services section of the weekly newspapers in his area and a coupon mailer he received, Roger identified 10 companies and approached them about participating in cooperative advertising. They each paid him $400 for a total of $4000. He didn't pay anything to send out direct mail pieces to 10,000 people on his mailing list.

This was a win-win situation for all the businesses involved. They paid only four cents for each mailer, and it was sent to their target market—people who were looking for various financial services. Roger won because even though he had to put everything together, he was able to send out direct mail to 10,000 people at no cost to his mortgage company.

This approach may not be appropriate for your business, but there are a lot of creative ways for sending out a direct mail program at little or no cost.

You Can Get a Response Rate of More Than 100 Percent

Is it possible to get a draw rate of 100 percent or higher on your direct mail campaign? Yes. It may not seem possible at first, but let me tell you how it's done.

I consulted for Big Bend General Store in Fort Worth, which achieved a 125 percent draw rate. This technique is not easy, and it is unlikely that you will achieve the same results, but even if you get a 25 percent draw rate, you have a successful program.

Big Bend's target market was 1000 businesses within two miles of the store. We sent ten coupons good for a 25 percent discount to each business. We printed the name of each business on the coupons and sent a letter asking the business owners to disperse the coupons to their employees. Most of the businesses obliged and were happy to do so, because it gave them a chance to pass on an unexpected (and free) perk to their employees.

In this case, we sent out 1000 pieces of direct mail, but in actuality we sent out 10,000 coupons. If only one employee out of ten from each business used the coupon, this would represent a 100 percent draw rate and 1000 new customers. Think about how you could increase your customer flow if you used this technique and two or three people from each business used a coupon. This would produce a 200 or 300 percent draw rate.

For this or any other direct mail campaign to be effective, you must create an offer that grabs the potential customer's attention.

Provide space on the back of the coupon for customers to fill in their name, address, and telephone number. This will help you build your own mailing list. After you have a mailing list, you can send each of your customers five to ten coupons to give to friends and relatives.

As you can see from the letter in Sample 3.6, we also enticed customers to visit the general store with a drawing for a free item. Doing this encourages prospects to put their contact information on the back of the coupon.

HOT TIP

The best source of businesses to contact to advertise in your direct mailer is businesses that advertise in other direct mailer packages, such as Valpak and the yellow pages coupon mailers.

Getting Paid from Your Direct Mail

When Terry attended the monthly tenants' meeting of the shopping center association of which he was a member, he had only one direct mail program running. Other business owners who had space in the shopping center tried to get Terry to divulge the secrets of his increased business. He asked me for the best way to politely tell them this was confidential information.

I explained to Terry that he didn't need to keep his direct mail program a guarded secret. In fact, he could take advantage of the other owners' enthusiasm and at the same time make even more money for his business.

At the next meeting of the business owners, Terry proposed that other businesses could participate in his marketing plan for $400 for each direct mail campaign. Business owners had to create an enticing offer and have their own coupons printed. Twelve business owners participated in the plan with Terry. Because the business owners saw how Terry's business had increased, they knew his program worked, and they felt that the $400 was a good investment. Terry received $4800 from the business owners to participate in his marketing plan. He collected over $2000 of net revenues after expenses for each direct mail campaign.

There are companies that will pay you to include inserts from other companies in your correspondence with your customers, such as your monthly invoices, statements, and direct mail. You can also make a straight swap and have your inserts included in the other company's direct mail for free if you include that company's inserts in your direct mail. Two companies that offer this are:

Leon Henry, Inc.
455 Central Avenue
Scarsdale, NY 10583
1 (914) 723-3176

Monrynski & Associates
401 Hackensack Avenue
Hackensack, NJ 07601
1 (201) 488-5656

Sample 3.6 Direct Mail Business-to-Business Introductory Letter.

I would like to introduce you and your employees to Big Bend General Store.

I have enclosed ten coupons good for a 25 percent discount on your next purchase. We've taken the extra time to imprint these coupons with the name of your business, so feel free to tell your employees that this is a special benefit you have arranged for them.

The Big Bend General Store prides itself on having the largest selection of merchandise made in the state of Texas, and we always donate 2 percent of all net revenues to the Children's Hospital in Fort Worth.

We understand our customers' time is valuable, and we pledge quick checkout and friendly clerks to assist you with any needs, from a two-penny nail to nail polish remover.

When you and your employees use these coupons, you will be entered in a drawing to receive a Caribbean cruise. Don't hesitate! Stop in now so you'll be entered in our next drawing.

P.S. If you need more coupons, please contact me and I'll bring more to you.

Terry McNeil,
Owner, Big Bend General Store

While direct mail marketing takes planning and organization, it has proved to be one of the most effective ways businesses have to reach potential customers. Whether you send out postcards or letters or organize a local coupon mailing with other merchants, direct mail is one way to easily communicate with your customers.

CHAPTER 4

Telemarketing
The Personal Connection That Pays Big Profits

Several years ago, a friend of mine, Randy, bought a house in Oklahoma City. He had always dreamed of owning a house with an in-ground pool, but the house that he fell in love with did not have a pool. One day, as a surprise, his wife had a sales rep from a local pool company come out. The sales rep gave Randy a price on an in-ground, vinyl-liner, sand-bottom pool. Randy didn't really want a vinyl-liner pool; he wanted one of those gunnite pools. He called another company in Tulsa, Paradise Pools, and the company sent him a catalog. He opened the catalog and found exactly the model he had imagined. Paradise Pools didn't sell swimming pools; it sold swimming environments. The catalog showed boulders and ponds and waterfalls that were absolutely magnificent.

Randy decided that he wanted the model called Neptune. He called Paradise Pools and told the salesperson, "I got your catalog, I'm interested in a pool, so come on out." The salesperson replied, "Well, you know our pools

BUSINESS MYTH:	MONEY TREE REALITY:
A small business does not have the time to do telemarketing itself or the money to hire telemarketers. Potential customers do not like to be bothered by telemarketers.	Telemarketing is one of the most cost-effective and time-saving tools that a business has. It does not have to cost a small business anything. If telemarketing is done properly, potential customers will welcome your call.

are very expensive. We only put them into the finest homes. You live 90 minutes away, and I don't want to drive out there and waste my time unless I know you can afford it." Then he gave Randy a figure for what the pool would cost. That figure was $10,000 higher than the price quoted by the sales rep who had already been there. So what do you think Randy said to the salesperson on the phone? "Have a nice day. No, thank you. Good-bye." Then he hung up.

A week later, Randy saw an advertisement for gunnite pools by a company by the name of Blue Dolphin Pools. Randy called Blue Dolphin and said, "I'm interested in a gunnite pool. I spoke to a guy with a company in Tulsa and he gave me a figure that was ridiculous." The man with Dolphin Pools said, "Yeah, his numbers are crazy. But believe me, I can show you that a gunnite pool, based upon the fact that we guarantee our pools for a lifetime, and based upon the fact that it will never leak, and based upon the fact that this pool is going to last as long as you and that house last, is actually an investment. True, it might cost a few dollars more than a regular in-ground, vinyl-liner pool. But over the lifetime of the pool, it may actually cost you less, since you'll never have to replace the expensive vinyl liner. I'll be more than happy to come out and show you the options. We can custom design that pool, make it do whatever you want, and you'll be pleasantly surprised when you see how little the actual expense is for the investment."

Randy said, "Come on out." The guy came out and helped Randy visualize what life would be like for the family with the new pool. When the sales rep gave Randy a price, he was truly shocked. It was $1500 more than the price given by the company in Tulsa! Did Randy buy the pool from Blue Dolphin? After negotiating for a small discount—8 percent—he did. The point of this story is simple: A majority of small business owners think that telemarketing is only outbound calling.

> **HOT TIP:** *One of the most important things you can do in telemarketing is get the name and address of every person who calls in. This will enable you to build a mailing list of potential customers.*

Telemarketing also encompasses inbound calling. That's when a potential customer calls in to your business, say, for information or to ask a question. In fact, this is what most telemarketing consists of.

The first pool company lost a big sale because it tried to prequalify Randy over the phone. The Blue Dolphin Pool sales rep, however, knew the real value of every customer's call and took advantage of the opportunity to set appointments with everyone who called. By following through with the opportunities and treating every person who called as a potential buyer, the company succeeded in closing more sales. In fact, two years later Paradise Pools, with its snooty attitude, went out of business.

An inbound call is very similar to an outbound call (when a representative from your company calls a potential customer). The biggest difference is that with an inbound call, most potential customers are already motivated to buy from you.

How many times have you called a business ready to make a purchase only to be treated like a second-class citizen? Many business owners mistakenly think that if a potential customer is calling, that person is certain to make a purchase, no matter how he or she is treated. This is an error in judgment, as is proven every day when dissatisfied customers take their business and their money elsewhere. When potential customers call you, treat them with respect. Give them the reasons why they should do business with you, and act as if you are happy to hear from them.

It has been my experience that business owners believe that telemarketing is only making phone calls to sell something to people. In my view, telemarketing includes both outbound and inbound calls and is not used strictly for the purpose of making a sale. Telemarketing can also include calls made to thank a customer for visiting your business. How many times have you visited a business and then one or two days later had a representative from that business call to thank you for shopping there? If you're like most consumers, you've probably never had this happen. How would it make you, as a consumer, feel if someone called and said, "Hey, we really appreciate your business. If there's anything else we can ever do for you, don't hesitate to call or stop by."

I have heard many business owners say that they are too busy to call customers back. My philosophy, and what I tell all business owners, is that if you don't make the time to treat your customers well, you will have a great deal of free time on your hands when you go out of business. I have also heard business owners say they can't afford to hire a person to make customer service calls. I tell them they can't afford not to hire someone. This is one of the best and least expensive marketing tools available to all businesses.

A few years ago, the Bonanza restaurant in Dover, Delaware, had the largest sales volume of any Bonanza restaurant in the country. Now keep in mind that the population of Dover is only 35,000. How did this restaurant rack up such high sales figures when other restaurants in the same chain, with the same menus, located in cities with hundreds of thousands or even millions of people had less volume? It's because this restaurant employed a full-time telemarketing person to call people who visited the restaurant and ask them how they enjoyed their meal. This type of customer appreciation leads to increased visits and great word-of-mouth advertising. It also enables the restaurant to find out if the customer was dissatisfied with any aspect of the visit. If so, the restaurant can deal with it before the customer spreads any negative publicity around. This form of telemarketing is almost the only marketing this particular Bonanza does. I would be willing to bet that it is still the largest-volume Bonanza restaurant in the country.

Telemarketing Can Make Your Business Successful from Your First Day of Operation

Jimmy Ross had worked in the restaurant business for more than twenty years. He had held every position from busboy to dishwasher, from cook to assistant manager—and even manager. Jimmy had always wanted to open his own restaurant, but he never felt that the time was right until the restaurant he was managing closed down.

Jimmy had saved up for the right time, and now that time had come. He spent three months making preparations. He found the perfect location, arranged for supplies and equipment, and hired and trained employees, including two telemarketers. The two telemarketers started working thirty days before the grand opening date. Jimmy was nervous about failing, and he wanted the restaurant to be full of hungry people on the day of his grand opening. He wanted to have so many customers that night that they would line up down the sidewalk. Isn't this every business owner's dream?

Telemarketing a Freebie

In order to make this happen, Jimmy had to contact potential customers weeks in advance. He felt that his best chance was to appeal to families, so he started a promotion that would entitle a child to receive a free meal with each paid adult meal. He printed up coupons and wrote a telephone script for the telemarketers. The script in Sample 4.1 can be adapted to fit almost any business.

> *By working faithfully
> eight hours a day you may
> eventually get to be a boss
> and work twelve hours a day.*
> *—Robert Frost*

Sample 4.1 Telemarketing Script to Invite a Potential Customer to Your Business.

> *Is John available? John, this is Amanda Lucas with Truffles Restaurant. The reason I'm calling is to personally invite you to our grand opening on June 1.*
>
> *As our guest, you will receive a free kid's meal with each paid adult meal. Our menu includes items such as steaks and seafood, salads and pasta, truffles and cheesecake. We guarantee that our service and food will be to your liking.*
>
> *May I send you a menu with the coupons? Is your address still 1245 Marydale Avenue? Great. I'll send that out, and I hope to see you June 1. Thank you for your time.*

This script is simple and straightforward. You don't need anything fancy or necessarily unique. After all, these days, common courtesy and simple sincerity can be quite refreshing. Here are a few telemarketing secrets you should know:

1. Never ask for the potential customer by his or her last name. For example, don't say, "May I speak with Mr. Kavanaugh." This is a sure sign to the person on the other end of the line that you are a telemarketer, a salesperson, or a bill collector. Instead, refer to the person by his or her first name.

2. If you sell to businesses and you do not know the name of the owner or contact person, simply ask the person who answers the phone, "Is the boss around?"

3. Tone is extremely important in telemarketing. Do your best to sound upbeat and cheerful when you make calls.

4. Never pause or hesitate in the middle of the script to ask, "How are you today?" This question will evoke an immediate response. Most people will put up their guard because they will know that you are calling to try to sell them something.

5. Present the potential customer with an offer that will make it worth the customer's time to listen to you and give you his or her business. Remember, free is one of the most excitement-generating words in the English language.

6. Make potential customers feel that they are part of a select group, that they are special.

7. If someone tells you she or he is not interested, ask if you can send some information in the mail. Most people will have no objection to receiving something in the mail. This will give you a reason to call back and ask if the person received the information and if there are any questions.

8. If the person you are calling is rude or negative, do not reciprocate. Be courteous, no matter how difficult it is. The best response to this type of behavior is to thank the person for his or her time, hang up, and move on to the next person.

9. Do not take any caller's rejection personally. This is probably one of the most important telemarketing rules. To be able to do this type of work, you need to have thick skin.

10. Smile, smile, smile. The person on the other end of the line will see it.

Telemarketing

Whether you as the business owner make calls or you hire someone to do it, make sure these rules are understood and followed.

In the case of businesses with direct sales, such as home improvement companies or insurance agencies, telemarketing is used to set up appointments. The script used is considerably different. Sample 4.2 gives an example.

Sample 4.2 Telephone Script for Sales-Oriented Businesses.

> Is John there? John, my name is Dave Matthews, and I am calling because you have been selected to be a show home for AAA Exteriors' revolutionary siding and windows. Being a show home means that we will install beautiful siding and windows in your home. We will give you some of the windows absolutely free and a substantial discount on the siding.
>
> All we ask in return is that you allow us to take before and after pictures of your home, let us put a sign in your yard for sixty days, and write a letter telling us your honest opinion of how the siding and windows have improved your home.
>
> You will also receive a gift certificate for a free dinner at either Pedro's Mexican Restaurant or Giovanni's Italian Restaurant, just for allowing one of our show home representatives explain the program to you.
>
> Would you prefer your free dinner at Pedro's or at Giovanni's? Great! I'll have our representative bring it out to you. Is tomorrow morning at 10:00 convenient, or is 6:00 tomorrow evening better?

This script works well. Even if you are not in the home improvement field, it will give you an idea of how to approach potential customers on the phone.

Telemarketing to Niche Groups

Jimmy Ross also identified specific groups of people and set aside a special day at the restaurant for each group. For example, he had a Senior Citizens' Day and a Government Employees' Day. He used niche marketing, which is covered in another context in Chapter 3, Direct Mail.

Both of Jimmy's telemarketing representatives went to the public library, found the city directories, and looked up the names, addresses, and phone numbers of members of select groups, such as senior citizens, government employees, state employees, doctors and nurses, teachers, and police officers. For detailed information on using the city directory as a resource, see

Chapters 3, Direct Mail, and 9, Third-Party Endorsements. The telemarketers used these lists to call and invite people to the restaurant for their special day during the grand opening week.

Jimmy offered each special group a 25 percent discount. This plan worked so well that he ended up setting aside a few days every week for specific groups. Obviously, other people could eat there on those days, but they did not receive the same special discounts. Overall, the telemarketing program helped Jimmy have a great grand opening and soon the parking lot was always full of cars. Everyone likes to eat at a good restaurant, and Jimmy's restaurant was obviously good. Sample 4.3 gives a script for niche groups.

Sample 4.3 Telemarketing Script for Niche Groups.

> *Is John in? John, this is Sara Barber with Truffles Restaurant. I'm calling because we are having a special celebration for all federal employees. Do you still work for the Postal Service? Great! As a federal employee you are entitled to receive a 25 percent discount off your family's meal each Tuesday evening at our restaurant. I would like to send you a personal invitation with a discount card. Do you still live at 4997 Fireside Drive? Great. I'll send it out to you today.*

Jimmy knew that having a successful business would take much more than motivating people to come in for a discounted or free dinner. He needed to make sure the customers' experience was enjoyable and invite them back again and again.

His main reason for hiring the telemarketers was to achieve this type of customer satisfaction and loyalty. By calling all the customers who came into his restaurant within two days to ask how the experience was and invite them back, Jimmy set himself apart from his competition.

In order to carry out this telemarketing program, the first step Jimmy took was to ask customers to fill out a customer survey card. In return, he offered them drinks free of charge. The survey card included questions about the customer, such as name, address, and phone number, and a rating of his or her satisfaction. The next step was to use the survey cards for calling the customers and inviting them to return to the restaurant for another special.

By having a telemarketing campaign based on customer satisfaction, Jimmy not only kept in constant contact with his customers and potential customers, he quickly gained a reputation in the community as a business owner who cared. Over time, Jimmy's restaurant earned such a good reputation that people from all over the state came in.

Easy as One, Two, Three

Tia Nicole owned a small retail store in Fort Worth, Texas, called Tia's. Her retail store offered a diverse range of products, from electronics, such as televisions and VCRs, to soft goods, such as dresses and jeans.

Her business had survived for five years but had never really thrived. For two consecutive years, Tia's profits decreased from the year before. Tia felt she needed to find a niche that her store would fill, something that would make it stand out and increase the flow of customers.

Over the last year or so, Tia had noticed that several companies in the area were offering to fix people's bad credit. This inspired her to put together a program to help people in the area reestablish good credit. The risk involved in such a program was high, so to protect her business from suffering large losses, she offered a store credit card that could be used at the store or to shop from her catalog. The customer was required to make a down payment up front with each purchase. The down payment percentage was between 15 and 35 percent, depending on the degree of bad credit.

In order to get word out about her program, Tia set up an inbound and outbound telemarketing department. She also decided to use a low-pressure three-step telemarketing approach. When people who had seen an advertisement called in, she would explain the basis of the program to them and offer to send out an application with more information. After a few days had passed, the telemarketer would call the potential customer back to see if he or she had received the application and information. The telemarketer would tell the potential customer about a special that week at the store if the application was returned that week.

With a three-step telemarketing program, you can increase the effectiveness of your marketing because you are not trying to sell anything on the first call. The objective on the first call is to inform the potential customer that you will be sending her or him something of benefit from your business.

The second step is to send the information to the potential customer. Finally, the third step is to make a follow-up call and invite the potential customer to do business with you. By the time you reach the final step, the potential customer is familiar with your company and is expecting your call.

The three-step telemarketing program is easy to implement and extremely effective. It can be used for nearly any type of business. Be creative and consider what you can offer that would motivate a potential customer to do business with you. The best part of the three-step program is that it is not based on selling as most people think of it. Instead, this program is based on offering. Do you see the difference? If someone calls to sell you something, it could be a turnoff, whereas if someone calls to offer you something, you feel special, grateful that the person thought of you. A lot of it is related to the telemarketer's frame of mind. If telemarketers think they are calling potential customers in order to sell something, they will have a lot of anxiety and will not do as well as if they are calling potential customers to offer something.

Dialing for Dollars—How to Make Telemarketing Pay through Reciprocal Marketing Programs

About a year after Tia started her telemarketing program, Ellen Kominsky, a friend of hers, decided to open a comedy club next door. She leased the space, furnished it, hired employees, and bought supplies. Like a lot of first-time entrepreneurs, she soon realized that she had enough money to pay the employees and other bills for the first month, but she did not have any extra money to pay for marketing. She was frantic when she called Tia to ask what she should do.

Tia wanted to help her out, but she did not want to help her out for free. She felt that Ellen needed to pay her own way. She offered to have her three telemarketers promote the comedy club at the same time they called for Tia's. Ellen agreed to pay $300 a week to Tia. When the telemarketers called customers about Tia's, they would also mention that the customers would receive a free ticket for two to the comedy club. The comedy club made money from the food and drinks the customers would buy, and Tia had the salary of one of her telemarketers paid by the comedy club.

Tia soon realized that she had stumbled on a great opportunity to get the salaries of her telemarketers paid, to give potential customers a package of great benefits, and to increase her business.

She approached several surrounding businesses. She offered to include their businesses in her telemarketing program for $150 a week plus expenses, such as postage, printing, and envelopes, which were split equally between the

Telemarketing

participating businesses. The participating businesses agreed to give a discount to customers who took advantage of the offer. Tia ended up with a total of 10 businesses participating. She made $1500 a week from the other businesses and paid her three telemarketers $900 a week.

In this situation, everybody won. The other businesses had three telemarketers promoting them. Tia made $600 a week for organizing everything, and she increased her business. Using this money-making marketing program, Tia dramatically increased the number of customers coming into her store because of all the benefits she offered. In addition, she had started a second business that was bringing in significant profits on its own.

Are results like these easy to achieve? No, they are not easy, but they are possible. If you are a business owner or are planning to start a new business, you must put away your personal fears and be confident enough to approach people. Every business is involved in sales in one way or another. Other business owners will be receptive to your ideas if you can demonstrate how your plan will benefit their business. Of course, you don't have to solicit other businesses to participate in your marketing programs. You can focus your efforts completely on your own business.

Reciprocal marketing programs are great for many businesses. You can agree to promote a business for free if that business agrees to do the same for you. Cooperative marketing is also possible. With cooperative marketing, the cost of marketing is split among the businesses participating.

Whether or not you solicit other businesses, your business will profit from the increased sales these programs create. You can make a profit from the program, or you can increase your sales even further by joining with other businesses in your area in the quest for new customers. If you pool your resources with eight or nine other businesses and work together, you can do a far more effective job of promoting all of your businesses than an outside source would ever do.

CHAPTER 5

Print Media

How Newspapers and Magazines Will Make Your Business Famous

Like many other rural and outer suburban areas throughout the country, the land south of Fort Worth, Texas, is dotted with mobile homes. Buying a mobile home is the only way that many people can afford to be homeowners. Furthermore, in Texas it seems almost to be the traditional way of life: a pickup truck, a farm, and a mobile home. Clichés aside, selling mobile homes can be a lucrative business, though not always highly profitable.

Carrie Harper had worked for Alliance Mobile Homes for over three years. Every day was nearly the same: in at 8:00 A.M.; sales meeting until 8:30; sales calls until 10:00; and then taking her turn at showing homes and writing up credit applications. By 9:00 P.M. she could count on only three things—-aching feet, a stack of credit applications (mostly denied), and fifteen minutes to make it home before her kids were in bed.

Late one night, Carrie lay in bed beside her sleeping husband, trying her best to sleep and trying to imagine herself in a different job. With each tick of the clock, which sat inches away on the nightstand, Carrie came up with another reason why she should make a career change. Sure, the money was okay, but every day she had to face the frustration of losing sales because of her

BUSINESS MYTH:	MONEY TREE REALITY:
An ad for a small business will never be noticed among all the big corporations' advertisements.	Small businesses can take advantage of advertising techniques that big corporations don't.

customers' bad credit. The previous month she had had over fifty sales, but only one approval. Something had to change. Then she had a breakthrough idea. She knew exactly where to start searching for a new approach to getting customers approved.

The next day, Carrie excitedly ran to the mailbox to get the *Bargain Post*, a local classified newspaper that came every week. She raced back to the house, opened the paper on her dining table, and searched every column for ads on credit repair. Carrie knew that if she could find a way to help her customers get a better credit rating, she would have more approved sales, and that meant more commissions.

One month into her new plan, Carrie was more discouraged than ever. She had checked out at least ten of the credit repair companies that were advertising and found that most charged between $1500 and $3000 for their services. Upon further investigation, she also discovered that many of these companies were scams; they simply collected their fees and did very little in return.

Then Carrie's husband, Dan, came home with some good news and an idea to help her. He had answered an ad in the *Bargain Post* for a manual on credit repair. He laid the manual on the coffee table, giving Carrie a wide grin.

"Maybe this will help," he said, then gave her a wink.

She picked up the manual and began reading. Soon she learned that as many as 50 percent of credit reports contain errors. She also learned the process for disputing errors. She knew there had to be a way to help her customers with their credit without charging up to $3000. It made no sense to her to charge such a large amount to people who obviously could not afford it. Carrie learned how to order a credit report. She started by ordering a copy of her own. Once she received it, she noted the errors and went to work to see if it was really possible to clean it up. Sure enough, in thirty days she had her report back. Everything had been corrected, and the corrections had vastly improved her rating.

Next, she set about working on the credit reports of her mobile home customers so that they could get approved and she could improve her commissions. She charged only $95 for the credit repair. It didn't take long for Carrie to discover that the demand for credit repair far exceeded the demand for mobile homes.

People started calling her at the mobile home dealership to fix their credit. So she decided to do what many people do when they're bitten by the self-employment bug. She took a deep breath, dove in head first, and started her own business.

Carrie started a credit repair company. She went into it with her eyes wide open. She knew that it wouldn't be easy and that the odds were against her, but she also knew that if she could provide a high-quality service at a low price, the rewards could be great.

> **HOT TIP:** *Find out what the deadline date is for the magazine you want to advertise in and call the magazine one or two days before the deadline. If there is remnant (unsold) space available, you will be able to negotiate a deep discount.*

One approach for making a new business stand out and be successful is to find a niche product that people need and want, preferably a niche with a large potential customer base. You also need an effective marketing plan that takes little cash. Carrie understood these business marketing components and applied them to her new business.

She decided to start her business part-time while she continued to work at the mobile home dealership. She got an answering service to answer calls twenty-four hours a day, and she ran an advertisement in the *Thrifty Nickel*, a weekly shopper. The answering service cost about $55 and the ad cost $36.50. Carrie invested less than $100 to start her business.

Carrie chose print media, such as the *Thrifty Nickel*, to get the word out about her new business. This let her run an advertisement immediately and target the customers she wanted to reach in a cost-effective way.

In newspapers, classified advertising gives you the ability to list your service in various categories—home services, stereos, video games, furniture, musical instruments, and pets, to name just a few. Carrie advertised in the financial services section.

Magazines are a little different. You should advertise in the one that focuses on your target market. For example, if your business sells golf equipment and supplies, you might advertise in *Golf Digest*. If you sell computer equipment, you might want to advertise in *Computer User* magazine. If you want to franchise your business, you could advertise in *Entrepreneur* or *Successful Franchising*.

You can run a display ad or a classified ad. In most cases when you first run an ad in a magazine you have never run one in, you should start out with a classified ad with a border around it.

Typically, you want to keep the advertisement basic and to the point. The ad Carrie created was basic, but it also did something important: It touched people emotionally. This is the first key element of creating your ad, finding a way to touch the reader, either through emotion, through humor, or by invoking their senses.

As is often said, when you sell steak, you don't sell a cold piece of beef, you sell the sizzle. You want a potential customer to taste it, smell it, hear it, and feel it. You want your customer to imagine how much her or his life will be improved by purchasing your product or service.

Carrie could have run the ad as presented in Sample 5.1. That ad certainly describes the service she was offering. But where is the sizzle? Sample 5.2 shows the ad she ran instead.

Sample 5.1

BAD CREDIT

We can remove bad credit from your credit report.

Call us at xxx-xxxx.

Sample 5.2

DON'T LET BAD CREDIT RUIN YOUR LIFE

We can help you clear up errors in your credit report so that you can get that home, car, or major purchase you've been dreaming about. Guaranteed results.

Don't hesitate, call our 24-hour hotline now for our special offer.

XXX-XXXX

Print Media | 109 |

Notice how this ad is constructed to touch the reader emotionally. It gives the reader a vision of what life could be like with Carrie's service. Three other vital aspects are covered in the ad:

1. It tells the readers that they are important, that is, they can call twenty-four hours a day.

2. It spurs them to action by telling them that if they act now, they will get a special offer.

3. It eliminates the readers' risk because the service is guaranteed.

Carrie ran this ad in the financial services category of the *Thrifty Nickel* and had a successful response. More than fifty people called her answering service in the first week. She returned their calls and set up appointments to explain her service to them in more detail. To cover her additional costs and to make a profit, she also raised her rates to $145 for a single person and $195 for a couple. The first week she made ten sales and over $1400, which isn't bad for an initial investment of less than $100. Eventually, Carrie got such a good response that she could afford to run similar ads in the mobile home, automobile, and houses-for-sale sections of the *Thrifty Nickel* and the daily newspaper.

COOL RESOURCE: For advertising in Shoppers nationwide, contact National Mail Order Classified, P.O. Box 5, Sarasota, FL 34230, or The National Marketplace at 1 (800) 525-2272.

How to Make the Important Choices

When using print media to market your business, you need to determine the best place to run your ad, whether to run a classified ad or a display ad, and how large the ad should be. A display ad is a minimum of one column inch. If you have a retail business, you may want to run a display ad or put an insert in the paper. If you are unsure about what type of print media is best for your business, start off with a small classified ad rather than spending more on a display ad.

There are techniques you can use that will enable you to get your business into the paper for free. It is even possible to get paid to promote your business in the newspaper.

Carrie ran her ad only in the *Thrifty Nickel* for the first three months. At that point, she decided to expand her business, but she didn't want to increase her expenses. Here's what she did.

Generate Customers with Free Publicity

One thing that many large companies do to generate customers and goodwill toward their businesses is send out press releases or press kits to various newspapers. One of the appealing aspects of press releases is that you do not have to be a well-known company to generate publicity. As long as you have a story that is interesting, newsworthy, and timely and you know how to format a press release, it is more than likely that your story will be picked up by newspapers in your area. Keep in mind that when you send press releases, you do not have to limit your scope to newspapers. Other media, such as television stations, radio stations, and magazines, are also potential targets for press releases. In this chapter, I discuss the print media, but you can use the same format and techniques discussed here for other media as well.

What Is Newsworthy?

How do you determine if what you have to say about your business is news that is worthy of printing? You make it so. Large companies do this every day. If you are writing your press release around the time of a special occasion or holiday, then gear it toward that holiday. For example, at Christmas Carrie sent out a press release about how much debt consumers incurred during the holidays. In another she wrote about how many consumers are still paying on credit card bills from the Christmas holidays three to five years before. Both of these press releases were printed because they were newsworthy and timely.

> **COOL RESOURCE:** One of the best ways to reach syndicated columnists and television and radio producers is to advertise in the Radio-TV Interview Report. For more information, contact Bradley Communications at 1 (800) 989-1400.

One good way to get a press release published is to come up with a "list of ten." In other words, send out a list of Ten Best, Ten Worst, or Ten Reasons for doing or not doing something. Carrie sent out a press release titled "The Top Ten Reasons Why Americans File Bankruptcy." Her list was published in every newspaper to which she submitted it.

No matter what type of business you own, there are a hundred different angles for stories you can create to get publicity. How many people outside the fashion industry had heard of Mr. Blackwell before he came up with his best-dressed and worst-dressed lists? Now their release is a major event every year. The Blackwell List is published in *People* magazine, *USA Today*, and newspapers across the country. How did Mr. Blackwell become the expert on the best and worst dressed? He made himself the expert through the correct use of press releases.

Here are just a few of the ideas that businesses we have helped came up with:

- A used car dealer did a press release on scams run by used car sellers who present themselves as private owners. These unscrupulous folks would roll back speedometers and use trickery to hide engine damage. The press release listed ten warnings when shopping for used cars. Not only did it bring his own car lot more business, but the newspaper eventually paid him to do a regular car column.

- A beautician did an article called "Ten Common Practices That Can Damage Your Hair." This led to a series of six articles that established her shop as the place to go for healthy and beautiful hair.

- A small local market concerned about a food poisoning scare in the town it served wrote a press release about preventing similar problems at home. Thereafter, the owner of this store became the expert that newspapers, television, and radio stations called any time there were stories circulating about any food-related subject.

What is stopping you from doing exactly the same thing for your business? Nothing. Once you get published, instantly you're an expert. At least you can be considered an expert if you know what you are talking about.

Using press releases can be an extremely effective marketing technique if carried out correctly. It is a well-known fact that a glowing article about your business will bring in more business than an advertisement. Because of this, some companies write articles about their businesses and run them as advertisements. While this may be more effective than a normal advertisement, it will not bring the results that a regular article can produce. For starters, doing the article as an ad says that it is a paid advertisement. When we see these ads, we feel sorry for the company that had to resort to that type of advertising. We consider it an obvious sign that the company either isn't legitimate or needs to hire a better public relations person. It's been our experience that, in general, people are much less likely to read an article that is a paid advertisement than to read a genuine article.

The Best Publicist for Your Business

When I talk to business owners about using publicity to promote their businesses, they are usually very gung-ho about it until they find out how much effort it takes to write a news release and make the follow-up calls to editors and producers. At this point, some business owners ask me to recommend someone who can do it for them. In a few cases I will recommend a publicist, but in most cases I refuse. The reason is quite simple: The best publicist for any business is the person who owns and runs that business. Who knows more about your business than you do? In the majority of cases, no one.

If you're like most entrepreneurs, your business is like a child. You suffered the pain of birth, you watched it grow up, and it sometimes stumbled, but it always made you proud. You may feel that you need help writing a press release because you don't believe that you are a writer, but in reality the objective of a press release is to generate enough interest that an editor or producer will call you. I know that you can think of some aspect of your business that will generate excitement.

COOL RESOURCE: Run a classified ad in over 300 newspapers by contacting American Publishing Company at 1 (800) 475-3121.

Formatting a Press Release

When you send out a press release, you need to format it properly in order for the newspaper editor to give it credence. If you don't do this, in most cases the editor won't even look at your press release long enough to notice whether the story is newsworthy or not.

It is best to double-space your news release. Editors do an unbelievable amount of reading every day. You want to make your press release as easy as possible on their eyes. Editors also need the space to make notes about your material. Sample 5.3 is a model press release that you can use as a guideline.

A press release should be no longer than one page. The main objective is to generate enough interest in your business that an editor or producer will call you to get more information and write a feature article.

> **HOT TIP**
>
> *Send out a press release offering something free, like a free report. This will help you in two ways: It will leave the impression that your business is willing to give, and it will help you build up a mailing list of potential customers.*

Elements of a Press Release

Letterhead. The letterhead should include the company name, address, phone number, and fax number on standard 8½ x 11-inch paper with black ink.

News Release. Write news release in the upper left corner in bold type with black ink.

Contacts. Contact names and phone numbers should appear in the top left corner under news release.

Headline. The headline should be in bold type and should give the story angle.

First Paragraph. The first paragraph should tell a brief story. In this way, if nothing else is published, this story will highlight the main reason for sending the press release.

Sample 5.3 **A Model Press Release.**

Jack's Cajun Restaurant
123 Main Street
Anytown, NY 12345

NEWS RELEASE
Jack Jones
1 (111) 222-3333

For Immediate Release

**FIRST CAJUN RESAURANT IN ANYTOWN
TO HOLD GRAND OPENING**

Jack's Bayou Restaurant, the first Cajun restaurant ever to open in Anytown, has set October 1 as the date of its Grand Opening. Jack Jones, the owner of the new restaurant, is a previous resident of Anytown and has been head chef at the Blue Bayou Cajun Restaurant in New Orleans for the past five years. Jack promises us a Grand Opening unlike anything Anytown has seen before. Red Willie, a Cajun band, will be playing from 7:00 P.M. to midnight. Kids eat free on opening night.

Janice Erickson of the New Orleans Restaurant Association commented: "Anytown is extremely lucky to have someone of Jack Jones's caliber opening a Cajun restaurant in their city. He is a very well known chef in New Orleans. He is one of the best Cajun chefs New Orleans has ever had."

For more information or reservations, contact Jack's Bayou at 111-222-3333.

30

Body. The body of the release should give the editor or producer all the details on your product or service. The goal is to be able to answer all the questions about the product. The body should include the following information:

- How the product or service was developed
- What market the product or service is intended for
- How consumers will benefit from the product or service
- Where consumers can purchase the product or service

Testimonial. Include a testimonial from someone who has used your product or service, preferably someone who is well known and influential in your community.

Concluding Paragraph. The concluding paragraph should describe how to get product samples or more information about the product or service.

Notation. The number thirty at the end of the release indicates the end of the press release.

Elements of a Press Kit

If you want to send out more information than a press release allows, you can use a press kit. This gives you the opportunity to release more information about you, your company, your mission, and what you want the public to know about your business. Following is a section-by-section description of a press kit.

Pitch Letter. The first thing the editor will see is the pitch letter, and it should be an attention grabber. It should be personalized and typed or printed in black ink on 8½ x 11-inch paper. It is a sales piece that is meant to arouse the editor's interest and prompt him or her to investigate further what you are writing about.

Press Release. The press release describes your product or service in greater detail than the pitch letter. It should provide enough newsworthy information to allow the editor to write a story directly from the release.

Backgrounder. This gives a short history of your company and information about it. The backgrounder profiles the key contacts at your company. Write Backgrounder in the top right-hand corner.

Business Card. A standard business card should be included with a press kit.

Photo(s). Photos or slides of your product can support the press release and help make the story of your product or service more compelling.

Testimonial. You should include a one-page collection of quotes and comments from customers, suppliers, or anyone else who has a positive comment on your product or service.

Fact Sheet. All technical or pertinent information about your product goes in the fact sheet. Fact Sheet is written in the top center of the page.

Folder. The folder that holds all the materials in the press kit should be a basic folder. Your company name or logo should be printed on the folder in two colors. The folder needs to have an insert on the inner left or right side where your business card goes.

COOL RESOURCE: Reach a circulation of over 3 million readers all over the United States by contacting the National Marketplace at 1 (800) 525-2272.

You can get press kit folders printed at most office supply stores and through NEBS. NEBS is a company that specializes in printing invoices, door knob hangers, letterhead, business cards, purchase orders, and much more. For an inexpensive alternative, buy plain press kit folders, available at Office Depot for a reasonable price, then print color labels (2½ x 3 inches) and affix them to the front of the folder.

> **HOT TIP**
>
> *Start your own in-house advertising agency. Print up letterhead and business cards for the agency. This will immediately save you 15 percent on advertising.*

Following Up

After you send out a press release or press kit, it is time to make follow-up calls. See Sample 5.4 for an example of a follow-up conversation. You may need to call an editor or producer several times before he or she listens and takes notice of what you have to say. Be persistent! Don't give up. When you call, be prepared to answer any questions the editor or producer may have. Don't be intimidated. Here is a checklist that you should complete before you make the follow-up call.

- ❑ Have an agenda. Decide on the topics and the points you want to cover. Know ahead of time exactly what you want to say.

- ❑ Do your research. Find out from the receptionist at the newspaper, radio station, or television station the names of the proper contacts. Also research the periodical's deadlines, because that may affect the editor's availability and receptiveness, more so with magazines than with newspapers.

- ❑ Time is money. Write out what you want to say. Make a few practice calls before you call the contact to ensure that you have down exactly what you are going to say.

- ❑ Make the call. When you call the contact, don't waste his or her time; get right to the point. Who are you? Why are you calling? Tell the editor or producer the purpose behind the call and why she or he should pay attention to what you have to say.

- ❑ Take action. Ultimately, you want the chance to talk up your product, so try to get an in-person interview.

Sample 5.4 **Model for a Follow-up Conversation.**

> *Jack Jones: Is Peter Samuels in?*
> *Peter Samuels: This is Peter Samuels.*
> *JJ: Hello, Peter. This is Jack Jones with Jack's Bayou Restaurant. I recently sent you a press release about our grand opening. I am calling for two reasons. First, I want to make sure you received the press release and to see if you have any questions that I can answer about the restaurant or our plans for the grand opening.*
> *PS: Yes. I did receive that.*
> *JJ: Do you have any questions?*
> *PS: Not right now.*
> *JJ: The second reason I am calling is to personally invite you and your family to our grand opening celebration. We will be having the celebration on October 1 from 7:00 P.M. to midnight. We will have the band Red Willie playing, and we plan on having a great time for everyone. Can I put you down for a reservation?*
> *PS: I don't know if I'll be able to stay very long, but I should be able to at least make it for dinner.*
> *JJ: Great. I look forward to meeting you.*

If your press release is not for a grand opening or celebration, then your follow-up call will be slightly different. In this case, take the approach of a courtesy call to make sure the contact received the press release and to make yourself available to answer any questions. For this situation, you would use the first part of the sample follow-up call.

Editors get hundreds of press releases every week. If you want to be successful in getting an article written about your company, it is imperative that you get past all the clutter they see. Making follow-up phone calls is a potent tool.

It also helps if you are creative. For example, send your press release with a gift basket or in a poster tube. Make the press release stand out, and you increase the chances of it getting noticed.

Get Paid to Be Published

When you send out news releases and talk to writers, editors, and producers, try to establish a relationship with each person. If you establish a good rapport with these people and you believe in your own abilities, it is possible for you to have

Print Media

your business in the newspaper for free every week. You can even get paid to promote your business in the newspaper. Approach the editors of each newspaper about writing a weekly column that will benefit their readers. You may have to spend several months talking to them before they agree, but it will be worth the wait. Tenacity is a key attribute in making your business succeed. You need to be persistent to break down the barriers that stand in the way of your success.

> *Even if you are on the right track, you'll get run over if you just sit there.*

It is difficult to get a column accepted, but it is possible. You need to be an expert on the subject you're covering, and picking a subject that is timely will improve your chances of the column being accepted. Take a creative approach to your subject and try to make the column not only informative but fun to read as well. If you approach your subject from an angle that hasn't been used before, you will have a better chance of seeing your column in print.

Carrie Harper approached several papers in her area, including the daily newspaper, the weekly shoppers, and newspapers geared toward senior citizens, women, and small-business owners. She offered to write a question and answer column about credit and debt for four weeks, without pay. Carrie's offer enabled the newspapers to run a new and timely column without any risk and also to see by people's responses how popular the column was. Within thirty days, Carrie was getting over a thousand letters per week and her column was in several newspapers. Even the daily newspaper asked her to do the column once a week. In less than a year, Carrie was making over $800 per week writing her column, and her credit repair business had doubled because she also included a little blurb about her business at the end of each column.

COOL RESOURCE: *To buy unsold space in* Time, Newsweek, *or other magazines for pennies on the dollar, contact Media Networks at 1 (800) 225-3457.*

Carrie saw the huge potential for her business and took it to the next level. She decided to try something new. Instead of getting paid a small amount from a weekly shopper, she figured out a way to make more money from the column. She agreed to write her column in a weekly shopper for free. In exchange, the shopper gave her one free page to use however she wanted. She started a financial page and sold ads to credit card companies, banks, car dealers, and other companies that made a commitment to help people with credit problems. Of course, she also had a large ad for her own company, and she made over $500 per week from the other advertisements.

Expand Your Market Area

It wasn't long before Carrie wanted to expand her business to encompass a larger geographic area. She wanted to run ads and articles in the surrounding states asking people to call her 800 number. She would then send out information to them, and if they liked the services she offered, they would sign up and send in a check. Carrie decided to run ads in weekly shoppers and regional ads in *Time* and *Newsweek*.

> **COOL RESOURCES:**
> - To locate major columnists who can write about your business, contact the P.R. Profit Center Database at 1 (800) 669-0773.
> - For a great PR firm that doesn't charge until it gets results, contact Annie Jennings Public Relations, 1 (908) 281-6201 or www.anniejenningspr.com.

Most people do not realize that you don't have to spend thousands of dollars to run an ad in *Time* or *Newsweek*. You can spend a few hundred dollars to run a regional ad. Carrie bought a full page of unused space in both *Time* and *Newsweek* and resold some of the space to the same companies that were running ads in her shopper financial services section.

Again, she ended up running an ad promoting her own business and was paid to do it. I think it is obvious by now that you don't need to have a lot of money to market your business. It is more important to be creative and persistent, and to know how to use marketing techniques to your advantage.

> **HOT TIP:** *To promote your business in newspapers and shoppers for a very low cost, give the newspaper a gift certificate from your business that it can give away to readers in exchange for a free ad.*

Use Time and Temperature Phone Numbers

Carrie built her business from scratch, literally from an idea, to over $3 million per year because she was extremely creative and was willing to be open to anything that would bring in customers. Most of the techniques she used were effective.

One of the unique ideas Carrie had was using the time and temperature service to promote local businesses. Most business owners do not realize that they can get their own time and temperature telephone number. Carrie bought a computer for less than $2000 and then sold 15-second commercials to six other businesses for $200 per month each. Next, she traded space with a local newspaper to promote the time and temperature telephone number. When people called in for the time and temperature, they would hear a 30-second commercial promoting Carrie's business and 15-second commercials promoting the other six businesses. The ads that were sold to the other businesses were rotating ads that would run every third call, so Carrie's 30-second ad and two other ads ran on every call.

Carrie made over $1200 per month and did not even have to pay for newspaper ads because she gave the newspaper an ad on her time and temperature number in return for space. Since this is a unique form of advertising, Carrie didn't even have to approach other business owners about advertising on her number. They heard about it and contacted her.

The Anatomy of an Ad

When you run an ad, whether you are paying for it or not, you must grab the reader's attention. The ad will not bring in customers if no one reads it.

The heading of your ad should always be centered, bold, and in caps. Two or three words are all you need. When appropriate, use power words, such as attention, warning, stop, or beware. Address readers according to the newspaper category, such as investors.

> **COOL RESOURCE:** To syndicate an article you write about your business, contact JSA Publishing, P.O. Box 37175, Oak Park, MI 48237; American International Syndicate, P.O. Box 46004, Bedford, OH 44146; or Crown Syndicate, P.O. Box 99126, Seattle, WA 98199.

The body of the ad should resemble a consumer message rather than a sales pitch. Keep the ad simple, and limit it to around twenty-five words. It can be beneficial to read the ads of your competitors to see what you like and don't like. The important aspect of the ad body is to have something that gets readers' attention.

The ending of the ad should always prompt the reader to action. Give readers a reason to act now, as opposed to waiting to act later. Make them feel that if they don't act immediately, they will miss out on something special, such as a reduced rate or a freebie.

The tag line, which is the very last line of the ad, should tell the reader exactly what to do: make a call, go to a store at a certain address, or mail in a certificate.

Never run a classified ad with the intention of having the reader order the product from the ad, with one exception: If your product costs less than five dollars, then you can use the classified ad as a one-step marketing tool. For all other products and services, the classified ad is a two-step marketing tool.

Step One. The idea behind the classified ad is to make contact. It's a screening process, a way to filter out everyone except people who are interested in your product or service. No matter what type of business you own, the classified ad can be used to get potential customers to reply with at least a name and address, and hopefully also a phone number.

Step Two. When the reader responds to the ad, you send out more detailed information that he or she can use to assess your product or service and decide whether to order it. You can simultaneously build a mailing list this way.

When Carrie ran her ads in various states, she received over 1000 calls per week. She sent information to the respondents, and they signed up for her services by mail. She built up her mailing list and sent out information every seven to eight weeks to the people who had not replied to a previous mailing. Keep in mind that although respondents may not order your product after the first mailing, they may order it after subsequent mailings. With each of her mailings, Carrie varied the letter, the offer, and the terms. She ended up sending out eight different mailings, but she got an acceptable response rate with each mailing, even though she was sending to the same people who had not yet ordered. It was profitable for her to do this because the response rate remained approximately the same whether the mailing was the second or the seventh. See Chapter 3, Direct Mail, for further details on sequential mailings.

> A shopkeeper was dismayed when a brand new business much like his own opened up in the storefront to the left of him and erected a huge sign that read *BEST DEALS*. He was thunderstruck when another competitive enterprise opened up on his right and announced its arrival with an even larger sign reading *LOWEST PRICES*. The shopkeeper was on a panic until he got an idea. He put the biggest sign of all over his own shop. It read *MAIN ENTRANCE*.

Get a Free Yellow Pages Ad

There is a very good chance that when you start your business, you will have to wait several months for your listing to appear in the yellow pages. This shouldn't be a major concern, because if you are planning to get most of your business from the yellow pages, you will be sorely disappointed. What's more, it is possible to get free yellow pages advertising immediately.

Before you start your business, check out your competition in the yellow pages. Call them to find out about their products, services, and prices. By doing this, you will be putting yourself in the customer's position, seeing things from her or his point of view. You may discover gaps in your competitors' services that you could fill, or any number of other facts that can give you an advantage.

Along with all this information, you can also find out which companies have telephone numbers that have been disconnected. Call your telephone company and arrange to take over one of these numbers. With any luck, you will find at least two or three disconnected telephone numbers, and one of those companies will have a sizable yellow pages advertisement. Bingo, you have a free ad in the yellow pages. When people call on that assumed telephone number, make sure that they know your business name and address.

Beat the Competition with Its Own Money

If your business is like most, you are in an industry in which your competition spends a ton of money on advertising or marketing. Maybe you are just starting your business, you have a small business, or for other reasons you don't have an advertising budget equal to your competition's. My advice in this situation is to use your competition's advertising as your own.

Eric Blankenship had owned Family Circle Pizza in Norman, Oklahoma, for several years. Eric had cultivated a profitable business until a disaster visited. A nationwide pizza delivery chain came into town and bombarded Norman with coupons, newspaper advertising, and huge yellow pages ads. Eric couldn't afford large ads in the yellow pages or display newspaper ads.

Eric thought through his situation carefully and decided that the only way he could compete with the national chain was to use its money to market his business. How did he do it? He took out small ads in local shoppers and 30-second commercials on the radio stating that anyone bringing in a yellow pages ad or a newspaper ad from any of his competitors would get three pizzas for the price of one.

This marketing tactic worked better than Eric could have imagined. Consumers looked for competitors' ads just for the purpose of taking them to Family Circle Pizza. Six months later, it was extremely hard to find a yellow pages ad for any of Eric's competitors. Of course, these competitors were still spending thousands of dollars a month for ads that weren't there. They spent large amounts on newspaper ads, but they got little response, because here too, the people of Norman were taking the ads to Family Circle Pizza to get three pizzas for the price of one.

> **HOT TIP**
> *Contact magazine editors about running ads on a per-inquiry basis. With this arrangement, you do not pay in advance for your ad. You only pay for the responses you receive. So you do not have any financial risk.*

Sarah Harper had run a successful hair salon at the same location for many years. She didn't do any advertising to speak of because she had built up a great repeat customer base. Then a $7 haircut chain moved in across the street

Print Media

and Sarah began to lose business. At first she was worried and upset, not sure how to handle the situation. Then she took the simple approach of putting a large sign above her salon and running a small ad in the local newspaper and shoppers that read, "We fix $7 haircuts."

Within ninety days, Sarah had increased her business above her normal average month. The franchise had a huge billboard out front and ran huge ads that brought customers to the area, but Sarah's simple sign that said "We fix $7 haircuts" helped convince customers to come to her shop instead. Within two years, the franchise closed up and moved to another location.

> **COOL RESOURCE:** To get a listing of newspaper editors, go to the public library and look in Gales Source of Publications.

The question all small business owners ask is: Can I compete with the national chains? Absolutely! You can! You can use their large marketing budgets to promote your business.

Print media can be a wonderfully expressive and profitable way to market your business. The key is to gear your print campaign toward your type of customers. For some businesses, a display ad will work. For others, a classified ad is best. Some businesses need to give a freebie to motivate potential customers to walk in the door, and some products or services are unique enough that the only incentive the potential customer needs is intrinsic.

Only you can decide which type of print media best suits your business. You may need to try different angles until you find one that works for you and your business. Also, keep in mind that print media can work hand in hand with other types of advertising, such as radio or television ads.

> **COOL RESOURCE:** To put inserts in newspapers nationwide, contact Quad Marketing/Newsamerica, 1290 Avenue of the Americas, New York, NY 10104, 1 (212) 603-6000 or 1 (800) 462-0852; or Valassis Inserts, 36111 Schoolcroft Rd., Livonia, MI 48150, 1 (313) 591-3000.

News Syndicates

Copely News Service
123 Camino de la Reina
Suite E250
P.O. Box 190
San Diego, CA 92108

Editors Copy Syndicate
3803 Pine Oaks Street
Sarasota, FL 34232
1 (941) 366-2169

Exclusive Press Syndicate
108 East 66th Street
Suite 6A
New York, NY 10021

New Wave Syndication
P.O. Box 232
North Quincy, MA 02171
1 (617) 471-8733

What's Up Information Svcs
1200 Ashwood Parkway
Suite 575
Atlanta, GA 30338
1 (404) 671-0200; fax: 1 (404) 671-0110

Whitegate Features Syndicate
71 Faunce Drive
Suite 1
Providence, RI 02906
1 (401) 274-2149

Womens International
News Gathering Svc (WINGS)
P.O. Box 33220
Austin, TX 78764
(distributes radio news by and about women)

CHAPTER 6

Television
The Medium That Can Make Your Business Successful

As a graduation present, Jim Mitchell received a joke book entitled *101 Reasons Why Lawyers Are Better Dead*. Jim had graduated from law school. He was young, idealistic, and determined not to be the type of lawyer that had inspired the book. He was ready to do his part to make the world a better place, but because he was fresh out of law school, he couldn't afford to offer his services for free. He needed to earn a living to support his growing family. Jim decided not to work for a large law firm, because he didn't want to spend his days in that type of greedy environment. He made plans to start his own firm, which meant he would need to find a way to let the public know about his services and what made him unique.

Having grown up in Los Angeles, Jim knew he didn't want to open his law practice there. He had spent the previous summer in Dallas, Texas, as an intern at a law firm and had grown to love the people and the area. He moved his family and his new law practice to Dallas.

After a few months, it was obvious to Jim that if he was going to make enough money to support his family and pay off his student loans, which totaled over $50,000, he needed to get better known. He felt that if the public

BUSINESS MYTH:	MONEY TREE REALITY:
Television advertising is beyond the reach of most businesses.	More and more small businesses are learning how to use television so that it is not only affordable, but profitable.

knew that he truly cared about people and wanted to help them with their legal problems, he would be inundated with clients. The question remained, though: How could he achieve these goals with absolutely no marketing budget?

> **COOL RESOURCE:** Subscribe to **Response TV Magazine**. This includes information on television commercials, infomercial production, consultants, telemarketing, fulfillment companies, and more. Response Television Magazine, 201 Sandpointe Avenue, Suite 600, Santa Ana, CA 72707, 1 (800) 346-0085.

I'll never forget the day I met Jim Mitchell. We had come to our daughters' school for Profession Day, I to talk about being self-employed and Jim to talk to the children about being a lawyer. Afterward, we both gravitated to the back of the room, watching the children line up for snacks. We began talking, and I could tell from the first words out of his mouth that Jim believed that I could help him bring in clients without sacrificing his principles. We continued our talk during a meeting the next day. We mapped out a strategy that would help Jim get his name out to the public and at the same time allow him to help people who could not otherwise afford legal help.

Most people are unaware of the fact that it is extremely easy to get on television for free. In this day and age, every major city has cable television. In fact, a majority of small towns now have cable television available. Often, when a franchise agreement is made between a cable company and a city, the cable company is required to provide a local access station. This is a station and channel set aside for the use of the citizens of the community.

Anyone is allowed access to the station to talk about any issue or topic he or she chooses. In fact, you are responsible for the filming, script, production, and editing of your show. You are in charge of every aspect of putting your show on the air. You are given free use of a studio and the cameras needed to film the show. This is not as difficult or as scary as it might sound. Most cable companies have free classes that will train you in every aspect of producing your show. The classes are also a great place to meet other people who will be interested in helping you film and produce your show. There is one downside to doing a show on local access: You are not allowed to blatantly advertise your business. However, you will be able to get your name out to the public.

Jim Mitchell enrolled in the classes and decided to produce a legal forum on his local access channel. Each week he discussed a different legal issue. He asked the viewers to write in with their legal questions, and he answered a few of them each week. This enabled Jim to build a mailing list of potential customers, and it also built up his reputation as an attorney who truly wanted to help others.

Of course, most local access stations don't have an enormous viewership, so it is a good idea to market your program, especially if its topic is unique. Jim printed up brochures and put them in convenience stores, grocery stores, laundromats, and other places all over town. He also wrote press releases and sent them to the local newspapers, and articles were written about his show.

When *Reality Law* debuted, Jim had a good response from the viewers and received a considerable amount of mail. The day after the debut, three new clients contacted his office. Each week, more and more people tuned into *Reality Law* and learned about various legal issues. Jim had such great success that he was soon asked to put together a weekly legal advice show on a cable network.

> **HOT TIP** *Do not use the in-house production crew to film your show. It is usually less expensive to find an independent producer.*

This is an opportune time to be self-employed, if you want to promote your business on television. With the advent of cable television and satellite television, the advertising rates for this medium have fallen drastically. In most major cities you can buy an hour of time on a cable network for $150 to $300. Given this fact, why pay for 60-second commercials when you can have your own television show and promote your business as much as you want? With a little luck, you'll become a celebrity in your community.

After some time, as his confidence increased, Jim took the plunge and produced *Reality Law* for a cable network. He bought airtime and a cable station for $300 per hour and spent approximately $2000 to produce each program. Before the show aired, Jim contacted various businesses and associates and sold ten sponsorships at an average of $300 each. The bottom line on Jim's activity was this: He sold sponsorships for a total of $3000 per week and spent $2300 per week for airtime and show production. After expenses, Jim had a profit of $700 per week and he was promoting his own law practice.

By starting out on a free local access station, Jim gained experience in producing his show and built a good reputation, so it was easy for him to get businesses to sponsor *Reality Law* when he took the show to a cable network.

No matter what type of business you own or plan to start, you can use this marketing technique to promote your business and get paid for doing it. Here are a few examples of how this marketing program has been put into use:

- A restaurant owner started a cooking program to promote his restaurant. The program became so successful that he finally sold the restaurant and had his show picked up by national television.

- A craft shop owner put together an arts and crafts television program. Today she is making over $200,000 a year endorsing products in addition to running these shows.

- An auto repair shop owner produced a program on car buying and car maintenance. Today, he also has six service centers where customers pay $50 to have cars they're considering buying checked out for mechanical problems.

This marketing program can be effective for any type of business if you are creative. I know one business owner, Dave Anders, who bought five minutes of airtime and created a series called *Business Spotlight*. He kept one minute of his airtime to spotlight his own business, sold three minutes to other businesses, and used one minute for an introduction to the show. Dave's marketing program was more expensive than some because he put *Business Spotlight* on a network station. However, he still ended up making over $2500 per month in net profit.

HOT TIP *Give your product to a cable auction show in exchange for some publicity about your business.*

Business owners liked the concept of *Business Spotlight* because the way Dave produced it, it seemed to be less an advertisement than an endorsement of various businesses. It goes without saying that before Dave spotlighted a business, he thoroughly checked it out to make sure that it had a good reputation, quality products, and a reasonably high level of customer service. Dave even went so far as to visit each business to witness firsthand how it treated its customers. It wasn't long before Dave had a waiting list of businesses seeking to be spotlighted. Ultimately, Dave was able to extend this concept into a radio show as well.

> **COOL RESOURCE:** Contact a company that will help you do an infomercial, such as Inphomation Communications, 1 (410) 649-1000; National Media, 1 (800) 504-5004; or Positive Response, 1 (818) 380-6930.

Jason Burrell owned a small car dealership in Fort Worth, Texas. He tried to treat all customers the way he would want his mother to be treated, with honesty and fairness. Jason had a generous return policy and often would take a car back if a customer had a serious problem with it within sixty days. He firmly believed that everyone who bought a car should know that it could be depended on to get the buyer to work, to take the kids to school, to get to the grocery store, and to do whatever else the buyer needed it to do. Jason viewed himself as an important cog in the machine that was his community.

Jason's own childhood experiences had influenced his ethics in business. When he was fourteen, his parents bought a car and in less than thirty days, it threw a rod and was no longer drivable. They still had the car payments and no warranty; consequently, they could not afford to purchase another car.

Within a few weeks Jason's father lost his job, and eventually the family had to move into a homeless shelter because they couldn't afford to pay the rent on their apartment. No wonder, then, that Jason considered it important that a person purchasing a car get one that was, above all, dependable. The only problem with this personal philosophy was that it cut into his profits. Many times, the cars he took as trade-ins turned out to be less than mechanically sound. Instead of selling them in this condition, he had the repairs done and made certain that they were sound before selling them.

On the positive side, Jason did get a lot of business from referrals by previous customers. But he did not have a marketing budget to help generate new customers, and he could not foresee ever having the extra money for a serious marketing campaign.

One day, as Jason sat in his living room watching a movie, a car dealership commercial came on and sparked an idea. He didn't need money to sell his cars on television. He started a program called *Car Market* and put it on television for half an hour every Saturday. The idea was not only to sell the cars he had on his car lot but also to allow other dealers and individuals to offer their cars for sale. *Car Market* was an immediate hit.

> **COOL RESOURCE:** *For free advice, contact your local SCORE office, located at the Small Business Administration office, or contact The National SCORE Office, Small Business Administration, 409 Third Street, Suite 500, Washington, DC 20416.*

For less than the cost of an advertisement in most major newspapers, Jason offered to show a picture of a vehicle, describe it, and give the name and phone number of the person to contact, all for only $10. Within sixty days there were so many people wanting to put their cars on *Car Market* that Jason expanded the program to one hour and had 200 cars to display.

Needless to say, Jason sold many cars from his own lot. His business increased dramatically, and it didn't cost him a dime. Jason made about $1000 net profit per week after expenses from *Car Market*. He paid $1.50 for each picture to be transferred to tape for the show; he paid $300 for the television time on cable; and he paid $400 per week for a photographer to take the pictures. One thing that helped *Car Market* become a success was that Jason insisted that all the participating dealers sign a contract to guarantee for ninety days any car they advertised on *Car Market*.

Is this kind of show limited to selling cars? Absolutely not. You can adapt this marketing program to almost any type of business. Be creative and open to any ideas that might fit with this approach. We even know of a television program in which a family earns enough to support themselves by hosting an auction of all sorts of used items. My teenage daughter has nicknamed it the *Crappy Auction*, suggesting, perhaps, that not all the items auctioned are of the highest quality.

> **HOT TIP** *When promoting your business on television, offer the viewers something for free that pertains to your business, that they call in to get. This will facilitate the compilation of a mailing list of people interested in your business.*

Television

No matter what kind of marketing you are using now, you want to use it to your complete advantage and know that it is working to bring in new customers. When Jim Mitchell promoted his law firm on television, he tied it into direct mail and a telemarketing program. He offered viewers three free guides that he had written about common legal issues and questions: *Texas State Laws on Divorce and Custody; Is Filing Bankruptcy Right for You?*; and *How Workers' Compensation Laws Affect You*. Viewers of Jim's television program could order the guides for free by mail or over the phone. The viewers of Reality Law received a free benefit. At the same time, Jim increased his business and added to his mailing list.

> **HOT TIP** *A marketing campaign is not a single event or contact. That's why it's called a campaign.*

This use of complementary multiple marketing programs helped Jim make the best use of all his resources. He learned what kind of information and help people needed from attorneys. This program enabled him to know if his marketing was successful and what types of television programs people would be most likely to watch.

I am always amazed when I see a company spending thousands or even millions of dollars on marketing without keeping track of which programs are working and which are not. Some national companies spend money on television, radio, or newspaper advertisements and then never ask customers what led them to buy.

> **HOT TIP** *Ask your customers how they heard about your business.*

The business owners who claim that their marketing programs are obviously working because people are coming into their businesses don't always realize that if they are spending $100,000 on one form of marketing and $100,000 on another form, maybe only one of those campaigns is working and they are wasting half of their marketing budget. These business owners could double or triple their business if they devoted all their marketing budget to the precise method that is most effective. In Jim Mitchell's case, he knew through long-term tracking that using all three marketing media at the same time gave his business the best results.

When Jim hires a new employee, the first thing he does is hand the employee that joke book, *101 Reasons Why Lawyers Are Better Dead*. The cover is frayed and the pages of the book are beginning to yellow, but the common perception that lawyers are untrustworthy and greedy still comes through clearly. Next, he leads the new employee to the west wall of his office, where there are literally hundreds of pictures of his clients. He explains to the employee that these people are the reason the law firm exists, that these people are his boss. Often the employee will remark that he or she has seen this person or that on *Reality Law*. Jim nods his head and begins to tell the new employee the rest of the story of how *Reality Law* began.

CHAPTER 7

Radio
Talk and Make Money

Jeannie Owens had worked for the State of Kansas for more than fifteen years, but she had always dreamed of being self-employed. After all those years of slaving away for someone else, she decided to take the plunge and start her own business. She had always been interested in health and nutrition. She had looked into buying a franchise, such as a General Nutrition Center (GNC), but since she had only $35,000 to put into a business, she decided against it.

While buying a franchise would have increased Jeannie's chances of success, she had studied and investigated the health and nutrition field for several years, and she thought she knew everything she needed to know to create a successful nutrition business. She discovered that most of the employees at a majority of other health and nutritional businesses were just cashiers, with very little product knowledge. In visiting the stores, she had overheard many conversations in which a customer wanted to know about a particular product, and the employee was unable to answer the question.

Jeannie vowed that this would never happen in her business. She diligently studied the benefits of every product she planned to carry, and she knew how

BUSINESS MYTH:	MONEY TREE REALITY:
It is expensive to advertise on the radio, and the response rate is low.	You can get paid a substantial amount every month to promote your business on the radio and be known as an expert in your field. Consequently, people will search you out to do business with you.

important this kind of information was to her health-conscious customers. She decided to stock only products from companies that were willing to put on product training seminars for her employees so that they would be knowledgeable about all the products that she stocked. She knew that if she could build a reputation for having knowledgeable clerks and excellent customer service, her business would be a success.

She decided to lease space in a popular shopping mall even though the rent was much higher than that in a strip mall a short distance from her home. She had visited both locations at least a dozen times, and she saw that the foot traffic in front of the mall space she planned to rent was at least ten times greater than that in front of the strip mall.

Jeannie definitely put a lot of thought, time, and effort into what she thought was necessary to open a business. But she didn't plan for one of the most important aspects of opening a new business—marketing. Jeannie had a disease that afflicts many new business owners: the McDonald's complex. As mentioned in the Introduction, many new business owners assume that just because they open their doors, customers will flock in on their own. If you are afflicted with this disease and do not overcome it, your business will fail, just as Jeannie's almost did.

I met Jeannie through an advertisement she placed in the business opportunity section of the local newspaper. She had been in business for only three months, and she was trying to sell the business in order to recoup at least some of her investment. She had great ideas and intense dedication, but she had spent all her money on inventory, rent, and salaries, without setting aside any money to bring customers in the door. She had no marketing plan whatsoever. Consequently, she was planning to sell out so that she wouldn't be totally broke.

After talking to Jeannie for an extended period of time, I realized that she was probably the most knowledgeable person about health and nutrition products that I had ever met. I believed that once people were aware of her vast knowledge, she would have an endless flow of loyal customers who would be grateful for her knowledge and helpful nature.

The question was how to make the general public aware of Jeannie's vast knowledge and do so without spending a lot of money that she didn't have.

Together, we decided that the best approach for her was to use the radio. I am not talking about advertising on the radio, I am talking about something much better. Radio is a powerful medium if you know how to use it. It is a medium of repetition. To succeed with it, you must use it consistently. If you are planning to advertise on the radio for one week and you expect a booming response, you will be sorely disappointed. You can have an ad run on the radio fifty or sixty times on a weekend or during the week and get very little positive response, but if you run an ad consistently for several weeks, you will start to see results.

Radio is not for the faint-hearted. If you have a recognizable name in the marketplace, radio is a great way to keep your name out in the public consciousness. If you are a new company that no one has heard of yet, then it will take a while for the public to trust you enough to respond to your radio advertisements.

If you decide to run an ad on the radio, the best time is what is called "drive time." This is in the morning when most people are going to work and in the afternoon when most people are coming home. These are also the most expensive times to advertise.

> **HOT TIP**
>
> *Always remember to negotiate with radio stations. If you buy an ad for drive time, ask the station to throw in two ads at other times for free. The station will negotiate because radio stations know that once an advertising slot goes unsold, that revenue is lost forever.*

Jeannie could not afford the time or money necessary to run an extended radio campaign. But working together, we came up with something much better. Instead of her buying 60-second time spots for ads, we developed the idea that she would put on a one-hour show about health and nutrition once a week. As an expert on health products, she had information that many listeners would tune in to hear. What's more, she had contacts with companies that produced health products and would pay to sponsor her to go on the air with her own program.

Through her study and research, Jeannie had become an expert on the subject, but getting the general public to be aware of that was a challenge. Word of mouth from customers who came into the store was good but slow. With a radio program, she could make her expertise known to thousands of people every week.

Most people are under the impression that the only people that have talk shows are nationally known celebrities and experts. Do you think that Dr. Laura, Rush Limbaugh, G. Gordon Liddy, Dave Ramsey, or even Jerry Springer started out nationally? No. They began locally and worked hard to make their programs heard nationally. There are a few nationally known names that started out nationally, but there are fewer than you might imagine.

A majority of talk radio stations have slots available and will be receptive if you have an interesting idea, a personality to match, and the money to pay for airtime. The idea is usually the hardest thing to come up with. If you can come up with a good idea, the money for your show will flow to you. And if you are worried that airtime for your program would be way out of your reach, think again!

Jeannie contacted the talk radio stations in her area and made a good connection with a program manager who was receptive to her idea. Once she had chosen a radio station, it was time to negotiate for the best available time slot, the best possible financial terms, and the number of commercials she would be allowed to sell to her sponsors.

At the end of the negotiations, she ended up with a Saturday afternoon time slot, for which she would pay $150 per week for the airtime. She was given eight minutes of commercial time that she could resell for whatever reasonable price she wanted to. The radio station was able to sell an additional eight minutes airtime. So she actually would be talking for only forty-four minutes of each one-hour show.

Granted, this is the cost for airtime in a medium-size town. But even in a larger city, airtime can be quite reasonable. For example, a Los Angeles FM station charges $500 for the same time slot reaching considerably more than five times the listeners. Prices will vary greatly, of course, but don't dismiss this as being impossible for you and your business.

Once Jeannie had the agreement signed, she contacted the companies that she felt were potential sponsors. Jeannie was smart enough to realize that if she did not find sponsors, she would still have a good deal. The $150 she paid for her one-hour talk show was extremely cheap for the exposure she would receive.

We wrote short scripts for her first three shows and put together a direct mail package to send out to potential sponsors. However, the first step was to determine who her potential sponsors were and to make a list of them.

Of course, the obvious sponsors were the manufacturers of the health products she stocked in her business, but she also contacted other businesses, such as a health food restaurant and a massage therapist.

She was pleasantly surprised at how receptive and excited other businesses were about being a sponsor. Even though she was not a professional advertising salesperson, she sold six minutes of sponsorship for an average of $150 per minute within ten days. And she kept the other two minutes to promote her own business. In other words, she was paying $150 per week for the airtime, but the sponsors were paying her a total of $900 per week to sponsor her show. So she was netting $750 per week to promote her own business and similar related businesses. She also became known as a health expert, and whenever a newspaper or a TV station discussed various health issues, it contacted her for her opinion. Talk about great free publicity!

Many talk shows start out exactly the way Jeannie's did—locally, then expand nationally. If Jeannie had done her show in ten similar-size cities, she would have made a profit of $7500 per week from promoting her business in those cities. Can you see how some radio personalities start out small and expand very rapidly? But Jeannie was not interested in having a national talk show. She only wanted to run a successful health and nutrition business in Wichita.

When you start out, you will need to devote two to three weeks to getting merchants who will sponsor your show. Once you have the sponsors, it will take an average of three to four hours per week to prepare each one-hour show. It also takes a large commitment from you because you have to commit to showing up every week on the day of your show. You get no days off or vacations, at least not for several months.

In Samples 7.1 and 7.2, you will find the phone script and direct mail package that Jeannie used with great success. You can adapt these to whatever business you are in or are planning to start.

Sample 7.1 Telephone Script for Approaching Sponsors.

> " Is the boss in? Great. Hello, Dan, this is Jeannie with the Health and Nutrition Forum. The reason for my call is that we are starting a talk show about health and nutrition issues that affect the public. This show will be on WKY radio and will be targeted to the audiences that you are trying to reach. We would like to fax or mail you information about this show because we would love to have you as a sponsor. We feel that your business would be a great fit with our show. Would you prefer that I mail or fax the information to you? Great. What is your fax number?
>
> We'll get the information package faxed to you today, and thank you for your time. "

This approach works very well. It is a soft sell, not meant to put pressure on anyone. You are calling a potential sponsor for the purpose of getting permission to send your information.

Sure, you could send the potential sponsor the information without calling first, but if the sponsor is not expecting the information, it will probably get thrown in the trash. Put "enclosed is the information you requested" on the outside of the envelope if you mail it and on the fax cover sheet if the information is faxed.

When you call first, the potential sponsor will be expecting your information and will be more likely to read it when it arrives. Give the sponsor a couple of days to look everything over and then call back.

Sample 7.2 **Direct Mail Package.**

INCREASE YOUR SALES
DECREASE YOUR MARKETING EXPENSES
HOW?

By targeting your advertising only to the consumers interested in your product.

Jeannie's Health and Nutrition Forum is a show for the consumer who is interested in learning how to be healthy.

We would like your company to be a sponsor.

I will be calling you in a few days to discuss this great opportunity with you.

The sponsors can provide you with their own radio commercials, or the radio station will usually do it for them for no additional charge. When you go on the radio, be sure to promote your sponsors with enthusiasm. They will appreciate it and be more likely to sponsor you for a longer period of time. Also, it is best not to ask a company to be a sponsor if you don't believe in its products or services. The money may be tempting, but it can hurt your reputation in the long run. Jeannie did very well. Her company really prospered, and she became known in the area as Jeannie Owen, health and nutrition expert.

There are excellent perks to this marketing program as well. Jeannie worked out a deal with one massage therapist to get a free massage once in a while so that she could say that her sponsor was her own personal massage therapist. Because of this, she could honestly bubble over with great recommendations for this massage therapist. She also talked to a health food restaurant to get regular free meals in exchange for her mentioning the restaurant and the health benefits of its menu items during her show.

Is starting your own talk show the only way to make money from promoting your own business on the radio? Absolutely not! A lot of business owners do not have the personality or the time to do a radio talk show, or they would rather promote their business on an FM music station. It is still possible to promote your business on the radio and get paid to do it.

> *Never be afraid to try something new. Remember that amateurs built the Ark and professionals built the Titanic.*

Dave Anders owned a martial arts studio in Minneapolis. The competition in that business is great in Minneapolis, and he wanted a way to separate himself from the competition. So, unlike his competitors, he did not require new students to sign a long-term contract. They could go on a month-to-month basis and pay only as long as they wanted to belong to his studio. He also gave all new students a free uniform. He ran ads in local newspapers and the response was good, but then his competitors began to offer the same things—and they had deeper pockets and started promoting their businesses on radio and TV as well.

Dave did not have the money for radio, but we were able to put him on there anyway. He had a lot of success, and it did not cost him a dime. We put together a business spotlight show in which various businesses would be spotlighted. Of course, the martial arts studio that would be represented would be Dave's Martial Arts Academy.

We negotiated with the radio station to buy five-minute spots for a 50 percent discount. We agreed to run the business spotlight fifteen times per week. Dave then sold three minutes of airtime to other companies and kept two minutes for himself. He paid an average of $25 per minute, or $125 for all five minutes. He then sold the three minutes for $75 per minute, for a total of $225.

He kept two minutes to promote his own business. In other words, every time the business spotlight was on the radio, Dave made $100 profit and his business was featured for two minutes. Since the business spotlight was on the radio fifteen times per week, Dave did quite well financially, and his business stood above the competition because his was the only martial arts studio spotlighted. It wasn't long before every opening he had for students was filled and he had to open a larger studio to accommodate more students.

What was really unique was that the business spotlight did not sound like a commercial. It sounded as if the businesses that were featured were specially selected. Consequently, businesses clamored to be featured on the show.

Which would you rather do, pay for your ads or get paid by others to promote your company and your products and at the same time become known as an expert in your field? If you follow the steps outlined in this chapter, you can become an expert too, and get paid to be on the radio.

CHAPTER 8

The Internet
The Superhighway to Success

"It already delivers more mail than the U.S. Post Office, can deliver news to more homes than any daily paper, and is emerging as the shopping center of the next century, but those accomplishments are dwarfed by what many see as the Internet's role in the future global economy. Like automobiles, broadcast, telephones, and other globe-shrinking leaps that preceded it, the Internet is expected to launch an economic quantum shift. World Wide Web–based commerce is expected to explode to $220 billion by 2001, almost one percent of the global economy, according to the research firm International Data Corp."

This quote is from a Reuters news article dated December 2, 1997. Three years later, the prediction that Web-based commerce will reach $220 billion appears to be right on schedule. Clearly, the Internet is a force to be reckoned with. Home-based businesses can use the Internet to compete with giant corporations if they know how to take advantage of the opportunities this revolutionary communications network provides.

Almost every important invention has caused economic pain for certain businesses. Television shoved newspapers out of first place as the most vital source of news. In the fifteenth century, the printing press itself made scribes, who copied everything painstakingly by hand, obsolete.

BUSINESS MYTH:	MONEY TREE REALITY:
A small business cannot afford to get a Web site, and even if it could, it could not compete with the huge international companies that have Web sites.	Getting a Web site is relatively inexpensive and will enable any small or home-based business to compete with any company, large or small.

Now, as the next millennium begins, the Internet is leaving some businesses extremely vulnerable. Since the Web is becoming such a powerful force, in advertising and in retailing, businesses both large and small need to learn how to take advantage of the opportunities it offers. Some businesses are better able to make full use of this system than others, of course. For example, selling small items such as books or software through the Internet makes a lot more sense than selling mattresses or refrigerators, but even these can be advertised and sold this way.

"The biggest challenge facing small businesses in the digital age is not technology, but a combination of inertia and a lack of marketing clout," says Geoffrey Ramsey, a statistics analyst at eMarketer, a New York company that tracks Internet marketing trends, research news, and statistics online.

As you may already know, small businesses represent 98 percent of all businesses in the United States, but most of these are way behind when it comes to embracing Internet technology. Considering that any small business can go global and compete with the huge national chains simply by building a Web site, it is foolish not to have at least some visibility on the Web. Even if you feel that, given the type of business you are in, you will never sell your product on the Web, it is still vital to have a presence there so that you can inform your customers about your company. Although you may not provide this minimal presence on the Web, rest assured your competitors will.

In many parts of the country, communication via the Web is so prevalent that having or not having an Internet address is considered a measure of how established you are in business. So think of your presence on the Internet as being something akin to having a listing in the yellow pages. In this day and age, potential customers go to one of these two places to find goods or services like yours. You can't afford to ignore either one.

There are currently over 5 million Web sites—some personal and some commercial. You hear about all the success stories and the overnight sensations, but you don't hear about all the failures, the millions of Web sites that get little or no business. Even the Web sites that get a lot of hits are not guaranteed to make a profit. Amazon.com is famous for selling hundreds of millions of dollars of books, but currently the company is still running in the red. How can you make your Web site stand out? How can people find you? With all this competition, how is it possible for your business to be successful on the Internet?

To grasp how best to use any new technology, we need to be able to go inside it. What's it all about? What is it capable of doing that previous technologies can't? What are its strengths and weaknesses? How can you make use of it?

The Internet combines many elements of all previous forms of communication: It offers graphics, the capacity for printing out material, a capacity for sound, and the capacity for two-way communication. Potential customers can read about you and your product or service, see a photo of you, and even talk to you. All of this gives you the ability to introduce your business to potential customers not just in your own town or state but the world over. Moreover, you can reach more people at a lower cost than ever before.

The Web in a Nutshell

Think of the Internet as the world's largest book. Each page in the book is a Web site. The Internet comprises millions of pages/Web sites created for thousands of different reasons. Web sites are created for business, for hobbies, such as collecting Beanie Babies or amateur rodeo riding, and even for personal use, to exhibit information about an individual's life or interests. The Internet has no boundaries and can be reached from any country by any person who has a computer, a modem, and a phone hookup. The bottom line is that it gives you the potential to market yourself and your business to people all over the world. And the best part of using the Internet in marketing is that the cost of at least having visibility is minimal compared to other marketing media.

What the Internet Can Offer Your Business

Here is a list of things the Internet can offer:

- ***e-Commerce.*** The Internet can be used to sell products or services.

- ***Customer service.*** You can use the Internet to give customers information and a way to reach you with questions, complaints, suggestions, compliments, stories of how they use your product or service, support inquiries, billing inquiries, and cancellations.

- **Brand awareness.** It can support your company's ongoing campaign for brand awareness. Since the Internet is basically limited only by the imagination of the designer, you can display your products or services in any number of ways to enhance customer appreciation and desire or need.

- **Add-on sales.** If a customer buys your main product from you at a retail outlet, you can offer add-ons over the Internet. You can bring this to the attention of the consumer as part of the product information that was included with the initial purchase.

- **Tracking.** It is a great way to track customers and their individual buying habits.

- **Market advantage.** Being on the Internet can give your business an advantage over your competition. With an online presence, you have greater visibility than your competitors who do not have such a presence. Especially if you market to the twenty-five and younger demographic, the Internet is a sure way to make yours the business of choice.

- **Expanding contacts.** The Internet is an ideal way to gather customer information. One type of information about your customers that you can get from the Internet is contact information—name, address, phone number, and e-mail address. Offer your customers a weekly/monthly electronic newsletter in order to get their information, or set up a separate members-only section on your site that they must register for in order to enter. In the members-only area, give special information or discounts that the general public doesn't get to see. This enables you to learn your customers' buying habits, solicit their suggestions for new product lines or new add-on products, and have them rate the service or the quality of your products. You can even ask for referrals to other potential customers, collect demographic information, and ask visitors to tell you what they would like to see added to your Web site.

- ***A showcase for your products.*** The Internet is an excellent place to display your products or give detailed explanations of your services. Because the Internet is such a graphically based medium and so interactive, it can showcase your company as few media can. As an example, car companies can use the Internet to display their automobiles and all the attendant features that are available with each model.

How Does a Business Make a Profit from a Web Site?

Before setting up a site, all business owners should ask themselves at least two questions:

1. How can I have an Internet presence that is profitable?
2. How should my company approach and use this marketing medium?

There are three main ways to make money from a site:

1. Sell a product or service directly online. Your business, product, or service can be marketed to people all over the world, and the best part of using the Internet is that the cost is minimal compared to that of other marketing media.

2. Direct consumers to your retail outlets to buy. Give visitors to your Web site information about your products or services that are in your retail stores. Entice them to visit your retail outlet in person or make an appointment with you to describe your services.

3. Supplement your site with advertising from other companies. The name of the game is "hits." Promote your site to the masses and get a lot of visitors to your site and people will be throwing money at you to put their ads on your site or to be a sponsor of your site.

The major purpose of this chapter is to teach you how to draw visitors to your site. Having a good site is important, but getting people to visit your site is more important. There are many corporations that have spent hundreds of thousands of dollars to build a Web page that few people visit.

A perfect example of this is Levi Strauss. This company spent over $500,000 building a Web site and a year later laid off 3000 employees. Why? How is it that a company such as Dell Computer can sell over $1,000,000 of computers on the Internet every day, while a company like Levi Strauss fails so dismally? It is called promotion. Granted, maybe a successful Web site would not have saved those employees their jobs, but maybe it would have. It is what you do after a Web site is up and running that can make your investment either pay off or go to waste.

You have to drive visitors to your site. You need to have an informative and interesting site that entices visitors to return, but it is not necessary to spend $500,000 or anything even close to that figure. Content is the most important feature of a site. Include as much free information on your site as possible. Make sure your site includes information, links, and applications that your visitors won't find anywhere else. This will ensure that your visitors return and even tell others about your site. And never forget that each time someone visits your site, you have an opportunity to sell that person something.

Put a sentence at the beginning of your site suggesting that visitors add your site to their favorites folder or bookmark your site. If they do this, they will be able to return to your site with just a click of the mouse. This makes your site readily available for them to visit whenever they want.

Explore the Field

Before you use any new marketing medium, you need information on demographics, and you need to know how other businesses in your field have used that medium to either increase sales or widen brand awareness. The Internet is no exception. Do not try to use this marketing medium until you have a concrete reason for doing so.

What are your goals in using the Internet? Do not start a Web site just because other companies are doing it. I could give you a list a mile long of businesses that started a Web site thinking that it would dramatically improve their sales, only to be very disappointed when this didn't happen. We all hear about the successes of Amazon.com, eBay, and Priceline.com, but while these stories are true, and millions of people come to the Internet every day to shop, the Internet may not be the right choice for every business.

Before you spend the money to get your business on the Internet, you need to know why you're doing so and whether your expectations are in line with reality. Find out what other companies in your industry have experienced. I'm not saying there isn't room for creativity and inventiveness on the Internet, because there is, but first, do your homework. Do your research and make smart decisions.

Small, service-based companies can use the Internet to disseminate information about their service, their record of customer satisfaction, and their effectiveness. For example, a tax preparer might want to list how much money she has saved for her clients, or a literary agent could show how many books he has placed with publishers and the average advance he has gotten for the authors. For businesses like these, a Web site is like an electronic brochure, giving the visitor free information.

How to Design Your Web Site

Once you decide to go online, the first thing to consider is how to design your Web site. Will you do this work yourself, or will you hire someone to do it?

Hiring a Web Site Designer

Hiring an expert to design and launch a Web site is very common. Perhaps you lack the time and the knowledge to do it yourself. There's nothing wrong with that, but explore the costs and quality of design services in your area. Web site design can run from a few hundred to tens of thousands of dollars.

If you decide to outsource this project, remember that, obviously, not all Web site developers/designers are the same. You want to find the best one within your allotted budget. Ask for references, ask to see other sites the person has developed and designed—ones where you can talk to someone in charge to verify that this person really did design that site. Also make sure that the person you choose can explain the options to you and knows how to execute those options. Ask any prospective Web site developer if he or she will maintain or help maintain your Web site or at least teach you how to do it.

Designing Your Own Web Site

The other option is to develop, design, and deploy your own Web site. If you have a feeling for computers and an interest in learning, there are programs available that will let you design your own site. The main things you'll need are:

1. An Internet service provider (ISP) or some way to connect to the Internet.

2. Web site building software.

3. A Web site host, a company that allows you to put your Web site on its server—sort of like renting space, for a certain amount per month.

4. A domain name. Once you have picked out your domain name, check to see if it's available, and then pay to have that URL registered for a minimum of two years, which is currently $70.

Here are the top elements of Web sites that make people want to come back:

Interesting, unique, up-to-the-minute content. Following are some Web sites that do this well. Of the hundreds of sites dedicated to the rock band Pearl Jam, Five Horizons (fivehorizons.com) is the only one that has a comprehensive concert chronology, with notes spanning from 1989 to the present. The Weather Channel (weather.com) is the only site that has complete weather information, including forecasts and Doppler radar, for over 10,000 U.S. cities. Aging with Dignity (agingwithdignity.org) is the only site to offer a legal version of "Five Wishes," a living will document that is completely print-ready.

Easy navigation. What else makes Web sites stand out? Successful Web sites are designed in a simple, easy-to-follow format. This means that they are easy to navigate, easy to understand, and not bogged down by unnecessary clutter.

One-of-a-kind tools. Women.com has many tools to help business owners. Fastcompany.com has a huge business-related discussion group that is an excellent place to network your product or service, especially if you target business-to-business sales. The 'Lectric Law Library offers hundreds of free business-related legal forms that can be downloaded and printed. Hamiltonbook.com offers closeout and discontinued books at a discount of up to 80 percent.

Detailed information about a product or service. According to a survey by Dohring Company, over 50 percent of people surveyed planned to buy their next car over the Internet. The reason for this is that the Internet provides a way for consumers to get detailed information on the availability of cars, rebates, features, and warranties without having to deal with high-pressure salespeople.

The key is to figure out the best way to attract visitors to your site so that they will either buy your product or service or get more information about you that will make them want to do business with you.

Building your own Web site is not as difficult as it might seem, though if you are not familiar with Web sites at all, it can be time consuming and a bit frustrating initially. I recommend using Microsoft FrontPage. With a cost of around $200, it is well worth the price, and it works seamlessly with other Microsoft software, such as Word, Excel, and Access. If you don't know how you want your Web site set up, spend some time online looking at a variety of sites and note what you like and dislike about them. This will give you an idea of what is possible and what will be suitable for your product or service.

If you purchase Web site construction software, the book that accompanies it will help you to build the actual Web site. Here are a few tips:

- Clutter is a negative in Web sites. Limit yourself to what is necessary and do not give in to the impulse to put unnecessary graphics, text, or other applications on your site. It may be fun for you, but it will only annoy your visitors.

- Make sure contact information for your business is somewhere on the home or opening page of your Web site. You would be surprised how many Web sites do not even list the company's telephone number. Also, make sure there is an e-mail link on every page of your Web site.

- If your Web site has more than one page—and most will—make it easy to navigate from one to another. Make your site as easy to navigate as possible so that visitors can quickly find their way around.

Consider networking with other business owners by adding a discussion group feature to your site. While I won't go into detail here on how to do this, be sure to explore this topic in your software manual. Don't forget that forms or surveys are excellent ways to capture potential customers' contact information.

How to Attract Visitors to Your Web Site

You have created your Web site, and it is up and ready for visitors. The next issue you must address is how to direct people to the site. In other words, how do you market your site?

For starters, you put your Web site Uniform Resource Locators (URL), or Web address (www.the-asba.com), on your letterhead, brochures, business cards, and advertising.

Search Engines

Next, you will want to submit your URL to the many search engines so that people can find your Web site. You can submit your site yourself, in which case you can go to http://www.tiac.net/users/seeker/searchenginesub.html, where you can easily submit your URL to the major search engines. This is done by companies which, for a small fee, will set up your site on numerous search engines all at once. You can also pay for streamlined submission. This generally runs around $40. It saves you the time and effort of submitting it to each site individually. A good place to do this is www.submit-it.com.

The Internet

> **HOT TIP:** *Set up your Web site so that people can enter from any of a number of pages. For example, you may have a home page where most people would enter, but you may also have a library, events listings, bulletin board, chat room, an area to enter a contest, or a form for requesting a freebie or more information.*

At the time this is being written, the major search engines are:

Altavista	www.altavista.com
Excite	www.excite.com
Infoseek	www.infoseek.com
Lycos	www.lycos.com
Webcrawler	www.webcrawler.com
Hotbot	www.hotbot.com

Search engines take from four minutes to six weeks, and in rare cases longer, to list your home page. It can then take up to an additional six weeks for the search engine's content searchers, called spiders, to catalog the content of your entire Web site. To maximize the number of hits you get on your Web site, it's important that you learn all you can about search engines and what you can do to make sure that your potential customers can find you quickly and easily. Telling you everything you need to know about that would be beyond the scope of this chapter, but here are some valuable tips to get you started. If you are hiring a Web designer, look for one who has expertise in this area.

> **HOT TIP:** *If you register your site with Submit It!, that company will submit your Web site to 20 different search engines.*

How Search Engines Rank Your Site. As in naming your business, be sure to give your home page a title that will arouse curiosity and interest, but at the same time tell visitors immediately what your site is about. Make sure that the first paragraph on your home page includes keywords that indicate the content of your site. Keywords are words that people could or would use when searching for your site. For example, some of the keywords for The American Small Business Alliance are *entrepreneur, small business, home-based business, marketing, making money, getting customers,* and *business associations.* As you can see, a keyword can be one word or a two- or three-word phrase. Be sure you take the time to think of all the keywords that apply to your business and your site.

You can also get your business listed in subject-specific search engines. These are search engines that deal specifically with one category of listings. For example, if you own an insurance agency, you might want to list your site with the search engine Insurance Online (www.insurenet.com).

COOL RESOURCES:
- *For more information on designing your Web site for search engines, check out www.searchenginewatch.com.*
- *To review how your site ranks on search engines, check out Rank This! at www.rankthis.com.*
- *To find industry-specific search engines, go to www.search.com or www.sleuth.com. Both are search engines for search engines.*
- *If you want to get placed higher in Internet searches, contact Surehits.com at 1 (405) 232-2272. Their parent company is Cyberspace Communications Corporation.*

Internet Directories

The next thing you should do is get your site listed with the major directories. A directory is similar to the yellow pages, but only for the Internet. Some of the major directories at the time of this writing are:

Yahoo!	www.yahoo.com
The Yellow Pages	www.theyellowpages.com
The Internet Yellow Pages	www.index.org
Bizweb	www.bizweb.com
Rex	www.rex.skyline.net
Starting Point	www.stpt.com
Web 411	www.sserv.com/web411

Comfind. . . . . www.comfind.com

Eye on the Web . . . . www.eyeontheweb.com

Lexiconn . . . . www.lexiconn.com

Linkmonster. . . . . www.linkmonster.com

If you own a retail business, you should also be listed in some of the more popular virtual malls. A virtual mall is exactly what it sounds like: a single location on the Internet where there are a number of stores. While the explosion of this means of e-commerce has been huge, you can still find a nearly complete listing of virtual malls on Yahoo! Also, many business-oriented magazines, such as *Entrepreneur* and *Success*, have started their own malls.

If your business has a catalog, you should also be listed at:

Catalog Mart . . . . www.catalog.savvy.com

Catalog Link . . . . www.cataloglink.com

Exchange Links with Other Web Sites

Another way to drive traffic to your Web site is to do what's called a "link exchange." This can involve simply contacting complementary Web sites and asking each of them to put up a "hyperlink" to your site, in return for which you will put up one to theirs. Usually this consists of a brief description of your service and a highlighted address. By clicking on your address, the visitor is immediately sent to your Web site. This is a simple person-to-person exchange. Or you can go through a link exchange service, such as LinkExchange (linkexchange.com) or BannerSwap (bannerswap.com). These types of services will put your banner advertisement (discussed below) into a pool from which advertisements to be displayed on various Web sites are chosen. They are displayed in order. It's a form of Internet co-op advertising.

You can also pay to have your banner advertisement or some other ad put on complementary Web sites.

COOL RESOURCE: You can obtain free content for your site at www.aracopy.com or at www.certificate.net/wwio.

Contact Information

How will you know what type of traffic your Web site is attracting? It's important to know this because, just as with any other marketing you do, you want to know what is working and what is not. You want to know how the visitors to your Web site heard about you so that you can determine if the site is profitable for you and decide what changes need to be made to draw more visitors if it is not. You can use a counter, which literally tracks the number of visits to your Web site, or you can employ a Web site statistic service.

For commercial sites, there is a charge, but it is normally minimal, and some Web hosting companies provide this service automatically. With a statistic service, you will get detailed information about the people coming to your site, such as what time they visited, where they live, what type of ISP they're using, how long they stayed at your site, and how many pages of your site they viewed. This type of information will help you to track what seems to be of the most interest to the most visitors.

On your home page, offer a free electronic newsletter (e-letter) to visitors who leave an e-mail address. The e-letter can have articles about your industry and your particular product or service. Make sure that the articles show potential customers the benefits to them of using your product or service. If there are no benefits, visitors will not make a purchase.

COOL RESOURCE: *One of the best companies we have found to help you get set up to do e-commerce is E Commerce Exchange. You can reach them at 1 (800) 639-6644.*

One other way of getting information on the visitors to your Web site is to offer memberships in a group connected with your company that provides a service, a newsletter, or a discussion forum. The membership is free, and it gives registered members access to information or parts of your site that non-registered visitors cannot reach. In return for this, the visitors give you some basic information about themselves. You can ask for detailed information, but make most of it optional. At a minimum, require them to give you a user name and an e-mail address. Preferably, you'll require full name, e-mail address, and physical address. This may scare away some visitors, but it will also weed out those who are not serious about what you're offering.

Still another way to reach potential customers is to go to other business-related discussion groups, share in the topics, and post a message leaving the URL of your Web site at the bottom. This is called a signature; it usually consists of your name, e-mail address, and URL. It would look like this:

> Jennifer Bishop
>
> Jennifer@the-asba.com
>
> The American Small Business Alliance, the entrepreneur's resource center, www.the-asba.com.

Promoting Your Web Site

Web Site Promotion through E-Mail, Newsgroups, and Mailing Lists

Electronic mail (e-mail) is not only the fastest, most direct, and most popular form of communication today, it is also one of the best marketing tools available to businesses. Messages sent by e-mail are usually free, and unlike the case with standard mail, you can use e-mail to quickly and easily send the same message to hundreds, thousands, or even millions of recipients.

"You've got mail" is not just a movie, it is also a popular catchphrase for millions of computer users. Millions of messages go all over the world every single day in one of three forms: person-to-person, messages posted to a newsgroup, and messages sent to a mailing list. As with regular mail, people don't like to get unsolicited or unwanted e-mail, also known as spam. There are Web advertising agencies out there that will sell you on the idea that sending out unsolicited mail to millions of recipients all at once will bring you riches. In reality, it can bring you a lot of grief in the form of hate mail, and you can even get your Web site or domain name suspended. It is easy and much more pleasant to follow a few guidelines that will not get you in trouble, but will make your Web site successful.

The visitors to your Web site represent the best source for e-mail addresses. You can send out press releases announcing your new Web site and what it offers. It really helps, of course, if you can come up with an angle or hook that is newsworthy and timely. For more information on how to do this, read Chapter 5, Print Media. By all means, send your news release to the traditional media, such as newspapers and television and radio stations, but send it to online sources as well.

Some services that will send news releases to online services for you are:

PR News Target	www.newstarget.com/prnewstarget/htm
Internet News Bureau	www.newsbureau.com
URL Wire	www.urlwire.com/*4home.html
GINA Internet Wire	www.gina.com
Xpress Press	www.xpresspress.com

As you start to promote your Web site, it is a good idea to rent a list of e-mail addresses from a mailing list company and send your flyer or information to the people on this list. This is not the same as sending junk mail because a lot of the people whose names are on these mailing lists have expressed a desire to receive certain types of information. As an example, if you own a pet store, you can rent a list of people who have animals and want to receive information about products for their pets.

Here are some list companies you can contact:

American List Counsel	www.amlist.com
Edith Roman Associates	www.edithroman.com
SRDS	www.srds.com
Liszt	www.liszt.com
Reference.com	www.reference.com
Yahoo!	www.yahoo.com

If you want advertisers for your site, one place to begin is Web Site Sponsors (websitesponsors.com).

You should also list your Web site with several broadcast services. These companies will announce your site and get it listed in many directories. Some broadcast listing services are:

Add It!	www.liquidimaging.com

The Internet | 159

    Add Me!. . . . . www.addme.com

    Broadcaster . . . . www.broadcaster.com

    Central Registry. . . . . www.centralregistry.com

    Free Links. . . . . www.mgroup.com

    Incor's Free Classifieds . . . www.incor.com

    Quick Launch. . . . . www.quicklaunch.com

    Register It . . . . www.registerit.com

    Website Promote. . . . . www.websitepromote.com

    Promote One. . . . . www.promoteone.com

E-mail Newsletters

Be sure not to overlook e-mail newsletters as a place to announce your Web site. Most of the newsletters will want you to be a subscriber, but most offer a free subscription, so that shouldn't be a problem.

    Here are some e-mail newsletters and other sources:

    Newsurfer Digest . . . . www.netsurf.com/NSD/index.html

    Scout Report . . . . www.scout.cs.use.edu/scount/report

    Net Happenings www.mid.net.80/net

    Postmaster Direct . . . . www.postmasterdirect.com

    Web Promote . . . . www.webpromote.com

    TargIt . . . . www.targit.com

    Internet Newsletter Library (www.newsletter-library.com) provides links to newsletters covering over 500 topics.

    Newsletter Access (www.newsletteraccess.com) features over 5000 newsletters.

    Link Exchange (www.listex.com) features a list of e-mail newsletters that are interested in exchanging advertising.

> **COOL RESOURCES:**
> - *Pubnet (www.olympus.net/keefe/pubnet) offers hundreds of links for Internet and real-world publicity.*
> - *U.S. All Media E-mail Directory (www.editpros.com) is a list of e-mail addresses, phone numbers, and mailing addresses for members of the media.*

Newsgroups

There are literally thousands of newsgroups that you can submit your Web site to. A few of them are:

Biz.americast	Misc.news.internet.announce
Biz.comp	Biz.marketplace.international
Biz.comp.misc	Biz.marketplace.services
Biz.entreprenur	News:comp.internet.net-happening
Biz.marketplace	News:misc.intrepreneur
Misc.entrepreneur	News:tnn.internet

To find the various newsgroups, you need to type in keywords of what you are looking for and start searching. Keywords might include *announce, marketplace, business, commerce, developer, industry, sales, profit, small-business,* and *entrepreneur*.

Attracting Increased Business with Contests and Giveaways

Offering something for free is a great way to build traffic to your Web site. With the exception of sex, free is the hottest word in the English language. It doesn't matter what you want to give away as long as it has some perceived value. It could be a newsletter, a book, a television set, or a trip to the Bahamas. A giveaway is a way to build traffic to your Web site. It provides people with a reason to visit your site and gives you something to promote. When you are giving something away, you will not have any trouble finding people who are willing and able to help you promote it. It makes no difference whether it is an outright

The Internet

giveaway to all the visitors to your site or a contest that only one person will win. It is easy to promote your contest or giveaway and therefore your site. There are hundreds of sites that give away freebies that will help you promote your site; some of these are listed here:

Virtual Free Stuff . . . . www.dreamscape.com/franhvad/free.html

The Contest Catalog . . . . . www.contest.catalogue.com/contests

Free 'N Cool . . . . www.freencool.com

Contest Guide . . . . www.contestguide.com

Thread Treader www.4cyte.com/threadtreader

Get Free Banner Advertising

If you have surfed the Web, you have probably seen hundreds of banner ads. Banner ads are display ads that are normally at the top of Web pages. Most companies that use banner advertising are paying hundreds or even thousands of dollars for their ads. What many of them don't realize is that they can get these same ads for free. In fact, there are even Web advertising agencies that will sell advertising for you on your Web site if you have enough traffic.

You can get free banner ads on other Web sites by agreeing to a banner exchange. A banner exchange is similar to a co-op ad. Every time you display another company's ad on your site, you receive a credit, and then, based on the number of credits you receive, your banner ad will be displayed on other Web sites. The great thing about this arrangement is that when you are a member of a banner exchange group, the management of that group tracks when and where banners are displayed throughout the network. The group management will also give you statistics on how many times your banner was displayed and how many times someone clicked on the banner to visit your Web site.

Designing an Effective Banner Ad

Even if you get your banner displayed at thousands of other sites, it doesn't do you any good if no one clicks through to your site. Therefore, it is important to make your banner ad as effective as possible. Here are a few design tips for your banner ad:

- Animated ads pull considerably better than static ads.

- Put the words *click here* somewhere in the banner to make it easier for the viewer to visit your site.

- Add bold colors, such as green, yellow, and orange, to attract attention to the banner.

- Change the banner ads frequently.

- Make your ad simple. This way it will load faster, thereby creating a longer impression time.

- Use attention-grabbing words, such as *free, win,* or *new*.

> **HOT TIP** *If possible, pay for keyword banners on hot sites. Some search engines will sell keywords linked to your banner ad. If the keyword is entered by someone using the search engine, your banner ad will come up.*

Exchanging Your Banner Ad

Before you can exchange your banner ad, you must become a member of a specific banner exchange group. This usually involves filling out detailed paperwork on yourself, your business, and your Web site. After you complete the membership process, you will be given an html code that you can add to any page on your site. The purpose of this code is to display the banner advertising of other exchange members. After you receive the html code, the next step is to submit your banner to the exchange. Following are a few of the banner exchange groups:

    LinkExchange . . . . www.linkexchange.com

    Smartclicks. . . . . www.smartclicks.com

BannerSwap . . . . www.bannerswap.com

LinkTrader . . . . www.linktrader.com

Cyberlink Exchange 2000. . . . www.cyberlinkexchange.usww.com

This completes the chapter on marketing on the Internet. We have discussed many different techniques and resources, but in reality, we have not even scratched the surface. The Internet is such a vast innovative tool that we could write two or three books about it and still not cover every possible technique. We have covered as many of the important and basic techniques and resources as feasible in the limited space available here. We hope the information in this chapter will help you get started with your own Web presence.

Remember, there are thousands of other techniques and resources waiting for you to discover or even invent. To be successful at marketing on the Internet, it is important for you to search and research to find the methods that will help you use this powerful tool to reach your present and future customers.

CHAPTER 9

Third-Party Endorsements
Setting Up Your Own Endorsement Organization to Send You Customers and Increased Profits

The Chicago Bulls were playing. James Quinn escaped the pressures of his business long enough to plant himself in a seat at The United Center as the second quarter began. He wanted to see the Bulls win. He wanted to know that someone could win. James Quinn's business was in the toilet, swish, and going on down. So that night he watched the Bulls and tried to forget how frustrating it is to own a business.

The game was frenzied and the crowd was rowdy, but his mind kept wandering back to that familiar little store off I-55 where he had spent twelve hours a day for the last six years. Jordan scored, and jumping bodies surrounded James Quinn. As the crowd settled down, he began to notice all the advertisements surrounding him. Nike was there, of course, along with IBM. AT&T and Sprint were at opposite ends of the arena with large color-on-white banners. Coke had its ads splashed everywhere.

Endorsements—what a concept! Mr. Quinn wondered if Michael Jordan would endorse Quinn's Golf Center for a vastly reduced fee. No, that would never happen, but Quinn's Golf Center sure could use some hype.

BUSINESS MYTH:	MONEY TREE REALITY:
It is impossible for a small business to get an endorsement from an association and for the association to send a small business its members as customers.	It is extremely easy for a small and even a new business to set up its own association in order to get an endless flow of customers.

There are many business owners like Mr. Quinn, who are seeking advice for getting customers in the door. For Mr. Quinn, I recommended a third-party endorsement approach. It worked out well for him, and the costs were minimal. His new customer count grew by 40 percent in the first six months.

What Is a Third-Party Endorsement?

Simply put, a third-party endorsement is one legal entity or business recommending another to prospective customers. Entities that can give third-party endorsements include labor unions, banks, nonprofit organizations, credit unions, industry associations, and any other established organization that the public sees as reliable and trustworthy.

Think of all the shoes Michael Jordan has endorsed and sold for Nike, or all the Pepsi Michael Jackson has moved off grocery store shelves. For most small businesses, such as department stores, restaurants, insurance agencies, home improvement companies, attorneys, and accountants, there are no famous athletes or organizations lining up and waiting to endorse them. However, there are organizations that the public trusts that could be pinch hitters.

A perfect example of a well-known third-party endorsement company is the American Association of Retired Persons (AARP). The AARP routinely sends letters to members recommending specific insurance companies. Because of these letters, some members believe that the AARP sells insurance. The AARP is not an insurance company; however, it gets approximately $250 million per year in fees for endorsing certain insurance companies and other business products.

The AARP receives this money for referring its members to those insurance companies and other businesses. Imagine that! Companies pay a quarter of a billion dollars every year just for the right to use the AARP name. In turn, consumers purchase the insurance because they trust the company recommended by the AARP.

Put yourself in the position of a senior citizen in need of a Medicare supplemental insurance policy. If you received two letters, one from the ABC Insurance Company and one from the AARP, recommending the XYZ Insurance Company, which insurance plan would you purchase? Most seniors pay attention to the AARP's recommendations. The reason is simple: The AARP is a niche association that shares a common interest with senior citizens. It focuses on satisfying the needs of seniors. It is an organization that seniors recognize and trust.

> *You are the engine that*
> *propels success.*

This association is not the only one that endorses businesses. There are two ways you can get endorsements. First, you can approach established organizations and ask them to endorse your company in return for a percentage of your profits. I have used this approach with much success. In other chapters, I discuss ways I have done this with various organizations. Second, you can construct an organization. Creating an association can be an effective customer-generating technique. I prefer this method because it gives the business owner more control and in the long run produces more profit.

With a third-party endorsement program, it is simple to sell your product or service. People can be hesitant about dealing with a new or small business. Because these businesses are unfamiliar to the public, trust has not yet been established.

Human beings are creatures of habit. How many times have you driven past several Mom and Pop convenience stores to get to the 7-11? How often do you go to Wal-Mart or Kmart instead of a small locally owned department store? There is a concrete reason for this behavior—habit.

As the owner of a small business, you must break the public's habits. Customers need a reason to visit your business. The initial visit is the hardest to achieve. Once a customer walks through the door the first time, it is up to you to impress that customer. It is at this critical time that the customer decides to return or not. A third-party endorsement will bring first-time customers into your business. It overcomes a major obstacle, a potential customer's natural skepticism. When a trustworthy third party recommends a business, this gives customers a reason for breaking their habits.

Setting Up a Third-Party Endorsement Program

You can customize a third-party endorsement program to fit nearly any type of business. The first thing to consider is how to reach the customer. Open your mind. Put yourself in the customer's shoes. Consider things from the customer's point of view. Certain questions can give you insight into your target customer.

Keeping in mind all you know about the customers you are trying to reach, look at the questions on the customer profile for Quinn's Golf Center (Sample 9.1), which sells retail golf equipment and operates a small driving range. Sample 9.2 is a blank customer profile that you can photocopy to answer these questions for your customers.

The customer profile will help you determine several things about your current and prospective customers: who they are, the best places to find them, and how to reach them in an effective manner, all while promoting interest in your product or service.

Consider this: the information on the customer profile is potentially worth more than Michael Jordan's 24-karat Nikes! When you have completed the customer profile, you will have a profile of your target customers. You will know what they like and dislike, what occupies their time, what they read, where they go, and what you can use to grab their attention and get them walking through your door.

As a business owner, it is very important to know who your customers are. If you don't know everything about them, ask them to fill out a survey about their likes and dislikes, hobbies, and so forth. If necessary, give them a discount off a purchase to provide this information.

We all recognize that information is valuable, and we know that most successful companies began by gathering this kind of information. Gaining insight into what you need to do to bring in customers is vital. Once you have this information, you will be able to pinpoint a niche of potential customers on which to focus. It makes no difference whether you are marketing to farmers, plumbers, doctors, bankers, construction workers, nurses, government employees, or accountants. Once you have the information, you can clearly identify your niche. The key is to keep a narrow focus. Make potential customers feel special and recognize them as belonging to an exclusive group. The next step is to analyze the information and customize it to fit the product or service offered by your company.

When working with third-party endorsements, it is crucial to analyze the company and determine the best way to present the endorsement to a customer. Sample 9.3 is a business profile for Quinn's Golf Center. The questions will assist you in understanding how your business fits with a customer's needs. Sample 9.4 is a blank business profile that you can use for your own business. By answering the questions on the customer and business profiles, you can analyze your niche market and develop a marketing strategy.

Sample 9.1 Completed Customer Profile for Quinn's Golf Center.

CUSTOMER PROFILE

1. What are my customers' interests or hobbies?

   Leisure activities, travel, golf.

2. What sets my customers apart from other people?

   They are usually in an upper-income bracket.

3. What is the general income bracket of my customers?

   $50,000 to $100,000 plus.

4. Does the employment status of my customers affect my ability to sell to them?

   Yes. They are usually executives, lawyers, accountants, doctors, etc.

5. What type of magazines or local papers do my customers read?

   Golf Digest, Golf Tips, Golf Magazine, Wall Street Journal.

6. What percentage of my customers are homeowners and renters?

   Usually, they are homeowners.

7. In what general area do my customers live?

   Upper-income areas, by country clubs.

8. What can I offer that will cut through the solicitations my customers receive and make them take notice of my business?

   A referral from the Golfers' Benefit Association, which recommends Quinn's Golf Center and offers them The Directory of Golf Courses in the United States absolutely free.

Sample 9.2 **Reproducible Customer Profile Form for Your Business**

CUSTOMER PROFILE

1. What are my customers' interests or hobbies?

   _____

2. What sets my customers apart from other people?

   _____

3. What is the general income bracket of my customers?

   _____

4. Does the employment status of my customers affect my ability to sell to them?

   _____

5. What type of magazines or local papers do my customers read?

   _____

6. What percentage of my customers are homeowners and renters?

   _____

7. In what general area do my customers live?

   _____

8. What can I offer that will cut through the solicitations my customers receive and make them take notice of my business?

   _____

   _____

   _____

Sample 9.3 **Completed Business Profile for Quinn's Golf Center.**

BUSINESS PROFILE

1. How long has my business been in operation?
   2 years.

2. Where is a convenient location for my customers?
   Suburban areas.

3. What makes my business unique?
   An indoor putting range and computer driving range.

4. What needs does my business fill?
   In addition to golf equipment, we carry a large selection of golf wear.

5. What awards or accolades has my business received?
   None.

6. What is my business offering?
   Products needed by golfers. We have an extensive order system.

7. Do I have any vendors that can add credibility to my business?
   Yes, various golf equipment manufacturers.

8. What niche does my company market to?
   Executive men and women.

9. How do my competitors present their businesses?
   Competitors only have basic equipment.

10. What type of marketing has worked in the past?
    Newspaper advertisements.

11. Why did past marketing techniques fail or bring only minimal results?
    Not being focused; contacting many people who could not afford our products.

12. How does the community view my business?
    I don't know.

Sample 9.4 **Reproducible Business Profile Form for Your Business.**

> **BUSINESS PROFILE**
>
> 1. How long has my business been in operation?
>   _____
>
> 2. Where is a convenient location for my customers?
>   _____
>
> 3. What makes my business unique?
>   _____
>
> 4. What needs does my business fill?
>   _____
>
> 5. What awards or accolades has my business received?
>   _____
>
> 6. What is my business offering?
>   _____
>
> 7. Do I have any vendors that can add credibility to my business?
>   _____
>
> 8. What niche does my company market to?
>   _____
>
> 9. How do my competitors present their businesses?
>   _____
>
> 10. What type of marketing has worked in the past?
>   _____
>
> 11. Why did past marketing techniques fail or bring only minimal results?
>   _____
>
> 12. How does the community view my business?
>   _____

Think of yourself as an intermediary. On the right side is the product or service; on the left is the customer who needs this product or service. You are the bridge that can bring them together. What a moneymaker that bridge can be when it is built correctly!

Look at the profile of your target customer. Please remember that this is niche focusing, not discrimination of any kind. Now compare the customer profile with the business evaluation. There are aspects of the two lists that will correspond and seem naturally compatible.

> **HOT TIP**
> *A great way to reach a target market is to rent a list of people with professional licenses from the state. For example, you can contact the State Nursing Board to rent a list of all the nurses in your state.*

Mailing Lists—The Key to Third-Party Endorsements

Many companies sell or rent mailing lists. Mailing lists are available for nearly any subject or niche market. The lists are categorized according to specific criteria, such as occupation, age, income, hobbies, geographical area, and nationality. The local yellow pages is a good place to start when seeking a mailing list company. You can find the names of several such companies and tips for dealing with mailing list companies and list brokers in Chapter 3, Direct Mail.

As an example, if Quinn's Golf Center set up the Golfers' Benefit Association in order to increase sales, the association could rent a list of subscribers to *Golf Digest* magazine. This can be done one of two ways: by calling the subscription department of *Golf Digest* and asking if the magazine rents its subscribers' list, or by calling a mailing list company to rent the subscriber list for *Golf Digest* or other golf magazines. Often the mailing list account representative will be able to suggest another list that will be even more successful.

> **HOT TIP**
> *A list of magazine subscribers is usually the best list to rent if you are focusing on a particular niche market. Today there are magazines aimed at almost every niche group. A quick way to research magazines is an online resource called The Electronic Newsstand at www.enews.com.*

Here's something to think about: Instead of spending $15,000 for an advertisement in *Golf Digest* that will reach unwanted markets, you can spend $350 to rent a mailing list of 5000 golfers in your target area. Even if selling nationwide is your goal, it is a good idea to test the market before you spend $15,000 on a print ad in a magazine. Procter & Gamble and McDonald's always give products a trial run in specific areas and stores before releasing them to a broader market.

As mentioned in Chapter 3 with regard to direct mail, make sure you request names, addresses, and telephone numbers from the list company. You will need telephone numbers to do follow-up calls. Also, request the most recent list available. Companies keep lists for long periods, and if you do not specifically request an up-to-date list, you may get a high percentage of old addresses. That means that mail will be returned, which is a waste of resources and time.

On average, renting a mailing list costs between $70 and $100 per 1000 names. Most companies offer preprinted labels, which is convenient and time-saving. There is usually a minimum amount required to rent, normally 5000 names.

> **HOT TIP**
> *Try to get more for your money: Tell the mailing list company that you will rent the list if the company will give you additional names (1000 to 2000) for free. It never hurts to ask, and the worst the company can do is say no.*

When you receive the list, make a copy before peeling off the labels. If you have been supplied a copy of the list, put it in a safe place. You will need a hard copy of it later.

There are free options if renting a mailing list is too expensive. You can use the city directory, which is available at the public library in most cities. The city directory gives the following information: whether the individual is a homeowner and how long he or she has been so, the economic status of the area where the person lives, the person's employer, and the phone number and address. Once you have filled out and analyzed the customer profile, you should know enough about your potential customers to use the city directory to locate your target market.

> **HOT TIP**
> *If you use the city directory frequently, it is a good idea to lease it. This gives you easy access and saves time. Most city directories are also available in CD-ROM format.*

The customer profile for Quinn's Golf Center showed the need to target high-income areas located close to a country club or golf course. If Mr. Quinn could not afford to rent a mailing list, he could go to the public library and compile his own list. He could locate the streets in affluent areas and write down the names, addresses, and telephone numbers of the people who live on those streets. By doing this, he creates a mailing list that costs him nothing. A list of directory companies can be found in Chapter 3, Direct Mail.

With the list prepared or on its way from the mailing list company, you have the names of prospective customers, but there are still a few more considerations. So put on your Nikes, it's time to go out and become a professional endorsing association.

> **HOT TIP** *Once you have built up your own mailing list, you can create an additional source of revenue by renting out your list to other companies.*

Setting Up the Association Office

When you as a business owner set up a third-party endorsement association, there are two ways to ensure that potential customers are not misled. The first way is to have a second person legally set up the association. If you are on the board of directors of the association, mention this fact in any letters sent to potential customers. The second way is to use envelopes from the association so that potential customers are intrigued enough to open the envelope, but to have the actual letter printed on your business letterhead.

If a second person starts the association, that person could spend time on it and arrange for additional benefits, such as low-cost group health insurance, life insurance, travel benefits, and product discounts. (Be sure to check the laws on this in your area; they vary from state to state.)

Once I consulted for the owner of a Canadian business that sold to manufacturers in Canada and the United States. Her lawyer liked the association idea so much that he set up a manufacturers' association. He arranged for members to receive group health insurance, travel benefits, group advertising, low-cost long distance, and other benefits. He even set up cooperative discounting for members purchasing from one another and from outside sources. This program will work if it is carried out properly.

The association needs an address. If you have a second person set up the association and that person has a business address, use that for the association's address. If this is not possible, but the association cannot afford an office, there are other alternatives.

One affordable option is to rent a mailbox from Mailboxes Etc. or another mailbox rental company. These companies are always professional, and they offer other services, such as copying and faxing. The average cost of renting is around $40 for a three-month period, depending on the area in which you live. Some companies offer a bonus for renting for a longer time, such as a free month in return for a six-month rental. These are usually good deals. Any of the box rental services will suffice. Look for these companies in the yellow pages.

> **HOT TIP**
>
> *If you have a home-based business, use a mail service such as Mailboxes Etc. for the business address. This makes your business appear more professional and will keep unexpected visitors away from your home.*

Make sure that the mail service you choose has a street address and uses only one suite number. The address should look like this: Golfers' Benefit Association, 1011 Pennsylvania Avenue, Suite 302 (your box number), Des Moines, IA 50310. Do not use a suite number with two sets of numbers or even letters, as this is an instant clue to any customer that the address is that of a mailbox service.

One other word of advice on mailing addresses: Do not use a P.O. box as the address of your endorsing association. If you employ a P.O. box address, customers will automatically be skeptical. Don't make your job any harder. You want the association to be professional.

It is also a good idea to get an additional telephone line exclusively for the association. You will rarely get calls on this line, but it is still a good idea to have a separate telephone number. Offer customers a free membership in the association. Put a small percentage of each sale you make into the association's bank account. Use these funds to provide more benefits to the members.

Printed letterhead and envelopes purchased through a local office supply store or printer will cost around $100 for 500 copies and envelopes. If you want to avoid this expense and you have a computer or word processor, you can print the letterhead yourself and then make copies.

For a cheaper route on envelopes, purchase a self-inking stamp giving the name and address of the association. Stamp all the envelopes going out. It sounds as if this would take a long time, but it goes much faster than you might expect. You can purchase self-inking stamps from a stamp company (look for a listing in the yellow pages) or from an office supply store. The cost is $25 or less, and self-inking stamps last for years.

Remember that the goal is to create an association that is separate from your company. This may seem like a minor detail, but it could mean the difference between the third-party endorsement program you are launching being successful or being a waste of time and money.

Rule for Endorsing Letters—Simple Is Better

Now it is time to write the letter from the endorsing association. It has been my experience that the rule of thumb is simplicity. It is tempting to give all the secrets away, to divulge all the services your business provides. I advise against this approach. I have done both, a simple letter and a descriptive letter. A simple letter produces better results.

The endorsing letter has two specific purposes: to give credibility to the endorsed business and to introduce the customer to the business. The purpose of an endorsing letter is not to sell your product or service. This task falls to you once customers come in and you are face-to-face with them. The endorsing letter is an enticement to customers to come into your business and nothing more. It is similar to an introduction from a friend or word-of-mouth advertising. It tells a prospective customer that the business is a good company, one that the association is recommending.

When the customer receives the letter, he or she will be interested in the contents and open it immediately. Samples 9.5 and 9.6 show two letters that can be adapted to fit any business. One is from the Golfers' Benefit Association, the other from Quinn's Golf Center. Look over the two letters and decide which approach you prefer. Remember, it is important not to deceive the potential customer.

> **HOT TIP** *Endorsement letters should be no longer than one page. When writing the endorsement letter, keep these two words in mind: simplicity and enticement.*

Sample 9.5 **Model Endorsement Letter (from the Association).**

GOLFERS' BENEFIT ASSOCIATION
1011 Pennsylvania Avenue
Suite 302
Des Moines, IA 50310

Dear Stephen,

    The Golfers' Benefit Association is pleased to announce that we have made arrangements for you to receive a 20 percent discount card from Quinn's Golf Center, located at 1025 Main Street. In addition, if you stop in within the next seven days, you may try out their driving range free. You will also receive the book *10 Ways to Improve Your Golf Game* absolutely free with any purchase of $50 or more.

    Don't hesitate! Take advantage of these benefits offered to members of the Golfers' Benefit Association by Quinn's Golf Center.

Thank you,

Jessie Mendenhall

*James Quinn is on the Golfers' Benefit Association's Board of Directors.

Sample 9.6 **Model Endorsement Letter (from the Business).**

QUINN'S GOLF CENTER
1025 Main Street
Des Moines, IA 50307

Dear Stephen,

Quinn's Golf Center is pleased to announce that you are entitled to a free membership in the Golfers' Benefit Association. As a member, you can receive a 20 percent discount on all merchandise from our store.

In addition, if you stop in within the next seven days, we welcome you to try our driving range for free. The remarkable book *10 Ways to Improve Your Golf Game* is absolutely free with any purchase of $50 or more.

Don't hesitate! Take advantage of these benefits offered only to members of the Golfers' Benefit Association by Quinn's Golf Center.

Thank you,

James Quinn

Once, as an experiment, I tried sending out two different letters. Both letters came from the association, but one mentioned that the company's owner was on the association's board of directors and the other did not. I received an identical response from both letters. The reason is simple: Once you get customers' attention with a good offer, they will be interested in what you have to say.

A cynical person might look at the letter in Sample 9.5 and think that it is too simple, that no one would believe it or respond to it. That person would be wrong. Mr. Quinn anticipated some results from his letter, but what he got far exceeded his expectations. He got tremendous results from this so-called simple letter. You will have the same results if you put forth the effort and follow these easy steps to third-party endorsements.

> **HOT TIP**
>
> *If third-party endorsements prove to be a good customer-generating technique, send out letters every six to eight weeks. In most cases, repeat mailings produce the same response rate. Remember that you are actually renting the list of names, and so the mailing list company may have some of its own names on the list. The mailing list company may ask you to pay to rent the list each time you do a mailing.*

You can customize this letter to fit any product or service. The letter you send should:

1. Help the customer feel a part of a special and select group.

2. Entice the customer to patronize the business by offering a special reward or discount.

3. Encourage the customer to act now by rewarding immediate action with a bonus. (Overcome procrastination by giving the customer a reason for a quick response.)

> **HOT TIP**
>
> *When a customer comes into your business, have a drawing for a prize or a "request for a free gift form" for the customer to fill out. This can be the start of a mailing list of your customers. Use this list often to send out mailings—for example, a monthly new product and free offers newsletter or an "our specials" flyer or brochure.*

> *Only those who fail greatly*
> *can ever achieve greatly.*
> —Robert F. Kennedy

Some important considerations in customizing an endorsing letter to fit your business are:

- You always remember the words *simplicity* and *enticement*.

- The letter tells the customer that your business specifically fills her or his needs.

- The endorsing association is doing the customer a favor by recommending the business.

- The association is knowledgeable about the business and has decided to put its reputation on the line to endorse this business.

- The endorsing letter gives the customer an opportunity to take advantage of special status as a member of a unique group.

- This unique status of the customer is used to create an endorsement letter that fits the business.

- The letter tells the customer to expect service and value when coming to the business.

How many letters should you send out? Keeping in mind the steadily rising cost of postage, I recommend 1000 letters as a trial run. This number will help you track the percentage of your customers who have come into your business because of the endorsing letter. However, the number of pieces you should ultimately send out depends on your business and your financial situation. At the time of this writing, postage, printing, and envelopes for sending out 1000 letters will cost approximately $400.

Tracking the format, numbers, and results is important. Keep records on the type of letter, the number of letters, and the results—positive and negative. When you send letters to several niche groups, keep track of the results and determine which niche group brings in the best results. After compiling these results, focus on the most productive niche group.

This tracking of returns gives you the numbers you need to ascertain if the third-party endorsement program is (1) paying for itself and (2) increasing your profits. The profit calculation will depend on your type of business and the amount of markup. If your business has a high markup rate, there should be plenty of leeway for the cost of this program. If your business has a low markup, this program may not be the right one for you. If it is not, there are other customer-generating programs in this book that will suit your type of business.

> **HOT TIP**
> *When you send out a mailing, you achieve success before your product is ever seen. Your sales depend on your mailing package, not your product.*

How to Boost Results with Customer Follow-Up

After you have sent the letters, you need to decide whether you want to establish a follow-up program. You can follow up with a call, inviting the customer to visit your business. You may decide not to do follow-up and just depend on the letter to bring customers to your business. Personally, I believe in being proactive. How often have you received a telephone call inviting you to a local business? How would you feel if a theater called to invite you to see the newest hit movie and offered you a free bucket of popcorn? Most people would feel highly flattered. I would be willing to bet that you would see a movie that weekend, even if you didn't like popcorn.

> **HOT TIP**
> *If you send out more than 1000 letters, it is productive to vary the letter slightly. This will help you determine which letter approach and offers work the best. If you plan to send out 5000 letters, you could have five different letters and/or offers. Use five different extensions if the customer is calling or five different names on the letter if the customer is coming into your business. Doing this makes the results easier to track.*

Third-Party Endorsements

As a business owner, you may not have the time to make follow-up calls. If this is the case, hire someone to make the calls and pay that person an hourly wage. It is money well spent. When you hire a phone person, make sure to test that person out over the telephone to see how his or her voice sounds and how comfortable she or he is talking on the phone. Some people can sound very pleasant and controlled when speaking face to face, but once the telephone is in their hand, the entire situation changes.

Sample 9.7 is a script I composed for James Quinn and the Golfers' Benefit Association. As you can see, in this script, I took advantage of the opportunity presented and offered the customer one more reason to shop at Quinn's Golf Center. Mr. Quinn and I believed that if old habits were broken and customers came to his store just once, they would be very satisfied and would return regularly.

> **COOL RESOURCE:** You can purchase the National Directory of Mailing Lists, which is a list of over 15,000 mailing lists that are available for purchase. Contact Oxbridge Communications, 1 (800) 955-0231.

Sample 9.7 Telephone Script for Customer Follow-Up.

> *Is Stephen in? Hi, Stephen, this is _____, and I'm calling about a letter sent to you a few days ago from the Golfers' Benefit Association regarding a special discount at Quinn's Golf Center. Do you remember receiving the letter?*
>
> *Great! The reason I'm calling is to personally invite you to our store and ask if you have any questions about the discounts that you'll be receiving. We've got a fantastic promotion going this week; if you come in, you'll also receive a free gift. Our hours are 9:00 a.m. to 10:00 p.m. Do you have any questions? No? We look forward to seeing you, Stephen. Be sure to bring the letter in to get your free gift.*
>
> *Thank you!*

Third-party endorsements work for almost any type of business, whether it is a large or small company at a commercial location or out of your home.

I have helped various businesses make a lot of money with this technique. As an example, in 1992 I met Jean Hargrove, the owner of a home health aide business she ran out of her house. Her business was struggling, and she was ready to throw in the towel. Her clients loved her and she had a great reputation for making good client care a top priority, but several of her clients had passed away during the previous six months, and she had been unable to get new ones. Since she had less than $300 to generate new clients, Jean's business was in severe trouble.

We immediately put a third-party endorsement plan to work. An associate of hers set up an association, got a mailing address for the association, and went to the library and compiled a list of retired people from the city directory. Then Jean sent out a letter from the association and called people back a few days later. She spent less than $300 and in 60 days, she had fifteen new clients.

John James ran a small health insurance agency out of his back bedroom. He set the goal of building one of the largest insurance agencies in the country. To achieve this goal, he began by setting up an association for the self-employed. This association provided numerous benefits to self-employed business owners. It also enabled John James to build up his insurance agency so that within ten years he bought out the insurance company for which he had been selling.

Are these examples out of the ordinary? No. There is nothing to keep you from experiencing the same kind of success with a third-party endorsement program. By putting this program into action you will see how easy it is to do and how well it works.

> **HOT TIP**
>
> *When doing follow-up telephone calls, always ask for the potential customer by first name only. Do not ask for Mr. Jones or Mrs. Stephen Jones. The public is knowledgeable about the techniques of telemarketers. Using Mr. or Mrs. is an immediate clue to a customer that you are a telemarketer, and the customer will automatically put up his or her guard. If you use the customer's first name, the customer will assume that someone he or she knows is calling.*

Customizing This Program

From the examples in this chapter, it should be obvious that you can customize a third-party endorsement program to fit almost any business.

Here is a ten-step outline for third-party endorsements:

1. Determine and understand the target customer.
2. Decide on the niche focus.
3. Choose a name for the association.
4. Rent a mailing list.
5. Get letterhead and envelopes printed for the association.
6. Write the endorsing letter.
7. Send out letters to mailing list prospects.
8. Personally call customers and invite them to your business.
9. Create ways to make customers feel welcome at your business.
10. Smile when a customer walks in the door.

If you follow these ten steps, you can anticipate a substantial increase in profits. However, if this program is to be successful, it is vital that you be persistent. Third-party endorsements are effective, but this is only one program outlined. Reading this entire book will open other avenues of customer-generating techniques to add to your business arsenal.

CHAPTER 10

Associations and Organizations

Aligning Your Business with Labor Unions, Credit Unions, and Banks to Make the Business an Overnight Success

Priscilla Daniels has a best friend she calls Lou. Lou takes very good care of her. Lou also has a wide scope of influence in the community. He has many "best friends" besides Priscilla, and he helps every one of them. Not only that, Lou has connections at the best companies, and he helped Priscilla get a healthy raise last spring. Her raise was so good, in fact, that she bought a van for her family instead of the small car she had planned to get.

Two years ago, Priscilla had major surgery. Lou made sure that her employer paid for it. When Leslie, Priscilla's daughter, got braces during the summer, Lou made sure that this expense also got covered.

Priscilla tells everyone how great Lou is and that her life wouldn't be nearly as good without him. With Lou's help, Priscilla has accumulated over $50,000 toward retirement.

BUSINESS MYTH:	MONEY TREE REALITY:
People are independent thinkers; they don't like being told what to do.	The majority of people are followers. If the president of a labor union or some other association suggests that they visit a business, they will follow the recommendation.

Yesterday, Lou sent a note to Priscilla inviting her to check out a new business in town. Lou being her best friend, of course she said yes. After all he's done for her, how could she refuse?

Imagine that it's your business that Lou has suggested that Priscilla visit. If Lou recommends your business to Priscilla, do you think she will try out your products or services? Of course she will!

Who is Lou? To Priscilla and the millions across America like her, Lou is a trusted friend, nearly a member of the family. But who, or rather what, is Lou in real life? Lou is Priscilla's nickname for her labor union.

This chapter is about connecting your business to organizations and associations such as labor unions, credit unions, service clubs, professional guilds, banks, community associations, and trade associations. By establishing a relationship with an association, you build rapport with all the association's members. Think of this marketing approach as getting an introduction to a large number of people from a community and economic leader they respect and trust.

American consumers are influenced by associations in mostly positive ways. Using associations to introduce your business means deep market penetration. It gives you an opportunity to reach people who otherwise might be inaccessible to you.

The association and organization marketing technique will give you exactly the kind of marketing scope you need to either establish a customer base or increase your customer flow. The success of this technique hinges on your business being customer-friendly and a constructive element in the community. Keep this in mind as we begin.

> **HOT TIP**: *If you create a valuable benefit for a union's members, the union president will be more than willing to do business with you, because he or she will be a hero to the members.*

What Is an Organization or Association Endorsement?

In the simplest terms, an organization or association endorsement occurs when your business arranges, with the assistance of the group's leaders, to market its products or services to the members of that group. For example, you might make such an arrangement with a community group made up of local businesspeople who can use your product or service.

Associations and Organizations

With this technique, you capitalize on the close relationship between a group's leadership and its members. If an association or organization recommends your business, the chances are good that the members will trust you to be reputable and professional.

In order to get and maintain this type of endorsement, it is imperative that you come to the bargaining table ready, willing, and in a position to provide exceptional customer service and a quality product or service. Associations and organizations do not recommend a company unless they are confident that the business is sound, the products and services are of high quality, and the association's members will be treated with respect and generosity.

Many companies know that marketing through an association or organization is good for business, but they don't go the next step and consider this technique an effective way to cultivate prospective customers.

What does the organization that recommends you want in return? It wants its members to feel part of a special group and to receive select benefits that are not available to the public.

Recently, when driving around Oklahoma City, I saw two car dealerships with signs that said "Credit Union Members Welcome." These business owners believe that putting out a sign will draw customers who are members of an association. This approach, while passive and unimaginative, will bring in a certain number of customers. On the other hand, the car dealerships could take this approach to the next level by creating an alliance with the leadership of several local credit unions. Suppose credit union members received a letter from the president of the credit union with a certificate for a $500 discount on a new car at your dealership. How many then do you suppose would shop for a new car with you?

If you were one of these car dealerships, you would get more business from a recommendation letter than from a big sign in the front window of the showroom. The credit union earns appreciation from its members for passing on a $500 discount. The members receive a discount and better service because of their special status as a part of the credit union.

Using an association or organization endorsement can work especially well if your business is either new or new to the area. When an organization recommends your business, you become a friend of a friend, a company that is worthy and trusted. Breaking down the barrier of unfamiliarity and giving people a reason to consider you will increase the number of potential customers who come to your business. Once they walk through the door or pick up the telephone, making them loyal and happy customers is up to you. It goes without saying that it is up to you to treat a person so well that he or she becomes a lifelong customer. For more information on this aspect of customer generation, see Chapter 13, Charming Customers into Your Business.

> **HOT TIP** *Getting an endorsement from an association will bring your business instant credibility and profits.*

The Advantages of Marketing to Organizations and Associations

Marketing to associations will produce a great deal of interest in your product or service on the part of the prospects you contact. When I set up a program of this type for an insurance agency, it yielded over a 90 percent draw rate. (A draw rate is the percentage of prospects who respond with interest to your product or service.) While you need to customize this technique to fit your business, it is common to get a 50 percent draw rate from the members of labor unions, credit unions, and banks.

The second reason associations are a superb source for customer generation is the time this technique saves. This program is simple to implement and time-efficient because most organizations keep their member lists current and compiled in such a way that they can be easily used for mailings. Therefore, by contacting and establishing a relationship with a few key people, you can gain access to hundreds, and in some cases thousands, of prospective customers.

Another factor to consider when using an association marketing program is the public image of your company. If you choose to work with an organization or association that serves the community, that association's reputation will reflect on your business as well. Prospective customers will view your business as being aware of and interested in community involvement and betterment.

Three Versions of the Association Marketing Program

In the remainder of this chapter, we will cover the three main versions of an association marketing program: reaching customers through labor unions, credit unions, and banks. For the most part, the techniques introduced here are interchangeable from association to association. We will also discuss the process for setting up such a program.

As you read, remember that these techniques can be modified to fit any business and any type of organization or association. The only limit is your imagination and what is appropriate for your business. I chose to highlight these three key venues because they fit the needs of most businesses. Feel free to improvise and use the ideas and scripts presented here to fit the business and association scenarios that are compatible with your unique niche.

> **HOT TIP** *Labor unions will give you the best draw rate from your marketing campaigns.*

Of all the associations I have ever dealt with, labor unions have produced the best results. They offer a potential draw rate of over 90 percent.

In the United States there are approximately 5700 labor unions, from an anthropologists' union to a zoological workers' union. Out of all these possibilities, you can certainly find a labor union whose members will be interested in your product or service.

I have used this program for many types of businesses. One example that comes immediately to mind is a program I established for a restaurant.

Jerry Kirkpatrick had owned the Maple Square Restaurant for three months when he came to me for marketing advice. He wanted to cater to a mostly blue-collar clientele, but he was having trouble getting people to try his restaurant the first time. The location was good, but there were three other restaurants within two blocks. The other restaurants were well established, and Jerry couldn't get people through his door. He was running out of time and money. I consulted with him, and we agreed that a labor union marketing program would best fit his budget and reach the most prospective customers for his buck. After implementing this program, Jerry got better than expected results that helped him keep customers coming in at a regular rate. You will learn more about Jerry's success later in this chapter.

Credit unions produce the second best results. They provide a business owner with a unique avenue for reaching prospects, and they carry a certain air of self-reliance that may be appealing to your prospective customers. If your potential customers will be coming from one locale, using a credit union marketing program is an excellent choice.

According to the Center for Credit Union Research, today there are over 11,000 credit unions, with a combined membership of over 72 million people. How's that for a target market for your business?

According to the FDIC, there are over 10,000 banks in the United States. How many different banks do you drive by on a daily basis? Have you considered that banks could be an unmatched resource for generating new customers?

> **HOT TIP**
> *If you plan to work with banks, you will have better luck in small towns than in large cities. Credit union marketing programs can be successful in either large or small cities.*

Some types of businesses do well with a bank marketing program. While this requires a slightly different approach and can be a harder sell initially, the results are excellent, since a bank's list of customers continually grows and comprises a wide cross section of a city's population. If your product or service has general appeal, a bank marketing program could be your answer to bringing in new customers.

After reading this chapter, it should be clear to you which type of program will be best for your business. Perhaps more than one of these techniques will provide good results. It is my sincere belief that you will experience success with these marketing programs if you follow them to the letter.

Examples of Association or Organization Endorsements

An association or organization endorsement program can be customized to fit almost any type of business. Whether you have an insurance agency, a movie theater, a day care center, or a retail outlet, this technique can work for you. There are literally thousands of different associations and organizations available to use with this program. If you consider what specific segments of the public are most likely to have a need for your business, it will become easy to find a complementary association or organization to approach.

If your business is a therapeutic massage center or spa, for example, then you would want to approach, say, a labor union whose members have physically strenuous or stressful jobs, or perhaps an association of professionals who like to treat themselves. On the other hand, if your business is an automotive repair shop with a wide appeal, you would want to use an approach that reaches a large number of people, such as a hospital's credit union or a secretaries' union.

A lumberyard owner selecting the members of a carpenters' local union would be an example of a good complementary approach. If your business sells computers, you could aim for members of the International Union of Technical Engineers. An office supply store might target members of the International Federation of Teachers. Perhaps your business has such wide appeal that you can sell your product or service to the members of all the associations or organizations mentioned above.

One important factor is to approach each association separately. Make each one feel that it has been specially selected as worthy of your individualized attention. Help each organization feel that you have given a good deal of consideration to the organization as a unique group and that you are interested in this organization because what you offer can be beneficial for the group's membership.

Setting Up the Association or Organization Endorsement

Step 1: Understanding Your Prospective Customers

As we've seen in other chapters, the best way to begin a new marketing program is to take a close look at your prospective customers. What desires and needs do your prospective customers have that your product or service can fill? For example, if you were selling and installing wall-to-wall carpeting, you would probably be wasting your time if you targeted an association of people who rented apartments rather than owning homes. A homeowners' association would be a much more fruitful prospect. What added value would entice a person to come to your business instead of to a competitor? Where do your prospective customers spend most of their time? What are their hobbies? How can they be reached?

Try to step into your customer's life and see the world through her or his eyes. As you answer certain questions, the picture of your prospective customer will get clearer and you will begin to know that customer better. You will come to clearly understand why that person would buy your product or service and what kinds of enticements might bring him or her to your business. Along with this valuable information, you also find out the best place to contact your would-be customers. Look at the questions and answers on the customer profile illustrated in Sample 10.1. (Sample 10.2 gives a blank customer profile that

Sample 10.1 **Completed Customer Profile for Jerry's Restaurant.**

CUSTOMER PROFILE: JERRY'S RESTAURANT

1. What are my customers' interests or hobbies?
   Leisure activities, bowling, spending time with family.

2. What sets my customers apart from other people?
   They are hard workers and family oriented.

3. What is the general income bracket of my customers?
   $10,000 to $30,000.

4. Are my customers blue-collar (laborers) or white-collar (professional or executive) workers? Will this affect their purchasing decisions?
   They are blue-collar workers. Value at a reasonable price is important to them.

5. Do my customers enjoy good benefits from their employers?
   No. They have basic benefits such as health insurance and a small life insurance policy, but no disability.

6. What percentage of my customers are homeowners and renters?
   They are probably half and half homeowners and renters.

7. In what general area do my customers live?
   Middle-income areas.

8. What categories of associations are good candidates to help me reach customers?
   Level 1 and Level 2 (the levels are explained later in this chapter).

9. What associations should I contact?
   American Federation of Teachers; American Postal Workers Union; Carpenters; AFL-CIO; Iron Workers Union.

Sample 10.2 Reproducible Customer Profile Form for Your Business.

CUSTOMER PROFILE

1. What are my customers' interests or hobbies?
   _____

2. What sets my customers apart from other people?
   _____

3. What is the general income bracket of my customers?
   _____

4. Are my customers blue-collar (laborers) or white-collar (professional or executive) workers? Will this affect their purchasing decisions?
   _____

5. Do my customers enjoy good benefits from their employers?
   _____
   _____

6. What percentage of my customers are homeowners and renters?
   _____

7. In what general area do my customers live?
   _____

8. What categories of associations are good candidates to help me reach customers?
   _____

9. What associations should I contact?
   _____
   _____

you can photocopy to answer these questions for your specific business and prospective customers.) The profile helps you determine several things about your current and prospective customers. For example, you can compile information about their interests, what type of unions they belong to, and whether or not pricing affects their purchasing decisions. The profile will also give you hints on what type of service and value your customers expect.

After you have completed the customer profile, the insight you will have gained will give you a general idea of which associations or organizations will work best for you. Keep in mind that this customer profile is only a guide to help you on your way to more thoroughly understanding your customers.

Step 2: Determining Which Association or Organization to Approach

There are two main categories of organizations or associations that you should consider when you are deciding which to approach with this kind of marketing program. First, look for organizations that naturally complement your business. Look at the examples given elsewhere in this chapter for some initial ideas. Second, look at organizations that have a broad and general membership. I recommend choosing two organizations from the first category (those that complement your business) and at least one from the second (those with general membership). Working with three organizations simultaneously is enough to make the program successful, and yet the amount of resources required will not be overwhelming.

> **COOL RESOURCE:** *Learn how to sell to the government by contacting Penton Publications, 1100 Superior Avenue, Cleveland, OH 44114, 1 (216) 696-7658; or Panoptic Enterprises, P.O. Box 1099, Woodbridge, VA 22193, 1 (703) 670-2812.*

When you compile a list of associations, the first place you should look is the yellow pages, under the headings of Associations, Labor Unions, and Credit Unions. If a union you are interested in is not listed in the yellow pages, you can call the national headquarters to get the address and telephone number of the local closest to you.

If you have a computer, you can also search through major search engines, or check into the Big Yellow electronic version of the yellow pages to find contact information.

Associations and Organizations

COOL RESOURCE: *Big Yellow can be found at www.bigyellow.com.*

Following is a list of unions along with an indication of the income level of the majority of the members. In general, Level 1 represents annual incomes up to $20,000, Level 2 represents annual incomes of $20,001 to $40,000, and Level 3 represents annual incomes over $40,001.

Union	Telephone	Level
AFL-CIO.	202-637-5000	2
American Federation of Government Employees	202-737-8700	2
American Federation of State, County, & Municipal Employees	202-737-1736	2
American Federation of Teachers	800-238-1133	2
American Postal Workers Union	202-842-4233	2
Bricklayers International.	202-783-3788	2
Carpenters	202-546-6206	1
Electricians	202-833-7000	3
International Brotherhood of Electrical Workers	202-728-6280	3
International Union of Operating Engineers	202-429-9100	3
Iron Workers Union	202-529-6226	2
National Association of Letter Carriers	202-393-4695	2
National Post Office Mail Handlers	202-466-2927	2
Firefighters Association	202-737-8484	2
Federation of Teachers.	703-451-6840	2

Fraternal Order of Police 800-367-6524 2
Sheet Metal Workers 877-769-4273 2
United Auto Workers 202-828-8500 3
United Food & Commercial Workers 202-223-3111 1
United Transportation Union 202-347-0900 2

Step 3: Choosing an Enticing Benefit

After you've determined which associations complement your business and you've compiled a list of associations or organizations to approach, the next step is to decide on the benefits that you can offer the members. Enticement is the goal. What product or service would interest the members of these organizations and entice them to patronize your business? Think about their motivation. Prospective customers can be charmed into your business if you give them a reason, offer an irresistible service, fill a unique need with your product, or furnish them with a tempting bonus or added value that isn't even associated with your business.

In the example of the Maple Square Restaurant, the place was new, designed to attract general laborers in the Kansas City area. With Jerry's consent, I arranged for endorsements from three labor unions. The enticing benefit we agreed upon was a free $1000 accidental death and dismemberment (AD&D) policy. For Jerry's target market, this enticement worked wonders.

At the time, a $1000 AD&D policy cost Jerry only about fifty cents. The entire association endorsement program benefited all the parties involved. The union got credit for arranging a free $1000 AD&D policy for its members. Jerry's restaurant now had a strong flow of customers. Customers came into the restaurant, ordered lunch or dinner, and picked up their insurance certificate on the way out. Granted, a few did not stay to order a meal; they just picked up the insurance certificate and left. The important point is that the Maple Square Restaurant became memorable because of the enticing benefit. The benefit got people into the restaurant, and that is a big step in the food service business. These people would certainly remember the restaurant and the free insurance policy and would come back for a meal.

For about a dollar apiece (including the cost of the policy, postage, and materials), Jerry was able to use an enticing benefit to spark interest in his restaurant. Once labor union members ate at the Maple Square Restaurant, Jerry won their loyalty with good food and reasonable prices.

I used this same $1000 AD&D benefit for Paul Boussard's Pinnacle Insurance Agency. This agency set up appointments with over 90 percent of the union members it called. Experience proves that this technique works.

> *Today's mighty oak is just yesterday's little acorn that held its ground.*

When choosing an enticement, put your creative abilities into high gear. A benefit can be something from your product line or something you get from another company. Consider an offer that appeals to your customer's sense of value and fun. Plan on spending some time on this step because your success will depend on your coming up with a benefit that is unique, something your customers don't have already.

You wouldn't want to give members of the Carpenter's Union a hammer, but you might want to give them a gift certificate to Builders' Square or Home Depot. You might even want to give them a gift certificate to an elegant restaurant so that they can take their spouses out for dinner in appreciation for putting up with their long hours and unpredictable schedules.

Step 4: Contacting the Association or Organization

So far, you have completed three steps in this program:

1. Understanding prospective customers
2. Deciding which associations or organizations to approach
3. Choosing an enticing benefit to offer the membership

The next step is to contact the association or organization leadership to present your offer.

> **HOT TIP:** *When sending a letter to an association, always keep it brief and to the point.*

In order to approach the association or organization correctly, you need to have the following information:

- The decision maker's (president or executive director) name
- When the president or executive director will be in town, so that he or she will be sure to receive your approach letter when you send it
- The mailing address of the organization or association

One telephone call can provide all the answers you are seeking. Call the association or organization and simply ask the name of the president or executive director, when he or she will be in town, and the mailing address.

In the case of the Maple Square Restaurant, we approached the Bricklayers Union local. We found out that Gary Thomas was the executive director of Bricklayers Union Local #234. We were told when Mr. Thomas would be in town, and we made a note of the mailing address.

It is critical to learn the name of the executive director so that the approach letter can be sent to him or her personally. It is a mistake to send an approach letter that is not addressed to a specific person. In a busy office, letters that are not addressed to a specific person may never get opened. In addition, the fact that you have the right name, with the correct spelling, shows that you've done your homework and have something worthwhile to say.

You want to be sure that the decision maker is in town when you plan to send the approach letter. This is necessary to ensure he or she will receive and read what you send. If the director isn't in town, the letter could be passed on to another person and never make it to the decision maker.

It is important to get the mailing address of the association or organization. Even if you have the address, verify that it is correct in case the organization has moved or receives mail at the post office. It is a good habit to verify addresses, even if you trust the source. Ask the person you contact specific questions, such as, "Does Ms. Jones receive her mail at this address?"

Step 5: Writing the Approach Letter

The approach letter is your way of introducing yourself and your business to the executive director of the association. In it, you want to outline how your ideas will benefit members and enhance the association's reputation. It also informs the executive director that you will be contacting him or her in a few days to discuss the details further.

Keep your approach brief and to the point. The head of any association or organization is a busy person who won't want to waste time wading through useless information. Keep the letter focused on these four points:

1. Who you are and what your business offers
2. How the association will benefit from listening to your ideas
3. How the membership will benefit from accepting your offer
4. When you will be calling to discuss the offer further

Now it is time to get the letter typed and mailed to the president or executive director. You want the letter to look professional. If your business doesn't have a letterhead, it is time to get one. There are a couple of alternative ways of getting letterhead. First, you can go to an office supply store (Biz Mart, Staples, Office Depot, etc.) or a print shop (Insty-Prints, Kinkos, Kwik Copy, etc.) and have letterhead stationery created for your company. You can also contact NEBS for stationery and paper products. There are literally thousands of graphics now available that you can use to produce good-looking business stationery at minimal cost.

The second way to get letterhead is with a computer. Software such as Microsoft Word, Works, or Microsoft Publisher comes with templates that let you make your own letterhead. There is also an excellent software package offered by Avery for creating business cards, labels, and even gift certificates. It costs about $40.

Read through the approach letter in Sample 10.3 and see how it is kept simple and hits on the four main points all approach letters should contain.

COOL RESOURCE: *Avery can be found at www.avery.com. The Avery site offers additional creative resources in an easy-to-use format, with templates, clip art, and many ideas for making office work easier.*

Sample 10.3 **Model Approach Letter.**

> Maple Square Restaurant
> 1234 North Star Road
> Kansas City, KS 60611
> 616-782-0543
>
> Mr. Gary Thomas, Executive Director
> Bricklayers Union Local #234
> 210 Main Street
> Kansas City, KS 60613
>
> Mr. Thomas:
>
> Greetings! I am Jerry Kirkpatrick, owner of The Maple Square Restaurant, located in the North Star Shopping Center. During the week of October 1 to 8, the restaurant is having a special union week. I would like to invite you and the members of Bricklayers Union Local #234 to my restaurant so that you can get acquainted with the staff and management. I believe you will find we pride ourselves on great food, fast service, and reasonable prices.
>
> We have arranged for the members of your union to receive a special benefit, compliments of the Maple Square Restaurant. In addition, I want to give you a free meal for you and a friend at Maple Square.
>
> In a few days I'll be calling to make arrangements to drop off your free meal coupons and to talk to you about the great benefits we want to offer the members of Bricklayers Union Local #234.
>
> Thank you,
>
> Jerry Kirkpatrick

Associations and Organizations

Step 6: Setting Up a Meeting with the Director

After you send the letter, wait about three days. This gives the director time to receive the letter and read it. This is the beauty of an approach letter—after receiving it, the director is expecting a call from you, and so from the time he or she says hello, you have a designated purpose for calling. Sample 10.4 gives a script (a guide) suggesting what you might say when you call the director.

Sample 10.4 Telephone Script Setting Up a Meeting with the Director.

> Is Gary around? Gary, hello; this is Jerry with Maple Square Restaurant. I recently sent you a letter about the restaurant, the benefits we would like to offer members of the union, and two free dinners for you. Do you remember receiving the letter? Great!
>
> I would like to set up a convenient time to drop off your free meal coupons and take a few minutes to tell you about the benefits available for your members. I have some time tomorrow morning at 10:00. Is that convenient, or would Wednesday afternoon at 3:00 be better for you?
>
> Great. I'll see you tomorrow at 10:00. And are you still located at 210 Main Street?

The conversation should be simple and to the point. Ask for the director by his or her first name. Try to approach the conversation with a confident attitude and think of the director as one of your friends.

Although many people are nervous about approaching customers on the phone, it is like many other things we are afraid to do—the more we face our fear and do it, the easier it gets. I've been in sales, marketing, and business for over 20 years, and I still get nervous. To a business owner, the telephone is a valuable tool. Remember, as a businessperson you have to be proactive and go after the business. Even a company as successful as McDonald's continues to be proactive and goes after business in many ways that aren't readily apparent. Granted, the McDonald's name is more likely to open doors and have customers flock in than the name of your business, but it wasn't always that way.

McDonald's started out as a small burger place in southern California. It had grown to half a dozen outlets before it was bought out by Ray Kroc, a malt machine salesperson. McDonald's had tough times too. Some weeks, the company couldn't meet its payroll, so a few of the office employees were paid with stock. McDonald's really took off when the company developed a marketing campaign that I still remember: hamburger, fries, a Coke, and change back from your dollar. Today, McDonald's is extremely successful because it doesn't sell food, it sells fun.

> **HOT TIP**
>
> *Using NEBS products can save you time because NEBS offers complete office paper systems, including stationery, billing, invoicing, accounting, payroll, invitations, orders, and shipping supplies, all personalized for your business. NEBS has many logos to accentuate your office paper system, and graphic artists are available to custom design a company logo for you. NEBS can be reached at 1 (800) 225-6380 or online at www.nebs.com.*

You should do the same thing. Don't be too serious. Have fun. Sell the organization on the benefits of doing business with you. If the director turns you down for an appointment, don't take it personally. There could be many reasons why your offer was declined, some of which may have nothing at all to do with you, your business, or your offer. Go on to the next organization. Remember: persistence, persistence, persistence. In a week or a month, call the director again. For more telephone presentation tips, see Chapter 4, Telemarketing. Once the director sets up an appointment with you, take a few minutes to pat yourself on the back; then get prepared for the face-to-face meeting.

Step 7: The Face-to-Face Meeting

Here are a few tips for the face-to-face meeting with the director. Sample 10.5 gives a script for this meeting.

Dress in the Same Type of Attire as the Person You Are Meeting. When I met with the president of the Carpenter's Union local, I dressed in blue jeans, knowing that this was the usual attire of the union members. If you are meeting with a banker, dress as the banker would—in a suit and tie. Of course, there are exceptions to this suggestion. If you are a stockbroker or investment adviser, don't wear blue jeans. You want to exhibit and maintain the professional image a suit gives when dealing with customers or business contacts. In general, however, this guideline will serve you well and, more important, make the person you're talking with feel comfortable. Years ago, when I dealt with farmers, I dressed like a farmer. I've even had several farmers tell me that if I had shown up wearing a suit and tie, they would have kicked me out.

Associations and Organizations

Pay Attention to What You Drive. What you drive to the meeting says a great deal about you. Don't drive a fancy new Mercedes or BMW. If you are meeting with a labor union director, don't drive any type of foreign car, since most unions have a "Buy American" policy. This single detail might give the union leader a bad impression and keep him or her from doing business with you. At the same time, don't show up in your cousin Albert's 1971 Plymouth Valiant, belching blue smoke and sounding like a cement mixer. If necessary, rent an appropriate car for the day.

Sample 10.5 Script for a Personal Meeting.

> *Gary, as I said on the phone, I'd like to invite you to Maple Square Restaurant. I've brought tickets for two free dinners for you and a friend. But, I have even better news. I want the union members to have a chance to try Maple Square, too.*
>
> *To show our appreciation to the members and the union, I have arranged for each member to receive a free $1000 accidental death and dismemberment policy. I want to send a letter to the members on union letterhead, signed by you, explaining how they can pick up the certificate for a free AD&D policy. You can write the letter, or I can write it. It doesn't matter to me. It depends on which you prefer and what is most convenient for you.*
>
> *I can either pick up the letterhead now and stop back tomorrow for your signature, or I can pick up the letter from you tomorrow along with the membership lists. Which is more convenient for you?*

Be Enthusiastic—Enthusiasm Is Contagious. When you meet with the director, greet him or her with a smile. Exude a positive attitude, and walk with a bounce in your step. In other words, be enthusiastic. Always remember that enthusiasm is contagious. You are there to deliver good news. Be friendly. Get to know the director a little bit and listen to what he or she has to say. I've seen entrepreneurs lose business because they didn't listen to a prospective customer or business contact. People need to feel that what they say really matters to you.

Establish Rapport and Offer the Benefits. After you've talked to the director long enough to break the ice and establish some rapport (you feel comfortable with him or her and vice versa), explain your ideas and the benefits you want to offer the association's members.

Sample 10.6 **Model Letter to Union Membership.**

Local Bricklayers Union #234
210 Main Street
Kansas City, KS 12345

Dear Jim Huxley,

    We are pleased to announce that the union leadership of local 234 has made arrangements with a local establishment, Maple Square Restaurant, for you to receive a $1000 accidental death and dismemberment policy absolutely free.

    Maple Square Restaurant is new to the community and serves a variety of mid-priced dishes. From October 1 to October 8 Maple Square will host Celebrate the Union Week. This is a perfect time for you to pick up your insurance certificate and while you're there, stay for lunch or dinner. I visited Maple Square and tried the chicken-fried steak. I had a great time. The food was good, and so was the service.

Gary Thomas
Executive Director

People today are more concerned with privacy issues than they once were, so the union president may not want to give out the membership list. He or she may prefer to send the letter out personally.

Step 8: Sending Out a Letter to the Members

After you get the letterhead from the director, it is time to type a letter to the union membership. Sample 10.6 provides an example.

Step 9: A Follow-Up Call to the Members

After the letter is sent out, you can either follow up with a phone call or let the letter do the work alone. Sample 10.7 shows a sample script for following up with a call inviting the union members to your business. If the union leader does not give you the members' phone numbers, then you can get them from information or expect a percentage of the members to show up.

Sample 10.7 Telephone Script: Follow Up with Union Members.

> Is Jim in? Jim, this is Jerry with Maple Square Restaurant. I am calling in regard to a letter that was sent from your union about the free $1000 accidental death and dismemberment policy you are entitled to receive from us.
>
> I am calling to personally invite you to my restaurant. I know that once you try Maple Square, it will become your favorite place to eat. So come by soon and pick up your certificate for the insurance policy and try out our daily lunch and dinner specials. Don't forget to ask for me when you come in so I can personally meet you and shake your hand.
>
> I hope to see you in the next day or two. Thanks for your time.

Step 10: Give Them What They Expect

You have made it to the last part of this marketing program. It is good to remember that marketing will generate customers, but it is up to you to make customers loyal to your product or service. By all means, make sure that the benefit you've promised is available for the association or organization members. Make a point of calling the executive director in a week or two to thank him for his help and see what type of feedback he's getting from the members. This is an excellent opportunity to monitor the response of your marketing program and to keep the contact current for proposing another member benefit offer at a later date.

Customizing This Program

As discussed in the beginning of this chapter, the same steps used for a labor union also work for credit unions, banks, and other associations and organizations. Follow the same steps no matter what organization you are approaching with this program.

Here is a summary ten-step outline for obtaining association and organization endorsements:

1. Find out about the needs and interests of your prospective customers.
2. Determine which associations or organizations to approach.
3. Choose an enticing benefit.
4. Contact the association or organization.
5. Write the approach letter.
6. Set up a meeting with the director.
7. Prepare for and attend the face-to-face meeting.
8. Send a letter to the members.
9. Make follow-up calls to the members.
10. Make certain that you fulfill your promise to the association and its members.

By following these ten steps, you can take your business, whether it is new or established, into a new sphere of customer generation. After reading this chapter, if you feel this marketing program would not work for your business, look over the other ideas and techniques presented in the book.

CHAPTER 11

Licensing
The One Technique That Will Triple Your Business and Give You Instant Credibility

John Crow ran a small but successful cosmetics company, Alexis Cosmetics, in Dallas, Texas, that was doing almost $250,000 of business per year. John couldn't break the $250,000 barrier no matter how hard he tried. Regardless of the marketing ideas he applied, he was stuck at less than $250,000 per year of business. Things had remained the same for four years, until one day John had a chance encounter with Christie Thomas, a well-known local model and a member of a musical group. She changed the direction of his company.

Christie was a regular user of Impassioned, an Alexis Cosmetics perfume, and she raved about it. She also liked the fact that Alexis was ecologically minded. For example, the company used only natural products and did not test those products on animals. It also donated a percentage of its profits to a few worthwhile organizations, such as Save the Rainforest.

In their conversation, John asked Christie if he could develop a perfume and name it after her. She quickly agreed, and their lawyers drew up the agreements. It wasn't long before John had a hit on his hands. The first year

BUSINESS MYTH: Only large companies have the clout to license a trademark or copyright.

MONEY TREE REALITY: A majority of the companies that use licensing are small companies.

after Christie's Passion came out, Alexis Cosmetics had revenues of over $1 million. This is one simple example of what the power of licensing can do for a business.

Another more recognizable example of licensing comes from the siding and replacement windows company American Remodeling (AMRE). Have you heard of this company? How about Sears Siding? Of course you have. Its commercials used to be everywhere—television, radio, newspapers.

> *A diamond is a chunk of coal that responded well under pressure.*

What most people do not realize is that Sears has never sold siding to anyone. American Remodeling went from being a small siding company selling locally in Austin, Texas, to being a nationally known company with sales of over $500 million per year in less than five years. How could the climb to financial success happen so fast?

American Remodeling licensed the name of Sears, a company with a reputation for quality products and customer-oriented service. Sears allowed American Remodeling to use its name in return for 15 percent of the gross. In other words, Sears was paid up to $75 million to let American Remodeling use its name.

American Remodeling charged as much as 50 percent more than other companies. Was the material or insulation that came from American Remodeling that much better than other companies? No, but people paid American Remodeling's prices because of the Sears reputation for quality.

What Is Licensing?

Licensing is the process of leasing rights to a legally protected entity, such as a copyright or trademark. The entity or property could be a name, such as Elvis Presley; a logo, such as the Microsoft logo; a likeness; a saying; a signature, such as Hank Aaron; or any combination of these.

The owner of the property is known as the licensor. For example, the Walt Disney Company owns the rights to Mickey Mouse. The renter of the rights (in most cases a manufacturer) is the licensee.

When a company wants to license a trademark for its product, it pays the licensor an advance, a guarantee, or a combination of the two, along with a royalty on every item sold. A guarantee means that the licensee guarantees the licensor a minimum dollar amount no matter how few items are sold. An advance refers to a guaranteed up-front payment when the contract is signed. In many cases, a company will guarantee a minimum amount and pay a part of that guarantee up front as the advance. The royalty rate is usually 10 to 15 percent, but it can be higher or lower. Normally, royalties are figured and paid every six months.

When Did Licensing Start?

There is a common misconception that licensing started in 1977, when the movie *Star Wars* was released. In reality, licensing began in the 1880s. Endorsements were made by celebrities, royalty, and the puppets Punch and Judy. Walt Disney's first license, for a school notebook based on Mickey Mouse, was granted in 1928, after Mickey's debut in *Steamboat Willie*. In the 1930s, celebrities, film and radio stars, and even comic strips were licensed.

> **COOL RESOURCE:** *If you have a product you would like to patent, you can get a free 30-minute consultation with a patent attorney by contacting The American Intellectual Property Law Association, 200 Jefferson Davis Highway, Suite 203, Arlington, VA 22202.*

Licensing can be extremely profitable. Davy Crockett merchandise generated $300 million of retail sales. *Star Wars* generated over $2 billion in sales. The Smurfs generated over $1 billion—not bad for a bunch of blue-skinned toons. How would you like to have a piece of any of these pies? It makes your mouth water, doesn't it?

Benefits to Licensors

As you might imagine, the major benefit to licensors is the financial reward. Of course, it doesn't do any good to make a profit from a trademark if the company licensing it has a shoddy product. Because of this, licensors are normally very careful whom they select to license their trademark.

A second benefit to the licensor is that when several companies are promoting products using the licensor's trademark, it helps market that trademark. For example, when a small company in Wisconsin started marketing the cheeseheads that you see in the stands at Green Bay Packers football games, it made many people take an interest in the Green Bay Packers and their other merchandise.

Another benefit to the licensor arises in the case of a movie, television show, or video. If the producers can presell the majority of the licensing rights, the advances can go toward the cost of producing the project. Look at what happened with the movie *E.T.—The Extraterrestrial*. Mars turned down the opportunity to show M&M's in the movie, but Hershey paid to put Reese's Pieces in it, and their sales shot through the roof overnight.

Licensing allows a company to make money from other product lines without taking any financial risk. The Elvis Presley estate makes much more money today by licensing than Elvis ever did when he was alive. How?, you may ask. Wouldn't you rather be a licensor and get 100 different companies to pay to market your product than try to come up with the money to manufacture those 100 products yourself? Licensing also opens up 100 more distribution channels for you.

Benefits to Licensees

The major benefit to a manufacturer who ties in with a licensed property is the instant consumer awareness that the trademark brings. If you own a company that makes T-shirts or towels, do you think you would make more money with nothing on your product or with a picture of Elvis? If you have a picture of Elvis on your product, you already have a base of customers.

When you become part of an established brand through licensing, you benefit from customers' awareness of the property. That awareness could include the perception of quality, educational value, or an upper-class image. Have you ever heard of the companies Weekend Exercise or Pagoda? How about Mikhail Baryshnikov or Dr. Scholl? Weekend Exercise licenses Mikhail Baryshnikov's name for a line of body wear and sells over $40 million worth of merchandise annually. Pagoda licenses the Dr. Scholl name and has sold over $120 million of foot products to date.

I am sure that you are familiar with the promotion that the Butterfinger candy bar did with *The Simpsons*. This promotion increased Butterfinger sales over 50 percent. A Pizza Hut promotion with *Eureka's Castle*, a Nickelodeon Television program, increased the customer count by over 70 percent.

Taking Advantage of Licensing

You do not have to be a large corporation to take advantage of licensing. The majority of companies that are licensees are small companies. It does help to have enough cash to pay the licensor an advance, but what is ultimately more important than that is what your company can bring to the table. Do you have a unique product, an unusual idea, or a large distribution channel? If you have a product with the potential for large exposure, a great idea for a product, or a lot of contacts to market the product, you may not need any up-front cash to seal a deal with a big-name licensor.

Another option you have is to bring a company with deep pockets to the bargaining table with you.

Getting Paid to Promote Your Company through Licensing

This is exactly what John Crow did. Christie Thomas wanted to promote Alexis Cosmetics, but she did not want an advance or even a guarantee from John. She wanted to be a part of Alexis Cosmetics because she liked the company and the quality of its products. John saw an opportunity to work with Christie and promote her along with Alexis.

John had several contacts in the beauty, fashion, sporting goods, and clothing industries. John found two companies, the first a clothing manufacturer and the second an exercise equipment manufacturer, that were also interested in licensing Christie's name. Each company agreed to give Christie an advance of $50,000, of which John was paid 15 percent, or $7500, for acting as her agent. John was paid a total of $15,000 up front and a continuing royalty rate of 15 percent of Christie's 15 percent (2.25 percent). This is a very unusual situation and you probably won't have this happen, but it shows you what can happen with some creativity.

John did not go into this situation blind. In the same way, you should know all you can about the ins and outs of the field before diving into the marketing techniques of licensing. John hired a licensing and trademark attorney and a licensing consultant to guide him through the entire process. I highly recommend that you follow John's example and make certain you have experts in this area to assist you.

Licensing is a sure-fire way to dramatically increase your sales, but it is also an area you don't want to go into alone. If you are serious about licensing, assemble a team that can advise you and guide you through its legal and business intricacies.

Getting Started in Licensing

You might be interested in being a licensor or being a licensee. The majority of small businesses are going to be interested in being licensees, because they do not own a trademarked property that will be of interest to enough people. For the purposes of this chapter, we will assume that you fall into the category licensee.

Step 1: Research

As a licensee, one of the most important things you need to do is research. It is knowledge that will determine how successful you are. It is obviously impossible to cover everything you need to know about licensing in one chapter, but I will cover the basics, including getting started, what licensors look for, resources you'll need, and a sample contract.

When you decide that you want to get into licensing, you must first determine what licensor best fits with your product line. For example, foot massagers and shoes make sense for Dr. Scholls, but furniture does not. There was a connection between the image of a model such as Christie Thomas and the product line of Alexis Cosmetics. Asking Arnold Schwartzenegger to endorse a woman's perfume would have been a different story. Many licensed product lines have failed because of a bad fit between licensee and licensor. It is vital to research the brand image of a property and carefully consider whether it is one that you want your company and products to be associated with.

If your target market is children, you wouldn't want your product associated with a sports figure who has been convicted of a drug-related crime (or any crime, for that matter). If you manufacture basketballs, you might want to license

Licensing

Michael Jordan's name. If you manufacture baseballs, you might want to license Mark McGwire's name instead. If you manufacture shoes, you might want to license both names. Do you think Nike would have sold as many shoes if the company had not licensed Michael Jordan's name? It is critical to find a licensable project that fits in well with your company's products and image.

Exclusivity. Some licensors grant exclusive contracts. However, most offer nonexclusive contracts or narrow exclusive contracts. An exclusive contract, if you are fortunate enough to get one, entitles you to be the sole manufacturer of a particular product. A nonexclusive contract entitles other manufacturers to produce the same product as you. A narrow exclusive contract gives you the exclusive right to market a certain product in a specific area or to manufacture the product with a prespecified type of material, while allowing other companies to market the same product in different areas or to manufacture it with different materials.

Even if you are not granted an exclusive contract, you should not be satisfied with being one within a large group of licensees. Research the company, ask questions, and make sure there are only a few companies offering the same line of products that you are offering.

Do Your Homework. After you have determined what product you are interested in pursuing, it is time to do some research. You need to learn all you can about the licensor and how its trademark will fit with your product. Here are some questions to ask:

1. Does the licensor have too many licensees offering the same product?
2. Is the licensor involved in more promotions than it can handle?
3. Can the licensor deliver on its promises?
4. Is the licensor actively involved in promoting its licensees?
5. How long has the licensor been in business?
6. Does the licensor have a long-term track record of dealing fairly with licensees?

Often a licensor will charge an additional 1 to 2 percent fee for advertising. This type of arrangement is usually a good thing for the licensee, because it enables the licensee to get national exposure.

There are several licensing industry newsletters and publications available that you can subscribe to. You might also consider attending any trade shows that may be in your area. One of the best newsletters I have seen is *The Licensing Letter*, published by E.P.M. Communications. This newsletter tells you what licensors are actively looking for licensees, who the best licensing consultants are, and what products are bringing in the most revenue.

> **COOL RESOURCE:** *You can reach E.P.M. Communications at 1 (718) 469-9330.*

E.P.M. communications also publishes other newsletters, such as the *Licensing Source*, a handbook that you can order, and two annual directories, *The EPM Licensing Letter Sourcebook* and *The EPM Entertainment Marketing Sourcebook*. E.P.M. also does consulting for licensors and licensees.

What Do Licensors Look for in a Licensee? In deciding whom to award a license to, licensors look for several things. The following are questions the licensor will ask:

1. Is the product a good fit?
2. Is it a unique product?
3. How large is the potential customer base?
4. Who is the target audience?
5. What distribution channels does the licensee have?
6. What is the licensee's track record?
7. Will manufacturing be done in-house, through a subcontractor, or through a sublicensee?
8. Is the licensee's sales force adequate to achieve the sales level desired?

9. Is the licensee capable of producing a new product line each year?

10. How many other licenses does the manufacturer hold?

11. Does the licensee plan to actively promote the brand, and subsequently the product?

12. Is the licensee financially stable?

These are all important questions that you, as a licensee, should be ready to answer. The licensor will also want references from companies that you are working with presently or have worked with in the past.

Step 2: Making a Presentation to the Licensor

Once you have determined that you can satisfactorily answer the above questions, it is time to approach a licensing consultant to make a presentation for you or to make one yourself. I highly recommend hiring a consultant. However, if you decide to do the presentation yourself, be prepared. You will need to give a brief synopsis of the property and have a presentation ready that will answer all the necessary questions and show the licensor why your company is the best of all the applicants to receive the license.

Hiring a Licensing Consultant. If you are new to licensing, a licensing consultant will offer you instant expertise. A consultant can tell you:

- How to negotiate contracts
- The current royalty rates
- What licensors are looking for in licensees
- How to identify the best licensors
- The best strategy to approach potential licensors

In addition to the above, licensing consultants also have developed contacts, and they can get you and your offer in to see the decision makers. Once you are in the front door, either you or the consultant can make a presentation.

Some consultants are paid a flat retainer, and some are paid an advance against a percentage of future sales (normally 1 to 2 percent of net sales).

Have you heard of Tae-Bo, the workout program created by Billy Blanks? The videos for Tae-Bo were released in August 1998, and in less than a year they had sold millions. The Century Sporting Goods Company, a small company in Midwest City, Oklahoma, was well aware of this craze and decided to take advantage of the public's interest in this product. Century signed an agreement with NCP Marketing Group in Canton, Ohio, the agent for Tae-Bo, to manufacture Tae-Bo apparel, such as kick-boxing shorts, tank tops, T-shirts, and baseball caps, along with equipment such as handwraps, gloves, punching bags, and water bottles.

Pokemon, the cartoon character that originated in Japan, is another licensing possibility that is making millions of dollars for numerous businesses. While it may be true that a high percentage of these opportunities are short-lived, it is equally true that millions can be made in a short time.

The only thing stopping you from following the same path as the people behind the stories above is a little knowledge and the foresight and persistence to make it happen. Sometimes an incredible opportunity can be right under your nose and you may not even see it.

When I owned a record company, I was talking to a public relations person about doing the publicity for one of our singers. This person happened to be the public relations person for Barney, the purple dinosaur. I had an opportunity, but I was blind to it. If I had been thinking, and aware of what was going on with Barney, I would have tried to negotiate a licensing agreement with Barney's creators for a record. I missed the opportunity, but someone else saw it and recorded an album that went on to sell several million copies.

Step 3: Signing the Contract

If you decide not to hire a consultant and you want to handle things on your own, I recommend that you hire a license and trademark attorney to assist you with the contract. I realize that many entrepreneurs—including myself—are stubborn and insist on doing everything themselves. For this reason, I've included a sample contract (Sample 11.1) that you can use as a guideline when you write your own licensing contract.

In most cases, the licensor will have its own licensing contract, but by reading this sample contract, you will get an idea of what should be in a contract and what to look for. If you are dealing with a company that has not previously been involved in licensing, then you can use this sample contract.

Sample 11.1 **Model for a Licensing Contract.**

LICENSE AGREEMENT

THIS AGREEMENT is effective as of _____ (hereinafter the "Effective Date") by and between:

_____ a corporation organized and existing under the laws of the State of _____, located at _____ (hereinafter referred to as "Licensor"), and _____, a corporation organized and existing under the laws of the State of _____ located at _____ (hereinafter referred to as "Licensee").

WHEREAS, Licensor is the owner of the trademarks and registrations thereof listed on Schedule A, which may be amended from time to time by mutual consent of the parties (the "Marks");

WHEREAS, Licensee desires to obtain a license from Licensor to use the Marks on products trademark is to be used on, solely in connection with the production, distribution, and sale of _____ Products (as hereinafter defined); and

NOW, THEREFORE, in consideration of the foregoing and of the mutual promises hereinafter set forth, the parties agree as follows:

1. Definitions

In this Agreement, the following terms shall have the meanings set forth below:

"Net Sales" shall mean the total of all charges invoiced by Licensee for sales of licensed _____ Products less the following items insofar as they are separately stated but included in the amounts invoiced to customers: usual trade discounts actually taken, returns, allowances, packing costs, insurance, transportation costs, customs duties and sales, use, import, export, and excise taxes.

"_____ Products" shall mean products to be used, produced, distributed, or sold by Licensee in conjunction with the Marks.

"Territory" shall mean the United States of America and its territories and possessions.

2. Term

    2.1 Subject to the provision of Article 10 herein, this Agreement shall continue in force for one (1) year from the Effective Date, and will be automatically renewed for periods of one (1) year each, unless either party gives notice of nonrenewal to the other party at least sixty (60) days prior to the end of any one (1) year term. Such notice will terminate this Agreement upon expiration of the then current term.

3. Grant of License

    3.1 Subject to the provisions of this Agreement, Licensor grants to Licensee, and Licensee accepts, a nonexclusive, nontransferable, personal license (with the right to enter into sublicenses only with producers of _____ Products and only for the sole purpose of producing and selling _____ Products to Licensee) to use the Marks in the Territory solely in connection with the production, distribution, sale, and advertisement of the _____ Products.

    3.2 Licensee shall not use the Marks other than as provided in Section 3.1 hereof.

4. Royalties

    A. Immediately upon execution of this Agreement, Licensee shall pay Licensor an initial fee of $_____ (_____ U.S. dollars).

    B. Throughout the term of this Agreement, and for any renewals or extensions of this Agreement, Licensee agrees to pay Licensor a royalty of _____% (_____ percent) of Net Sales of Products bearing the Licensed Trademark.

    C. "Net Sales" means gross sales less any returns, sales, use or value added taxes. Within sixty (60) days after the end of each semiannual period ending on June 30 or December 31, commencing with the semiannual period during which this Agreement becomes effective, Licensee shall furnish to Licensor a statement in form reasonably acceptable to Licensor, certified by a responsible officer of Licensee, showing the Net Sales of Products bearing the Licensed Trademark sold during such semiannual period; such fact shall be shown on such statement.

    D. Within such sixty (60) days, Licensee shall, irrespective of its own business and accounting method, pay in United States dollars to Licensor the royalties payable for such semiannual period as shown in the statement required by Section 4C. Such statement, together with the payment for the fees shown therein, shall be sent to Licensor at its address as follows:

_____

E. Overdue payments hereunder shall be subject to a late payment charge calculated at an annual rate of four percent (4%) over the prime rate (as posted in New York City) during delinquency. If the amount of such charge exceeds the maximum permitted by law, such charge shall be reduced to such maximum.

F. Licensee shall pay any tax (and any related interest and penalties), however designated, imposed as a result of the existence or operation of this Agreement, including any tax which Licensee is required to withhold or deduct from payments to Licensor, except (I) any such tax constituting an income tax imposed upon Licensor by any governmental entity within the United States proper (the fifty (50) states and the District of Columbia), and (II), if the aforesaid office of Licensee is relocated to a jurisdiction outside of the United States proper, any foreign tax imposed on Licensor or any of its subsidiaries if such tax is allowable as a credit against U.S. income taxes of any of such companies. In the case of taxes imposed pursuant to Section 4F(II), Licensee shall furnish Licensor with any evidence required by United States taxing authorities to establish that any such tax has been paid.

5. Quality Standards

5.1 Licensee agrees that the nature and quality of (1) all services and goods rendered by Licensee in connection with the Marks; (2) all goods produced, distributed, or sold by Licensee under the Marks; and (3) all related advertising, promotional, and other related uses of the Marks of Licensee shall conform to standards set by, and be under the control of, Licensor. All such uses shall require prior written consent by Licensor. Any different usage also shall require prior written consent by Licensor.

5.2 Licensee agrees to cooperate with Licensor in facilitating Licensor's control of the nature and quality of _____ Products, to permit reasonable, periodic inspection of Licensee's and/or sublicensees' operations, at reasonable times and with reasonable notice, and to supply Licensor with specimens of all uses of the Marks upon request. Licensee shall comply with all applicable laws and regulations and obtain all appropriate governmental approvals pertaining to the production, distribution, sale, and advertising of _____ Products.

6. The Marks

6.1 Licensee shall include the Marks on or with all _____ Products sold under the Marks and shall include all notices and legends with respect to the Marks as are or may be required by applicable federal, state, and local laws or which may be reasonably requested by Licensor.

6.2 Licensee acknowledges the ownership of the Marks by Licensor, agrees that it will do nothing inconsistent with such ownership, and that all use of the Marks by Licensee and all goodwill developed therefrom shall inure to the benefit of and be on behalf of Licensor. Licensee agrees that nothing in this Agreement shall give Licensee any right, title, or interest in the Marks other than the right to use the Marks in accordance with this Agreement and Licensee agrees that it will not attack the title of Licensor to the Marks or attack the validity of this Agreement.

7. Infringement

7.1 Licensee shall notify Licensor promptly of any actual or threatened infringements, imitations, or unauthorized use of the Marks by third parties of which Licensee becomes aware. Licensor shall have the sole right, at its expense, to bring any action on account of any such infringements, imitations, or unauthorized use, and Licensee shall cooperate with Licensor, as Licensor may reasonably request, in connection with any such action brought by Licensor. Licensor shall retain any and all damages, settlement, and/or compensation paid in connection with any such action brought by Licensor.

8. Indemnification

8.1 Licensee, at its expense, shall defend and indemnify, and save and hold Licensor harmless from and against any and all liabilities, claims, causes of action, suits, damages, including without limitation, suits for personal injury or death of third parties, and expenses, including reasonable attorney's fees and expenses, for which Licensor becomes liable, or may incur or be compelled to pay by reason of Licensee's activities or breach of the terms of this agreement, including but not limited to: (I) claims of infringement of any intellectual property right; or (II) product liability suits by direct or indirect customers of Licensee.

9. Termination

9.1 Licensor shall have the right to terminate this Agreement effective immediately upon Licensee's receipt of written notice from Licensor in the event of any affirmative act of written notice from Licensor, in the event of any affirmative act of insolvency by Licensee, or upon the appointment of any receiver or trustee to take possession of the properties of Licensee or upon the winding up, sale, consolidation, merger, or any sequestration by governmental authority of Licensee, or upon any breach of any of the duties and obligations of Licensee under this Agreement.

9.2 The exercise of any right of termination under this Article 9 shall not affect any rights which have accrued prior to termination and shall be without prejudice to any other legal or equitable remedies to which Licensor may be entitled by reason of such rights. The obligations and provisions of Articles 4, 6, and 8 shall survive any expiration or termination of this Agreement.

10. Effects of and Procedure on Termination

10.1 Upon the expiration or termination of this Agreement, Licensee agrees immediately to discontinue all use of the Marks and any term confusingly similar thereto, to destroy all printed materials bearing any of the Marks, and that all rights in the Marks and the good will connected therewith shall remain the property of Licensor.

11. Relationship of the Parties

11.1 The relationship of Licensee to Licensor is that of an independent contractor and neither Licensee nor its agents or employees shall be considered employees or agents of Licensor. This Agreement does not constitute and shall not be construed as constituting a partnership or joint venture or grant of a franchise between Licensor and Licensee. Licensee shall not have the right to bind Licensor to any obligations to third parties.

12. Assignment

12.1 This Agreement may be assigned by Licensor but shall not be assignable or transferable by Licensee without the prior written consent of Licensor, and any attempted assignment by Licensee without such prior written consent shall be void and shall constitute a breach of the obligations of Licensee hereunder.

13. Notices

13.1 Any notice, demand, waiver, consent, approval, or disapproval (collectively referred to as "notice") required or permitted herein shall be in writing and shall be given personally, by messenger, by air courier, by telecopy, or by prepaid registered or certified mail, with return receipt requested, addressed to the parties at their respective addresses set forth above or at such other address as a party may hereafter designate in writing to the other party.

13.2 A notice shall be deemed received on the date of receipt.

14. Applicable Law

14.1 This Agreement shall be governed by and construed in accordance with the laws of the State of _____, without regard to principles of conflicts of laws. Any case, controversy, suit, action, or proceeding arising out of, in connection with, or related to, this Agreement shall be brought in any Federal or State court located in _____ County and the State of _____.

15. Sublicense

15.1 No sublicense agreement into which Licensee enters pursuant to Section 3.1 of this Agreement may extend beyond the term of this Agreement. Licensee may not enter into any sublicense pursuant to this Agreement without the prior written consent of Licensor.

16. Modification, Amendment, Supplement, or Waiver

16.1 This agreement constitutes the entire agreement between the parties with respect to the subject matter hereof and supersedes all previous agreements, promises, representations, understandings, and negotiations, whether written or oral.

16.2 No modification, amendment, supplement to or waiver of this Agreement or any of its provisions shall be binding upon the parties hereto unless made in writing and duly signed by both of the parties to the Agreement. A waiver by either party of any of the terms or conditions of this Agreement in any one instance shall not be deemed a waiver of such terms or conditions in the future.

IN WITNESS WHEREOF, the parties hereto have caused this Agreement to be duly executed on the Effective Date.

_____ (Licensor)   _____ (Licensee)

Name: _____   Name: _____

Title: _____   Title: _____

CHAPTER 12

F.A.B.

How to Put Your Best Foot Forward by Stressing Features, Advantages, and Benefits

According to the Small Business Administration, 95 percent of business failures are due to a lack of sales. This well-known figure is not surprising. What is astonishing is the fact that people start businesses every day without any plans for how they're going to generate customers. No matter what your business, it is imperative that you have a coherent plan for making sales and bringing in new customers. A well-researched marketing plan not only will help you to stay solvent but will keep you on the road to success.

Recently, I had a lengthy conversation with a woman who had opened a beauty salon. She had spent over $25,000 on equipment and renovations to open her shop. When I met her, she was trying to sell the business because her profits were low and her customers few. She had spent her entire budget before she opened her doors, and she didn't have the money she needed for advertising or marketing. Fortunately, we were able put our heads together and come up with a marketing plan that was within her limited budget and is already bringing in a flow of new customers.

BUSINESS MYTH:	MONEY TREE REALITY:
Business owners must sell a product or service at a lower price than the competition in order to outsell them.	If you add value and quality to your product or service, you can outsell the competition, even if your prices are higher.

As the techniques in this book have already shown, you don't need a big budget to have a successful marketing program. But one thing is certain: No business can survive for long without a marketing plan. Your marketing plan is literally your map to success.

If I asked you to take a ride with me, the first thing you would notice is that my car is full of maps. I travel extensively, and it's important that I know how to get around, whether I'm in a big city like Houston or a small town like Wellston, Kansas. Without maps, we may arrive at our destinations, but we waste time and money getting there. Starting a business is much like taking a trip; you need to map out the best and straightest route to your destination, a business with an endless flow of customers.

> **HOT TIP**
> *The product justifies the price, not the other way around.*

One of the things many business experts and sales and marketing books emphasize selling is the features and benefits of your product or service. While the product is obviously important, there are several reasons why I disagree with this advice.

Here are some of the drawbacks of selling only features and benefits:

- Most of your competition sells this way.

- If you emphasize only features and benefits, then the only way to distinguish yourself from your competition is by advertising a lower price, which means a lower profit margin for you.

- If you emphasize only these two aspects of a product, you aren't doing anything to make your own product stand out from other similar products.

Instead of doing what everyone else does, you need to come up with some extra appeal that makes you stand out.

How to Add Advantages to Features and Benefits

In this chapter, you will learn to use the selling technique called F.A.B.—features, advantages, and benefits. This technique will help you surpass your competition by emphasizing quality instead of price, thereby increasing your potential profit margin.

Let me tell you a story about Robert. He became one of the greatest salespeople I know by using the F.A.B. technique.

One day, as Robert was making calls in the Midwest, he went into a department store. As he walked around the store, he was immediately impressed. The floor was immaculate, all the merchandise was beautifully displayed, and the help was courteous and friendly. In fact, Robert was so impressed that he decided to compliment the people who ran the store. He asked a clerk for directions to the executive offices, where he actually got in to see the store president.

Robert told the president, "You know, I've been all over the country and I'm a great salesperson. When I see an organization that's run as well as yours, I think it's only right that I come and compliment you. This is the finest run department store I've ever seen any place in the world. I mean, it's immaculate, the merchandise is beautifully displayed, the help is courteous, they're friendly, they're out there looking for add-on business, they're doing all the right things. It's flawless..." Here, Robert paused, and stared at the floor for a moment. "To be honest," he said, looking up, "there's only one exception, the sporting goods department."

The president, who was somewhat taken aback, said, "It's funny you should say that. Sales have always been weak in sporting goods."

Robert's eyes lit up. "You don't know me, I don't know you, but I want to make a suggestion," he said. "I suggest you put me in charge of the sporting goods department. You don't know what I can do, so you only need to pay me five dollars a week. I guarantee you that by the end of the second week, I'm going to have increased your sales by 30 percent. After that, you can bring me up to $1000 a week. I guarantee that at the end of a month, I'm going to double sales, at which time you double my income. The following month we will double sales again, at which time you double my income again. By the twelfth month, this will be the largest-selling sporting goods department in America. Then we can talk about a real compensation package based upon profits. How does that sound?"

> *The greatest pleasure in life is doing what people say you cannot do.*

The president thought it over. "Hey, the guy's going to work for five dollars a week. What do I have to lose?" He said to Robert, "Let's try it."

Robert took over the sporting goods department. Sure enough, at the end of the second week, sales were up 30 percent. Robert's salary went up to $1000 a week. At the end of a month, sales had doubled and Robert's income doubled.

Meanwhile, the president was looking at the reports and figures. He said, "This is incredible. What is this guy Robert doing to increase sales at such a high rate so quickly?" The president decided to take a walk down to see what Robert was doing.

Robert was talking to a man and holding up a fishhook. Robert said to the customer, "Sir, I can tell you're a person who knows real quality. You understand that in the long run quality always costs less because it lasts a lifetime.

"Let me point something out. These are not just any hooks; they're made out of titanium instead of steel, like most hooks." (The advantage: the hook's quality.) "That's the same material they use in airplanes, where they have the biggest stress. It's the strongest metal known to humankind.

"A fishhook made of titanium may cost a little more, but it will not warp or rust. You can catch a whale on these hooks."

The man says, "I'll take the hook."

Robert turned and picked up a package holding a spool of fishing line. "Do you know about this special line?" he asked his customer. "It's nearly invisible. Look." He opened the sealed package and held the line up to the light. "It's invisible in the water, yet it's made from a special nylon from Germany." (The advantage: the quality of the fishing line.) "This line can actually hold up to 800 pounds.

"True, this line will cost a few dollars more, but it will last a lifetime, so it actually costs you less."

The guy said, "I'll take the line."

Robert said, "Now, sir, with this wonderful hook and this wonderful line, you're not gonna put it on an ordinary reel, are you? I happen to have a reel here, made of the same steel that surgeons use in operating rooms all across the country. You know, scalpels have to stay sharp. Even though they're used hundreds of times and cleaned and sterilized repeatedly, they don't lose their edge because they are made from a special formulation steel." (The advantage: the reel's quality.) "The same factory that makes scalpels has made this reel. That's why this is the finest reel anywhere in the world, to go with the finest line and the finest hook."

The guy said, "I don't need to know the rest. I'll take the reel."

Before the man had left the store, Robert had sold him a box of hooks, a fishing reel, a new fishing rod, a landing net, a boat, and a motor. At the cash register, the man signed a credit card slip for $4500.

The president walked over to Robert and said, "Wow. That was incredible. To think that this guy stopped and was looking only to buy a fishhook, and you ended up with a $4500 order."

Robert said, "Fishhook? He didn't want a fishhook. He stopped by and asked where the restroom was. I said, 'Gee, have you seen the weather report? It's supposed to be beautiful this weekend. If you're not gonna be doing anything, why don't you think about going fishing?'"

I wanted to tell you this story to emphasize how an expert salesperson combines advantages with features and benefits.

Feature names the item:

- Facial cleanser
- Plant food
- Fishhook

Advantage stresses quality and value compared to the competition's product:

- Natural emollients imported from Brazil

- Scientifically formulated phosphorus balance
- Made of titanium, which will last forever

Benefit tells what the buyer will gain:

- Soft and clean skin
- Healthy plants
- A product that catches fish and will last forever

The advantage of a product accentuates its quality and value, thus justifying a higher cost. This makes the item more appealing, which means higher profits for your business.

Let's take another example. Suppose that a business specializing in replacement windows pitches its product using features and benefits alone:

> This window has nylon pile weather-stripping (feature), which increases the comfort level of the home and helps control utility costs (benefit). It also has an extruded aluminum frame (feature), which eliminates the time, cost, and aggravation of repairs and maintenance (benefit).

Compare that to a presentation adding the advantage element. In this second example, note how the advantages are used to compare the product to its competition:

> This window has nylon pile weather-stripping (feature). It will not rot like the cloth or canvas weather-stripping used by many other window companies (advantage). Not only will you enjoy the increased comfort level of your home, but you will also control utility costs (benefit) for many years to come. It also has an extruded aluminum frame (feature). It is more durable than the rolled aluminum used in inferior products (advantage). The benefit to you is the elimination of the time, cost, and aggravation of repairs and maintenance (benefit).

Which window is potentially going to bring in more profit? It doesn't take a genius to figure out that the F.A.B. technique can mean the difference between selling low-cost windows for $200 or high-quality ones for $800.

> **HOT TIP**
> *Never ask a customer, "How much do you want to spend?" Use the F.A.B. technique to establish the value of your product or service, thus making the price of secondary importance to your customers.*

What is it about the A factor (advantage) that adds so much power to your presentation? Unlike sales presentations that use only features and benefits, presentations using advantages sell the differences between your product and your competitors' products. Most people will agree that it's worth paying more for quality and value. No matter what product or service your business offers, look for the advantages, or the differences between your product and your competitors'. Then learn everything you can about those advantages and incorporate what you find into your presentation.

In this chapter, we have shown you how to use the F.A.B. program to sell products. The same techniques are effective for a service business. Ask yourself, what advantage does my service offer that my competition does not? When you have the answer to that question, you will stand above the competition. By doing this, your business will increase sales and substantially raise profits.

CHAPTER 13

Charming Customers into Your Business
The Secret to Getting More Business Than You Can Handle

In our house, the telephone is an instrument of work, not of pleasure. From an early age, our kids have known that the telephone is off limits. They know, but they don't always obey.

On Christmas break two years back, the kids were becoming restless. I'm sure every parent knows this phase: The presents are already old and boring, there is nothing on TV, and it is three days before school starts again. During these three days, the children adopt a mantra. It's very simple, and every child knows it: "I'm bored. There's nothing to do." Children may whisper, sing, scream, speak, throw themselves despairingly across the furniture, fight with their siblings, or stomp while repeating this mantra.

On this particular day, my kids were begging for something fun to do and I was two days behind schedule on a presentation that would yield over 15 grand if I could spend just a few more hours polishing it. I was on the phone all day, checking figures, rechecking suppliers' stock, collaborating with

BUSINESS MYTH:	MONEY TREE REALITY:
There will always be a flow of new customers. If I lose a customer, there will always be a replacement in the wings.	Every business is built or destroyed one customer at a time.

the graphic designer on the presentation. I had one final call to make—to the prospective client, begging him to give me one more day before he took his business elsewhere.

I grabbed some orange juice and took several deep breaths, mentally preparing to present all my reasons for the delay and the benefits I could bring to this client if he gave me a measly twenty-four hours. I made the call, trying to steady my voice and keep panic at bay while I mentally calculated all the bills I wouldn't be able to pay if this prospective client said no. He was in a good mood. He listened and said, "Uh huh," with all the appropriate conversational pauses. Things were going my way, and I was a master at sales and manipulation. Then I heard a sound that I didn't recognize at first.

Girls have a distinctive way of squealing, somewhat akin to fingernails scraping across a chalkboard. Any parent with girls will immediately know what I'm talking about and probably cringe. This was the sound I heard; all three of my girls were squealing into the telephone receiver. "What was that?" the client asked. Then the girls dialed a number and started talking about this boy Daniel and how cute he was. Immediately it all clicked for me, and I knew that they were trying to call Daniel and had no idea that I was on the phone with a potential client…maybe I should say a nonpotential client at that point.

I cleared my throat and said, "Hello." I heard a faint click, and I knew the phone conversation was back to my client and me. I spent the next few minutes trying to explain that I was working from home and that my children had broken in on our call.

I didn't get the account, and my children felt terrible. A few months later, that potential client went bankrupt owing several suppliers and contractors large sums. "This is great," I told my kids. "Look at all the money you saved me!"

> **HOT TIP**
> *If yours is a home-based business, set up a private work area. Make sure that everyone in your home knows what that room or area is for and what it is appropriate for them to do when you are working.*

While this story had a happy ending, it could just as well have been a disaster for me. The bottom line is this: If you work at home, make sure you don't compromise your professionalism. Have a business phone that is separate from the family phone, and if at all possible, have a separate space designated just for business. Don't put yourself in the position of losing good customers through false economy.

After the incident with our girls, we did several things to make sure that everyone in the house understood the importance of our business. We set up a more secluded office area, removed all extensions of the business phone from other areas of the house, and reemphasized to our children the importance of respecting our work hours. In a sense, all the members of our family now see themselves as part of the family business, each doing her or his part to make it successful. In other words, we cobratized our business. We made it customer-friendly.

What Is Cobratizing?

Have you ever seen a snake charmer playing a flute as a cobra in a basket follows the beat of the music and the charmer's every move? Think about how successful your business would be if you could charm customers into your business the way the snake charmer charms the cobra. In fact, you can charm customers into your business by making it customer-friendly. By using the techniques in this chapter, you will learn how to do this. I call this technique cobratizing, and if you do it, your business will be successful.

It does not matter whether your business is run out of your home or from a commercial location, you must cobratize it. In other words, you must make every aspect of your business customer-friendly so that you can provide the very best service possible.

How to Go Above and Beyond Customer Service

My wife and I lived in Texas for almost nine years. During this time, we had several businesses. At times we ran several vastly different businesses simultaneously, along with raising our family. Perhaps the only thing that saved our sanity was that we found a hotel that quickly became our weekend retreat. The entire building—six stories, with a pool/spa area, a large expansive courtyard, and an excellent view of Irving, Texas—was soothing and relaxing. When you walked into that hotel, it was as if every concern, problem, or care in the world immediately melted away.

For anyone with his or her own business, a retreat like this can be a lifesaver. Because of the important role the hotel and staff played in our lives, they became a model for our own customer service. First and foremost, the place was relaxing and beautiful. It was an oasis in the middle of a maddening professional storm. This hotel didn't go to great expense to make us feel welcome, but it made certain we got what we requested. The price was within our means and included full breakfast with made-to-order omelets. In the evening we received two free mixed drinks, and the waiters were polite and attentive without being intrusive. Each hotel suite had a spacious bathroom, two completely separate rooms, each with a bed and television, and amenities such as a mini-coffee maker and refrigerator (although these were small things, they added to our comfort).

Truly, this hotel was a thoroughly cobratized business. It charmed its customers and helped them to feel special, appreciated, relaxed, and satisfied. That kind of service can cost your business millions or nothing, depending on your organization, your customers, and your creativity. In this chapter I list eight rules for cobratizing your own business. If you follow these rules, you will discover that customers don't want the world; they want to feel safe, appreciated, and comfortable, doing business with an organization that appreciates their business and their loyalty. Truly, you can't go wrong by following the example of our favorite hotel in Irving, Texas.

The Eight Rules for Charming Customers

Rule 1: If You Don't Cobratize Your Business, Don't Expect New Customers.

While it's good to have models for how to do things right, it can also be valuable to look at examples of how things are done wrong. By becoming more aware of the worst examples, we sometimes gain insights into the subtle effects our actions can have on our customers. We all have our own war stories of bad business dealings. I want to relate a story that happened to me a few years back.

Being in the market for a good second car, I bought a car at the Jackie Cooper dealership in Oklahoma City. I paid the down payment, signed the papers, and drove off.

Six weeks later, when I did not receive my tags and documents, I called to find out what was going on. I was told that the dealer's original source of financing had filed for bankruptcy. The finance manager told me that the dealership was now working with another company and that a larger down payment was needed. I told the finance manager that I was going to hold the dealership to our original contract. When the dealership refused to honor that contract, I told the finance manager to forget the whole deal and have someone pick up

Charming Customers into Your Business

the car. I simply would not do business with people who wouldn't stand behind their agreements. The dealership did pick up the car but refused to return my down payment, saying that it was rent for the time I drove the car.

A local car dealership in Oklahoma City has steel reverse spikes running across their driveway. You can drive in, but if you drive out the same way, your tires are punctured. When you pull into this dealership, you are met by a valet who politely disappears with your car. The sales staff then hammers you to buy a new car from the dealership. Customers who don't buy a vehicle literally have to beg to get their car back. The psychology is simple fear: Consciously or unconsciously, you (the customer) feel stranded. You don't even know where they've taken your car. I'm sure there are many people who respond to the fearful voice inside them and buy cars from this dealer, motivated as much by fear as by their need for a new vehicle.

Car dealers complain that they have a bad reputation and do not understand why. Of course, not all car dealers treat customers this way, but enough of them do that people get nervous and stressed when they go shopping for a car. Would I ever return to either of these places to buy another car? Not on your life! The lesson here is a simple one. In my lifetime I will probably buy at least 10 more cars. Repeat business is like gold, and it is gold you can mine simply by treating your customers as you would like to be treated.

No matter how large or small your business is, if you do not show appreciation for your customers before, during, and after the sale, it is headed for failure. Sure, you may make an immediate sale here and there, but if you aren't going for long-term repeat business, the chances are good that your customers are not going to be talking you up to their friends either. Your business may survive for one year or for five years, but eventually it will fail if you do not make customer satisfaction a high priority.

It always amazes me how many businesses are set up from the very beginning to fail. There are simple things that business owners neglect to do, such as

- Putting a highly visible street address in front of the business.
- Putting a sign with the name of their business in front.
- Making sure that words on the sign, literature, or promotion board are spelled correctly. I've seen basic words misspelled, such as restaurant or retail. If you can't even spell restaurant, are people going to trust you to feed them?

Can a misspelled word keep customers away from your business? Yes. How can you charm and entice customers into your business if you are not professional enough to check the proper spelling of the words before you put them on your sign? Does this mean you can't be a successful businessperson if you don't know how to spell? No, of course not. But if you know that your spelling leaves something to be desired, hire someone to proofread whatever you put out to represent your business.

Ultimately, it is your careful attention to detail that charms customers to your door. And spelling is one of those details that stands out.

Unfortunately, neglect of the details is not limited to small companies. I have seen national chains, such as Kentucky Fried Chicken and Burger King, run promotions with misspelled words. I have seen neon signs at national chains with dead lights that were not repaired for months. This may seem like a no-brainer. However, as the public knows and every business owner should be aware, actions speak louder than any words. It is in the performance of the daily details that a customer determines how a business is run and the attitude of its owner toward the customers.

Rule 2: Customers Know and Remember Where They Are Appreciated and Where They Are Not.

One of my pet peeves is the business owner who doesn't provide a public restroom. Every business is willing to take the public's money. This is a given. Supposedly, businesses serve the public. But frequently, they don't have the one thing every person needs.

The 7-11 convenience store chain used to be guilty of this. What happened? The chain ended up filing for bankruptcy. That's right, the largest convenience store chain in the world filed for bankruptcy protection. Was it just because the chain did not have public restrooms? No, this was not the only reason, but it is relevant, because the chain's attitude toward customers showed in many different ways, of which failing to provide restrooms was just one. What's more, that attitude went all the way up to the executive offices. 7-11 did emerge from bankruptcy. Today, in most cases, these stores have public restrooms. However, most of the stores still are not cobratized. The restrooms are in the back storage area, and the clerks are often far from helpful.

Unfortunately, 7-11 is not alone when it comes to neglecting its customers. Restroom facilities are often a powerful indicator of a business's concern for its customers. When my wife, Jennifer, was pregnant, we stopped at a Church's Chicken in Fort Worth so that she could use the restroom. They refused to let her use it. When a woman is pregnant, it is not the time to block her way to the restroom. Six months later, the same Church's Chicken closed its doors and Popeye's Chicken bought the entire company.

By contrast, look at Love's convenience stores, which are normally located by major highways in the South. These stores have large, clean, easily accessible public restrooms, and they have expansive filling station areas, usually with 10 or more pumps. They provide hot food and the normal items you would find in a convenience store. The clerks are always friendly and helpful.

An associate of mine tells of a time he stopped at a motel in Fort Worth, Texas, to spend the night. He had a coupon from a coupon book for a $4 discount on a room at this hotel. The night clerk refused to honor the coupon. It was 1:00 a.m., there were two cars in the parking lot, and this genius refused to accept a $4 coupon! Did my friend stay there? Not on your life. Instead of making $35 on the room, this motel made nothing. The thing about the motel business is that once a room goes vacant for the night, the motel can never get that money back. It's lost forever.

If you're a motel owner, you should consider what I call tiered pricing. This means that as the night progresses, the room rate becomes increasingly negotiable. If it is 1:00 a.m. and you have 50 empty rooms, you should be open to negotiating a price for the next customer who comes through the door. When a potential customer walks in, asks the nightly rate, and turns to leave because he thinks it is too expensive, ask what that person would be willing to pay for the room. If you can make even a small profit from the room, you are further ahead than if you let the customer walk out the door.

A customer of mine recently shared the following anecdote. He bought a $16,000 boat, and the very first time he took it out on the lake, it literally started to fall apart. The boat dealership and the manufacturer refused to honor the warranty; each said that the other was responsible. What did they

BUSINESS MYTH:	MONEY TREE REALITY:
Customers will patronize a business just because the doors are open.	Customers need to be motivated to visit a business the first time. Business owners can entice customers into the business.

gain by refusing to satisfy a customer? The repair took about two hours. But for the sake of that two hours of labor, the dealer lost a customer's goodwill. You can bet your life that this customer didn't go back when it came time for his yearly tune-up. Nor did he buy his $300 fish finder from this dealer. What's more, when this customer's brother-in-law was in the market for a similar boat, he immediately warned him against purchasing it from this dealer. In fact, the boat dealer ended up losing a sale of $23,000—which was what the brother-in-law paid for his boat at a competitor's dealership.

Don't miss this lesson, since it applies to all businesses. The dealership appears to have lost only a few dollars, but in reality it lost a great deal more: It lost that customer's trust. Boat owners generally hang out with people who either own a boat or want to own one. What do you think the popular topic of discussion is? You guessed it—boating. A boat owner who is dissatisfied will tell everyone he meets about that boat dealership and manufacturer. This could translate into many thousands of dollars in lost sales, as it did in the above anecdote.

> **HOT TIP** *The best marketing any business can have is a satisfied customer.*

I could write an entire book about customer service and ways in which businesses make their customers feel either welcome or unwelcome. However much I want to focus on the positives, the negative examples are instructive since they remind us how easy it is to overlook the bigger picture. Don't lose sight of the fact that your goal is to charm customers and bring them to your business.

Rule 3: Evaluate Whether Your Business Is Cobratized.

Your business can compete and win against any competitor, including the national chains, if you make every single aspect of your business customer-friendly.

Every person who walks into your business or calls on the phone is important. Follow the golden rule: "Treat others the way you would like to be treated." The following are three major elements of contact with your customers. Go over these elements carefully to see exactly where your business needs improvement.

People. When a customer comes into your business, the first person that customer meets should ideally be one of your highest-paid employees. Why? The first impression a customer gets is a lasting one. What's more, that first contact

Charming Customers into Your Business

may be the only chance you have to make a good impression. Take advantage of this chance and ensure that customers are greeted by an employee who is courteous, satisfied, and happy to be working for you. Front-line employees, such as cashiers, clerks, greeters, and customer service representatives, should be willing to do whatever is necessary to give the customer a good impression. Every person who works for you should appreciate the fact that without satisfied customers, you might as well close your doors and send your employees home permanently.

If the first person your customers encounter is grumpy, in a bad mood, or resentful because she or he feels unappreciated, that person is putting out a bad first impression of your business. Similarly, the person who greets customers on the telephone should be personable, friendly, and helpful. Something as simple as having a live person answering the phone instead of a machine is enough to make customers comment on how nice it is to talk to a real person. It's easy to make your customers feel special, and in most cases, it won't cost you a dime.

Make sure everyone in your company knows how to treat potential customers, whether on the telephone or in person. The person who answers the phone should smile, be cheerful, and be well trained in terms of answering customers' questions or referring them to someone who can. The person answering the phone needs to convince callers that your company is worthy of earning their business. You never know how much business you may get from any caller, so treat every caller as if he or she is bringing you a million-dollar contract. You never know when this could be true.

When we started our home-improvement company, I called several banks and finance companies to set up financing for our customers. The first company I contacted did not give me the service I wanted or handle our customers as I wanted them to be handled. I kept calling different finance companies to find one that shared my philosophy of treating customers like gold.

Eventually, on my fifteenth call, I found Phillip Siebel, a loan officer at Banc One in Oklahoma City. I asked him several questions. He never said, "No, we can't do that." In fact, he had an extraordinary sense of the importance of customer relations, which he has maintained in dealing with every person I've referred to him. We have enjoyed a great working relationship ever since. When we first started working with Phillip, this particular Banc One office was a three-person operation. One and a half years later, the office has more than twenty-five employees. Phillip is now the manager, and his boss, Brad, was promoted to manager of three states.

We do a large number of consolidation loans and refinancings, so in some months we helped Phillip personally reach over a million dollars worth of loans. He has always let us know how appreciative he is of the business we bring to him. Are we the exception? No. This is the way Phillip and his Banc One office treat all their customers. This great attitude has helped that office grow and prosper.

Many businesses today think it doesn't matter whom they hire as long as the employee has a warm body. This attitude may get the job done in the short run, but in the long term, it can be your downfall. Set your business apart from the competition. Give your business an advantage. Offer the added value of employees with good attitudes. Pay your people a little more, give them bonuses, and send them on trips to reward them and show your appreciation. The extra investment in time and money will be worthwhile, as those employees will help increase your number of customers and your sales.

Once a person calls or visits your business, do whatever is necessary to turn that person into a lifetime customer. Never tell a customer no, for any reason. Selling is customer service, and customer service is selling. If a customer needs a product that is out of stock, don't treat that customer as unimportant. Instead, treat him or her like your friend. Special order the product, find it at another location, or even call a competitor to see if that competitor has the product in stock.

Unfortunately, when demand for goods and services exceeds the supply, courtesy is often the first casualty. Do not allow this to happen in your business, even if you find yourself in a hot seller's market.

> **HOT TIP** *The best way to sell a customer is to be empathetic. Relate to the customer and understand how she or he feels.*

Places. Take pride in your business, and let that pride show. Get a sign that expresses your pride and professionalism, and keep it properly maintained. If the sign needs painting, paint it. If a light needs changing, change it. If appropriate, get a movable sign (one with removable letters that lets you change what it says) for displaying your specials or promotions. Change your special every week and be sure to maintain the sign. If a letter falls off, replace it immediately. Someone once said, "Success is in the details." Of course you don't want to get buried by the details, but bear in mind that how you maintain your premises—be it your sign or the floor of your office—says to the customer, "This is the kind of service or product I provide."

Have a special that will entice people to come in. As an example, if you own a grocery store, you might put out a sign reading "Free Gallon of Milk. Come inside for details." When customers walk in, hand them a certificate for a free gallon of milk with the purchase of $25 worth of groceries.

Be creative. You know your business better than anyone else does. What could you do to charm customers into your business?

Things. Here are some easy ways to show customers that they are important:

- Have a public restroom.
- Offer them hot coffee and soft drinks.
- Provide snacks.
- Make the atmosphere extremely relaxed.
- Give people discounts for no reason other than just because you feel like it.
- After customers make a purchase, give them something free.
- If customers have to wait in a long checkout line, apologize and give them a freebie.

A friend of mine went into a convenience store one day to buy gas and cigarettes. There were five people in line ahead of him, and he was really losing his patience. If he hadn't needed to pay for the gas, he would have left. But when he got to the counter to pay for his purchase, the clerk apologized for the long wait and threw a disposable lighter in his bag for free, telling him that it was for his inconvenience. That lighter probably cost the store 39 cents, but with that gesture it bought my friend's loyalty for life. If you treat every customer with that kind of respect and service, you will be successful.

Cobratizing Evaluation Checklist

Outside of business
- ❑ The front sign clearly displays the name of the business and the street address.
- ❑ The promotional display is clean, accurate, and updated frequently.
- ❑ The parking lot is clean, spacious, and safe.
- ❑ The parking lot is well lit.

Inside of business
- ❑ The layout is easy to navigate, well organized, and easy to remember.
- ❑ Public restrooms are available, and there are changing tables in both women's and men's rooms.
- ❑ A water fountain and pay phones are available.
- ❑ Items are stocked as needed.

Employees
- ❑ They are dressed appropriately for the business.
- ❑ They are friendly, outgoing, and helpful.
- ❑ They are properly trained on all equipment.
- ❑ They are knowledgeable about the products and services offered.

Telephone
- ❑ It is answered by a person, not a machine.
- ❑ The operator is friendly.
- ❑ The operator knows other employees.
- ❑ The operator offers to assist callers even if they are not customers.

> **HOT TIP:** *It costs absolutely nothing to be friendly, but the return can be limitless.*

Rule 4: Satisfying Your Customers Starts with Knowing Them.

There are several ways in which you can gather information about your customers. When a customer decides to make a purchase, get the person's name, address, and birth date on a sales log. This record will let you provide customers with great service long after the sale. With proper information, you can send your customers promotion announcements, discount certificates, notices of holiday specials, and notes of appreciation for their business.

If you keep track of what each customer purchases, when similar merchandise becomes available, you can send a note saying that you have an item that might be of interest.

Rule 5: Anticipate What Your Customers Need before They Need It.

When it comes to charming customers into your business, you must be proactive. If your business is one that caters to children, such as a toy store or a bike store, and a parent brings children to your store, treat the children like important customers. For example, McDonald's gears its commercials toward the kids, not the parents. It is because of the children that McDonald's is the number one restaurant chain in the world. Consider how you feel when someone treats your child well.

> **HOT TIP:** *Don't have a single-invoice mentality. Get the follow-up information so that you can turn a one-time customer into a lifelong customer and friend.*

As part of this discussion of great customer service, training your employees properly, and targeting your sales pitch to the proper person, I would like to tell you a story. This is a story I am borrowing from *The Zen of Selling* by Stan Adler (AMACOM, 1998). This is a great book and I highly recommend it.

> *A few years ago, my daughter and I set out on a Saturday morning to buy a new bike for her. She had outgrown her old one, and this was to be our present for her tenth birthday. We started at a bike shop near our home. I remember Tracy pausing just inside the door of the shop, momentarily*

awed by the rows and rows of bikes. Then she spotted the one she liked and marched over to it with me in tow. As she stood with her left hand on the seat of the shiny red bicycle, a salesperson approached.

It had been a while since I shopped for a bike, and I tried to think of the right questions to ask.

"She seems to like this one. Is this a good choice for her?"

"It's a really good bicycle," he answered, looking over our shoulders at another customer coming through the front door.

"Well, what makes it good for us?"

"It's very popular; we sell a lot of 'em."

"But I'm wondering if it has the right features for my daughter."

"Well, how much did you want to spend?"

> **HOT TIP** — *Never ask a customer how much he or she wants to spend. It's a sure way to lose a sale.*

Tracy stepped back from the bicycle. I started to say something, then stopped. This wasn't making sense. "Actually," I said, "we're just looking today. Maybe we'll come back later."

The salesperson shrugged. "Okay. I'll be here when you're ready."

And over Tracy's protests, we left.

Later that afternoon, we bought the same bicycle at another shop not 15 minutes away. It was the very same model, and the price was probably the same, but there was one big difference: Paul.

When we entered the second shop, Tracy spied her bicycle and headed toward it. A smiling salesperson came over, introduced himself as Paul, and shook hands with both of us.

"I can tell you really like this one, Tracy," he said. "What do you like about it?"

"I like the color. Red is my favorite color. And I like the name. One of my friends has this same bike, but it's not red."

"Where do you think you'll be riding it?"

"Around," she answered, running one finger across the smooth anodized handlebars. "Maybe to school sometimes."

"How far is that?" Paul asked.

"It's not too far. Just a few blocks."

Without shifting his attention from Tracy, Paul quickly looked up at me and nodded understanding when I held up seven fingers.

"And do you ride on the street to get to school or on the sidewalk?"

"On the sidewalk. Except when I cross the street, of course," she said seriously.

"Of course," Paul didn't smile. Neither did I. "What kind of bicycle do you have now, Tracy?"

"A four-speed," she answered. "We're going to give it to my sister. It's still a good bike."

"Great! That's how I got my first bike, too—from my big sister. Tell me something: Did it take you long to learn to use the gears?"

We stayed there for the better part of an hour. Paul continued his friendly conversation with Tracy, drawing out from her information about how she would be using the new bike and what she liked and didn't like about her old one. She never stepped back from the red bicycle.

"How about you sit on the seat, Tracy," Paul suggested, "and let's see how this one fits."

The seat was too high. While he chatted with Tracy about his own experience with his bike just like this, Paul quickly adjusted the seat to her height and asked her to hop up again. She put both hands on the handlebars and moved one of the gear levers. Paul began explaining which levers moved which gears and showed her the correct gear combinations for most riding situations.

"I don't think I can remember all that," she said, frowning.

"Okay, I'll write it down for you."

And he did. He pulled out a small notebook from his back pocket and made a list of all the main points. He also went over the correct braking procedure and some safety tips.

"And if you forget any of this," he added, handing her a business card, "you can call me any time. Here's my number."

I'm sure my daughter had never had anyone give her a business card before. She held it carefully, with both hands, as we drove away.

In the car, along with a proud papa and a beaming 10-year-old girl, were a brand-new bike, a new helmet, and a tool bag with the name of the shop on it.

Since then, I have referred several people to that shop. Last summer, I bought a new bike for myself and had the opportunity to watch a repeat performance as Paul skillfully moved me from shopper to excited buyer. And he never once asked me, "How much do you want to spend?"

As you can see from this story, the first bike shop did not lose just one sale. It lost the initial sale, future sales to the same customer, and several referral sales.

If you could own one of these bike shops, which would you want to own? The first salesperson may not have received proper training, or maybe he was being paid minimum wage and didn't care about making the sale. However, look at how many sales the bike shop lost because of one employee's inability to make a customer feel special and satisfied.

Human contact is critical in every business. We all want to be treated as if we really matter. When we are made to feel that the businessperson's only interest is how much money we're going to leave with him or her, we're probably not going to become a loyal customer. Every aspect of your business should entice customers to visit, whether on the phone or in person. When a customer buys, that customer should feel good about the decision. All aspects of the customer's business experience with you or your company should reinforce the fact that he or she made the right decision. Every detail should be pleasant and consistent. After the customer leaves, you should keep in contact and continue to make that customer feel important, as if he or she were your only customer. This can be done by sending them correspondence thanking them for coming to your business or offering them special discounts.

> **HOT TIP:** *Resist the temptation to prejudge a customer. Some of your largest sales will come from the people you least expect, if you treat them well.*

It is very important that you as a business owner make a good first impression on your potential customers. It is equally important that you not judge customers on first sight. Never prejudge anyone because of his or her race, age, gender, status, or physical appearance. If a person comes into your business but doesn't buy anything, that person is still a customer. Treat that person as if she or he is worth a million dollars. Who knows, this person's business might be worth this much or more.

When I owned an insurance agency and was training a new representative, Dave Samuels, we had an appointment with a farmer. As we pulled into the driveway, Dave thought we should turn around and leave. The weeds were up to our waists, there was rusty farm equipment lying around, pigs were running loose around the yard, and the house was a tiny shack. We went into the house and treated the family as if they were important, and we walked out

Charming Customers into Your Business

with the largest insurance sale I ever made. It turned out that the farmer was very wealthy. He just didn't spend his money on material possessions.

A friend of mine, Jim, worked for a car dealership. One day a customer walked into the showroom. The man wore dirty overalls, his arms and face were filthy, and he smelled like pigs. Initially, Jim thought the man was lost and wanted directions, but when Jim went over to him, the man said that he was looking for a stripped-down pickup. Mostly to humor him, Jim didn't break off the conversation, but told the man that the only pickups currently on the lot were fully loaded. The man looked at the available models, found a red truck he liked, and told Jim he would take it. Jim asked how he wanted to finance it, and the man said he would write a check for the entire purchase. A bit stunned, Jim watched the man walk toward the door, saying that he would be back in an hour to pick up the red truck.

Thinking the check wouldn't clear, Jim called the bank. The bank representative told Jim the check was good up to seven figures, and if more was needed, he could have it transferred from another account! The man was a millionaire. Later, Jim found out that the man had been to five other dealerships to buy a truck, but no one offered to help him. Jim was the only salesperson who gave the man the attention he deserved. Within the following twelve months, the man bought thirteen more vehicles for his family members! How much money did the other dealerships lose because they prejudged a potential customer who looked as if he couldn't afford anything?

That kind of thing doesn't happen every day, of course. But can you afford to treat any customer like a second-class citizen, based only on physical appearance?

> **HOT TIP** *You can't expect life's best unless you're giving it your best.*

Rule 6: Set Up Your Business from the Beginning to Be Cobratized.

When you are in the planning stages of setting up your business, it is important to come up with a name that:

- Is unique
- Is easy to remember
- Tells everyone exactly what your business sells

I have driven by many businesses with interesting names that tell nothing about what they do. Given that I don't know what they do, what are the chances of my ever becoming a customer of theirs? The right name can help bring business in the door, so take the time to think up a name that fits these three criteria.

As an example, in Oklahoma City, there is a moving company called Budget Movers. What's so special about this name? Both words identify important aspects of the service the company offers: It's a moving company, and it doesn't charge a lot. When I needed some stock moved to a warehouse four years ago, I contacted the company. It was the least expensive moving company I could find. Two guys showed up in an ugly brown truck with hand-painted white lettering. In most businesses you would want the vehicles to have a professional appearance, but in their case, it worked better to look as if the company could not afford to paint the trucks in a professional way. Regardless of the outward appearance, the company did good work and charged well below the going rate. When I called Budget Movers again three years later, the company had eight trucks, all of which were painted that ugly brown with hand-painted white lettering.

Another good name for a moving company is Two Students and a Truck Moving. Why? It's different, it identifies the service being sold, and it gives a visual picture of students needing the work to pay their way through college. Apparently, down-to-earth names for trucking companies is a trend in this country. A friend who lives in a small northern California town tells of one called Two Guys with a Big Truck.

The only way these names might be better would be if they were A Budget Mover or A-1 Students Moving, because that way their listing would be at the beginning of the yellow pages.

As an example, if you were opening a gift store in Oklahoma City, you could name it Gift Emporium and be listed fifty-sixth in the yellow pages, or you could name it A Gift Emporium and be listed second. Which business do you think is going to get more calls from the yellow pages advertisement? Most people start at the beginning and never make it past the fifth or sixth listing. There are 167 gift shops listed in the Oklahoma City directory. No matter what kind of business you have, wouldn't you prefer to be listed toward the beginning?

When deciding on a business name, try to find a name that fits the business. I suggest never calling a business something like Johnson Enterprises. Enterprises makes the business appear to be small but trying to sound larger than it is. In most cases, the owners are showing their lack of business knowledge by using Enterprises as part of their business name.

> **HOT TIP:** *Your job is to show the customer a way to buy with satisfaction. Forget the selling. Let the customer do the buying.*

Rule 7: Cobratizing Means Surpassing the Competition.

Even though your business is starting out small, you can still compete with the big boys and win. In the state of Oklahoma, there is a small tire dealership called Hibdon Tires. Actually, the business isn't small any more. It sells more tires in the state than all other tire companies combined.

How does Hibdon do it? The company goes out of its way to give customers what they want—a no-hassle, guaranteed tire service. No matter what happens to your tires, if you get a flat for any reason, Hibdon Tires will replace it free, no questions asked.

The first time I shopped at Hibdon Tires, I didn't believe that the company would stand behind the product as advertised. I didn't believe it until I had a flat. In fact, the flat was caused by a road hazard that ruined the tire. Hibdon replaced it free without a hassle. Hibdon didn't have the prorated refunds that other dealers use. With such a generous warranty, why would anyone want to buy tires at any store other than Hibdon's? It's the only place I use. And guess which place I recommend to my friends and customers.

Rule 8: Don't Neglect Customer Follow-Up.

Businesses spend a great deal of money, time, and effort to generate customers, and then they make a huge mistake. Once a customer makes a purchase, the business owner believes the job is done. If you want to grow your business, think of that first purchase as just the beginning of your relationship with the customer. Be ready to service what you sell. Be ready to welcome every customer back whenever he or she needs other goods or services.

Once a person becomes a customer, let that person know that you appreciate his or her business. Stand above your competition. It's very easy to do. Less than 1 percent of all businesses ever make follow-up calls to their customers.

If a person has made a big purchase, such as a home improvement, a major appliance, a car, or furniture, make a personal call to that customer within 48 hours of the purchase to thank the customer and make sure that he or she is satisfied with the product or service and the way he or she was treated at your business. While you're not calling for referrals or more sales, you will invariably find that that is what you get.

Every business, including retail stores and restaurants, can gather useful information about its customers. Retail stores can give customers a 10 percent discount for filling out a quick form listing their name, address, phone number, and what they purchased. Restaurants can give customers a free drink with their meal if they fill out a similar form or a survey-quality form. Don't place the form on the table or counter. Instead, instruct the clerk or server to give a form to every adult at the table. Each of those adults may know people that the other people at the table don't know. By gathering information about everyone at that table and calling each of them, you are reaching more potential customers.

Some business owners don't like to make follow-up calls for two reasons:

1. It means more work.
2. They are afraid of confrontation with a customer.

The correct way to face each of these is as follows:

1. If you are afraid of hard work, go work for someone else. Self-employment is not for you.
2. If a customer has a problem and initiates a discussion when you approach him or her, it is to your advantage to deal with the problem immediately.

I would much rather have customers tell me about problems they are having with my product or service. Why? Because, if you know anything about human nature, you'll know that if they aren't telling you, they are telling all their friends

BUSINESS MYTH:
Customer service ends once the customer makes a purchase.

MONEY TREE REALITY:
Customer service does not end with a sale; instead, it actually begins before the sale and continues long after the sale is made.

Charming Customers into Your Business

and co-workers. Would you rather have that bad-mouthing going on or have that same customer telling everyone how you stand by your goods and services 100 percent?

Making follow-up calls is hard work and can be time-consuming, but the rewards are tremendous. If your business is large enough, you can hire someone to make the follow-up calls. Keep this resource in mind, and when you run a special promotion, call all the customers who you think would be interested. If follow-up calls are not appropriate or reasonable for your business, perhaps a note in the mail is. However you decide to do it, find a way to keep in touch and let your customers know you appreciate them.

Before you can treat customers in a way that makes them feel special and satisfied, you have to charm them into your business.

CHAPTER 14

Making Your Dreams a Reality

The One Secret You Must Know in Order to Succeed in Business

In the 1970s, there was a young guy who had just graduated from high school who was in love with movie making, enthralled with every aspect of the industry. One day he took a tour of Universal Studios. He rode on the bus with the open cars behind it and was driven around the studio. As a seventeen-year-old kid, he thought the tour was boring. It didn't represent the real motion picture industry—at least, not the one he wanted to see. He had an idea, and he slipped off the bus, unnoticed by the escort, and walked onto a set where a movie was actually being made. Walking around as if he belonged there, he was soon standing next to the director.

One of the things I teach people is to ask questions. The best friends of any businessperson are Who, What, When, Where, How, and Why.

This kid had never had any sales or business training, but he did get next to the director. "Why did you have them do that?" and "What was the reason

BUSINESS MYTH:	MONEY TREE REALITY:
To be successful in business, you must have a lot of startup capital	A lot of the most successful businesses today were started with nothing but a dream.

for that?" he asked. When people start asking you questions, what happens? You find yourself not only answering the questions, but also enjoying telling all the details. In the process, you begin to like the person asking the questions because we all like to talk about what we do and brag about our accomplishments.

The director started opening up to the kid. He told him all the reasons why different camera angles are used and how to achieve certain effects. Before long, the kid noticed that it was five o'clock and they were shutting down production for the day. The director said to the kid, "Steven, let me tell you, I have enjoyed having you here today. Any time you want to come back, just use my name and come back. I'd like to share with you some insight into how we make motion pictures." The director and Steven walked off the lot together, and the director had his arm around Steven. They walked past the security guard "Bye, David; see you tomorrow," the director said. "Bye, David," Steven chimed in.

The next morning, Steven got out of bed, grabbed his father's briefcase, emptied it, put his lunch in it, put on his best and only suit and tie, and went back to Universal Studios. He said to the security guard, "Hi, David, remember me? I'm with..." and named the director. He walked past security onto the lot. Every day Steven returned to the lot, walking around meeting people, asking questions, to the extent that everyone thought he belonged there. If you've ever been on Universal's lot, you've probably noticed that there are many empty trailers. Steven found one, cleaned it up, and started bringing furniture from home to outfit the trailer. He made a sign that read Steven _____ Productions and posted it outside the trailer.

At the end of the summer, Steven was in the lunchroom talking to one of the vice presidents of Universal. The vice president said, "You know, Steven, I haven't seen any of your work." Steven answered, "I'm working on a new project that I think is very promising. I want to prove that you can take amateurs that have never acted, with a budget that's small, and still do a short that's totally creative and engrossing. I want to prove that it's not really the amount of money that determines a film's success. I want to show that it's the individual doing it and his creativity that make a movie interesting. I want to prove that it's not necessary to have these multimillion-dollar production budgets that we're doing in order to have a good movie."

The vice president said, "That sounds interesting. When it's finished bring it to me; I want to see it."

When Steven returned home, he got on the phone and called all his friends, relatives, neighbors, and in-laws. He got them all together in a room and made a presentation to them about investing money in his production company to make this short film. He raised $10,000. With that $10,000, using his own friends as actors and shooting with equipment that was lying around, he went back and shot a short film that he had written. He then took the short to the vice president and showed it to him. The vice president was impressed. "That's an amazing example of creativity on no budget, very interesting."

Now Steven confessed, "Sir, I think it's only fair that I tell you I'm a fraud. I don't work here. I've been sneaking onto the lot. I wanted you to see what I'm capable of doing in film. I did this short with a couple of friends' money and no professionals, on my own."

The vice president said, "Son, I'm signing you to a five-year contract; go and get yourself an agent." With that Steven Spielberg started his career.

How many people have the courage to make their dreams a reality as Steven Spielberg did? Unfortunately, not many. Among the people who have made their dreams a reality are Michael Dell of Dell Computers, who started his business by calling people on the phone from his college dorm room to sell them computers. Now, Dell Computers is a thriving, multibillion-dollar company. Stephen Jobs started Apple Computer from his garage. He had many doors slammed in his face because no one believed in the potential of a personal computer. Stephen Jobs persevered and in the process created an entire industry.

Then there's Steve Case, who started America Online with a dream and a vision, and now is the head of a company with over 15 million subscribers. Wouldn't you like to own a business with 15 million customers, each paying you at least $20 per month?

What about Bill Gates of Microsoft? He is now the richest man in the entire world. Did he build Microsoft into the company it is today because he is smarter than you or I? If you were to talk to anyone who knows Bill Gates, and probably if you were to ask the man himself, it is not likely they would attribute his success to his level of intelligence. However, he is smart enough to surround himself with people who are extremely good at their jobs, who are intelligent, no doubt, but whose success is more likely attributable to other factors.

All of these successful people and others like them have one thing in common, the one thing that can make you a success: persistence. No matter how hard things got or what obstacles they faced, these people never gave up and never lost sight of their dream.

Several years ago I was talking with a multimillionaire, and I asked him why he was a multimillionaire and other people were not. What made him different? He told me that the difference between himself and other people was that the other people stopped trying after 100 failures, whereas he kept trying after 101 failures, 102 failures, 103 failures, etc. In other words, he never gave up; he kept trying until he succeeded. He was persistent. All successful people are persistent.

These are just a few examples of people that you've heard of who followed their dream. There are hundreds of thousands of other people who have made their dreams a reality; some of them you've heard of, some you haven't, some you will hear about in the future. Perhaps you will be a person who will inspire others by the success story you create.

Being a success doesn't necessarily mean making a billion dollars. It means making your dreams a reality, whether in business or in another area—for example, by being a teacher and role model for young people. Your dream is your own, and you are the only person who can make it a reality.

Recently I read about a survey in which the question was asked, "What is the most likely way that you could become a millionaire?" I was astonished that the survey showed that a majority of Americans believed that the only way they could become a millionaire was to win the lottery. This is a sad reaction. What most people don't seem to realize is that any person in the United States could retire with over a million dollars if he or she saved less than $100 per month, starting before the person turned thirty. In order to make your dream a reality, you must have a goal, a vision, an idea of exactly what you want. You also need to have a plan, a road map of where you want to be and how to get there. If you were traveling across country to a specific location, no matter how large or small your destination was, you wouldn't leave without a map. Without a map, you might reach your destination, but it's more likely that you would get lost. Even if you did reach your destination, it would take longer without a map. Not to mention figuring out how to reach your destination when you encounter road construction or detours along the way. Business is no different. In order to succeed, you need a goal and a plan, a map of how to get where you want to be and how to cross the unexpected detours along the way.

Making Your Dreams a Reality

Let me say this one more time: Never give up. Ever since I was eighteen, I have been known as Persistent Pat. I never give up. Being persistent is possible when you have a goal or vision and refuse to deviate from the plan to reach it. You will hit detour signs, and you will be told no. You will have doors slammed in your face. Don't allow discouragement to settle in on you and your dreams.

It is possible to be successful in business, but if you think it will be easy, you will be out of business in less than six months. You need to give your dreams every part of yourself: mind, heart, soul, hopes, time, and energy. It is hard work. Many days will be eighteen hours or longer. On those nights when you have several hours of hard work ahead of you, remember your dream, and keep in mind the road you planned out to make that dream a reality.

Always give your customers what they want, even if it means little profit for you on one particular sale. Take a long-term view of your customers and building customer loyalty. You may make a larger profit on the next sale, and then your sacrifice will have paid off. Treat your customers with respect and try to always say yes. If you don't have what the customer wants, find someone who does, even if it means sending that customer to a competitor.

Discover or invent a niche in your business. What do people want that no one else in your field is providing? Find out and fill that need. Will you be able to satisfy every single customer? Probably not, but at least make an attempt. In some of my businesses, I have had customers who still were unhappy after I gave them refunds. Thankfully, this type of situation is rare. I have been in various businesses for more than twenty years. In that time, I have had fewer than five people who weren't satisfied. That is a great record, but it is not good enough to satisfy me. As I have always believed and have always told my employees and other business owners, every business is built or destroyed one customer at a time.

I want you to be satisfied with this book. I hope you have learned a few things from reading *Money-Tree Marketing*. In fact, I hope you have learned a lot, but remember, you are the only one who can make your business a success; you are the only one who can turn your dreams into reality. Use your creativity and imagination. The techniques in this book can be a starting point, but you need to add your own ideas and come up with your own unique marketing techniques. And don't be afraid to try something new. If it doesn't work, remember that you can gain valuable knowledge from your failures as well as your successes.

We want to hear from you. If these marketing techniques have helped you or if you don't understand some part of the book, write to us. If you have unusual marketing techniques that have helped your business, please let us know. We would also like to know what aspect of business you would like to learn about—for example, starting a business, legal issues facing small businesses, or funding a business. We will use the input from our readers in our next book, covering the issues that most people requested.

Appendix

Joining the American Small Business Alliance

We would like to invite you to join the American Small Business Alliance. As a member, you will have access to consultants, marketing experts, lawyers, bankers, and other professionals who will assist you in starting or running your business. You will receive discounts on various business-related items. The membership is normally $35 per month, but if you mention this book, you will get a three-month trial membership for only $35. You will also receive a free copy of *Money-Tree Marketing* to give to a friend, relative, or anyone starting a small business.

Win a Free Business

We want to put you in business. If you want to own a business, here is the opportunity of a lifetime. We will assist someone to get started in a business chosen for that person on the basis of his or her talents and past experience. It could be a restaurant or a janitorial service or a retail shop. If you want to enter, send your name, address, phone number, the type of business you are most interested in starting, and an essay of 200 words or less on why you should be selected to win a business.

Free Marketing Consulting

If you already own a business and would like to have a free marketing coach to help you dramatically increase your business, here's your chance. We will select one person to receive personal consulting to help him or her grow the business. To enter, send your name, address, phone number, the type of business you own, and an essay of 200 words or less on why you should be selected.

Absolutely No Obligation

To enter either of these contests, there is absolutely no obligation to purchase anything or to get a membership in the ASBA. However, we do recommend that you join the ASBA if you are thinking about starting a business or if you already own a business and want to grow it, get advice on various issues, or save money on purchases for your business. As a member, you will also be entitled to attend seminars and classes regarding various business topics that are designed to help you increase your business. If you want to join the ASBA and enter either of these contests, send your name, address, phone number, and essay to:

> The American Small Business Alliance
> Membership & Contest Department
> 9608 N May Avenue Suite 301
> Oklahoma City, OK 73120

If you want to enter either of these contests, but you do not want to join the ASBA, send your name, address, phone number, and essay to:

> The American Small Business Alliance
> Contest Department
> 5830 NW Expressway Suite 225
> Oklahoma City, OK 73132

For more information on joining the ASBA, please send a legal-size self-addressed stamped envelope to the same address. Details on the contest and information on joining the ASBA can be found at our Web site, www.freesmallbusiness.com.

Thank you for taking the time to read *Money-Tree Marketing* and for being our friend in business.

Index

add-on sales, 146
address, 49, 97–98, 184, 200
addresses, 176, 200
advantage, 229–230, 242
advertisement, anatomy of, 121–122
advertising
   classifieds, 107, 108–109, 112, 122
   cookbooks, 22–23
   cooperative, 88, 89, 90
   direct mail, 29, 90
   and licensing, 216
   in newspapers, 107
agreements, 16–18, 218–224
alliances, see cooperative efforts
American Small Business Alliance, 261–262
appreciation, 30, 238–240
associations
   benefit selection, 198–199
   decision-maker contact, 199–206
   endorsements by, 188–190, 189, 192–193, 208
   marketing to, 190–192
   member contact, 205, 206, 207
   selecting, 190–192, 193–198

banks, 192, 208, 241–242
banner ads, 155, 161–163

barter
   auction shows, 130
   and direct mail, 90
   for meals, 37–38
   and newsletters, 12
   and printing, 22
   and radio, 141
   weekly shoppers, 120
benefit, 230
bird dogs, 37–38
birthdays, 68
brand awareness, 57, 146
brochures, 13, 15
business cases
   ad agency, 4
   attorney, 127–130, 134
   bicycle purchase, 245–248
   boats, 239–240
   bookstore, 21–22
   car dealer, 131–132
   convenience stores, 238–239
   cosmetic company, 209–210, 213–214
   credit repair, 105–110, 119–120
   gymnastics school, 33–34
   insurance business, 39–40
   long distance resale, 26–27
   martial arts studio, 141–142
   mobile homes, 105–111, 119–120

business cases *(continued)*
  mortgage broker, 80–88
  movie hopeful, 255–257
  movie theatre, 32–33
  nutrition store, 135–140
  pest control, 60
  replacement windows, 230
  restaurants, 7–20, 34–37, 37–38, 96–97, 99–100
  retail store, 89–90, 101–103
  sporting goods, 20–21, 227–229
  swimming pools, 93–94
business spotlight shows, 128–129, 142
business-to-business
  direct mail, 69–70, 76, 89, 91
  telemarketing, 98

catalogs, 73, 86, 155
centers of influence, 28–29, 32, 34–37
charities, 10, 11, 20–21
children, 8–9, 97, 245
city directories, 64, 99, 174
classified ads, 107, 108–109, 112, 122
cobratizing
  business name, 249–250
  checklist, 244
  and competition, 251–252
  customer appreciation, 238–240, 243
  examples, 235–238, 245–248
  first impressions, 240–242
  follow-up, 252–253
  and information, 245–248
  warranties, 239–240, 251–252
columnists, 110, 119–120
commercials, TV, 127–129
competitors, 30, 40–42, 123–124, 251–252

consultants, 217–218, 261–262
consumers
  and direct mail, 29, 58–59, 73, 74–75, 88–89
  objections, 85
contests, 160–161, 261
contracts, 16–18, 218–224
cookbook, 21–23
cooperative efforts
  direct mail, 88, 89, 90
  insurance, 39–40
  on Internet, 147, 152, 155, 161, 162–163
  referrals, 38–44
  telemarketing, 102–103
coupons, 37–38, 76, 89, 91
credit, 101–102
  for donations, 11
credit cards, 74
credit unions, 189, 190, 191–192, 208
customer base
  importance of, 2
  information about, 31, 168–170, 245
  and referrals, 26, 31–33
customer contact, 39, 40
customer-friendliness, 3, 45–46, 57, 95–96
  see also cobratizing; satisfaction; tips
customer profiles, 60, 61, 168, 169
customer service, 145, 242

decision-makers, 9–11, 12–13, 13, 200
direct mail
  advantages, 56–57
  business-to-business, 69–70, 76, 89, 91
  consumer response, 58–59, 73–74, 180

Index

cooperative approach, 88, 90
and emotions, 29
great words, 73–74
incentives, 65–66, 70, 75, 80–81, 82
insert service, 90
involvement devices, 74–75
vs. junk mail, 58
labels, 63, 69, 74
letters, 67, 70–71, 73–75, 83–84
list brokers, 62–64, 157–158
mailing lists, 62–65, 79, 89, 122, 180, 190
monitoring, 79–80
motivators, 71–72
odds of reading, 66–67, 68, 69–70
opportunities, 75–76
payment options, 82–83
postcards, 63, 67, 68
presorting, 76–77
to radio sponsor, 140
reading rates, 67
response rates, 88, 89
sequential, 82–87, 122–123
service bureaus, 77–79
target market, 59–62, 66, 71
and TV promotions, 133
directories
city, 64, 99, 174
Internet, 154–155
telephone, 250
discount cards, 13–14, 15–20
discounts
and cobratizing, 243
and direct mail, 76, 86, 87
and endorsements, 178
and fund raising, 10, 14
for magazine space, 107, 119
for niche markets, 100

and prospecting, 48, 49
and referrals, 36, 38, 45
for survey forms, 31
displays, 244
draw rate, 79, 82, 88–89, 190

E-mail, 157–160
emotions, 29, 72, 73
employees, 240–242, 244
endorsements
association for, 167–177
definition, 166–167
follow-up, 183
letter content, 177–182
mailings, 180, 181
ten steps, 185
tracking, 182
envelopes, 69–70, 74
examples
business profiles, 171, 172
business-to-business direct mail, 91
classified ads, 108
customer profiles, 60, 61, 168, 169, 195, 196
endorsement letters, 178, 179
letters to association, 202, 206
licensing contract, 219–224
press release, 114
sponsor flyer, 140
three step flyer, 87
exclusivity, 72, 189, 215

F.A.B. (sales technique), 227–231
facilities, 238–239, 242–243, 244
fear, 71
features, 226, 229

Index

fictitious name certificates, 49–52, 65
financing, 83
   see also credit
first impressions, 240–242, 248–249
flyers
   with bills, 74
   for prospecting, 50, 51
   for three-step incentive, 87
   for two-step program, 82–83
follow-up
   advantages, 252–253
   for direct mail, 84–85, 95, 100
   for endorsements, 182–183, 206
   for press release, 117–118
free samples, 9, 10, 97–98
fund raising
   commission rate, 12
   cookbook, 21–22
   discount cards, 13–14
   interview content, 11–13
   literature, 13, 15
   with other merchants, 14, 18–20
   phone contact, 9–11
   point of sale, 20
   rate setting, 15–16
   with schools, 8–11
   timing, 13

gift certificates
   for decision makers, 10
   in direct mail, 81
   for endorsements, 199
   and newspaper, 120
   for publicity, 12
   and referrals, 30, 37, 45, 46
gifts
   for birthday, 68

and cobratizing, 243
and endorsements, 179, 198–199
and press release, 113
and referrals, 38, 45
and TV, 132
to Web site, 160–161
golf, 20–21
government, selling to, 194
greed, 72
guilt, 72

handouts, personalized, 13
home-based business, 234

image, 190, 204
incentives, 65–66, 70, 75, 80–81, 82
infomercials, 129–131
information
   and classifieds, 122
   and coupons, 89
   about customers, 31, 46, 168–170, 245–248
   and direct mail, 56, 57, 64–65, 72, 74
   about fund raising project, 13, 15
   about licensing, 215–216
   about potential customers, 89, 94
   and telemarketing, 94
   on Web site visitors, 146, 156–157
informed prospecting, 47–52
informing mail, 58–59
insurance
   complementary businesses, 39–40
   as endorsement benefit, 198–199
   motivators, 71
   for sponsors, 21

Index

Internet
  directories, 154–155
  E-mail, 157–160
  newsgroups, 160
  signatures, 157–158
  see also Web sites
interviews, 204–205, 217–218
involvement devices, 74–75

labor unions, 187–188, 191–192, 197–198
letterhead, 176–177, 201, 206
licensing
  benefits, 211–213
  consultants, 217–218
  contracts, 218–224
  definition, 210–211
  exclusivity, 215
  information on, 216
  presentation, 217–218
  questions, 215, 216–217
lines, waiting in, 243
link exchange, 155
list brokers, 62–64, 158
literature
  direct mail, 29, 67–71
  for nonprofits, 13
  and prospecting, 49, 50, 51

magazines
  costs, 107, 124
  for target markets, 62, 63, 173
  Time and *Newsweek*, 119, 120
mailbox rental, 176
mailing list brokers, 62–64, 158
mailing lists, 62–65, 89, 122, 132, 173–174, 190

mailing service, 77–79, 90
mail order, 82–83
marketing
  to associations, 190–192
  description, 10, 133
  money-tree, 4–6
  monitoring, 133
marketing plan, 4, 228
McDonald's complex, 1–2, 136
monitoring, 79–80, 133, 182, 245
motivation, 4, 71–72
multilevel marketing, 28

names
  business, 249–250
  personal, 249–250
National Marketplace, 116
NEBS, 204
negotiation
  with list broker, 64, 174
  with print media, 107, 120, 124
  with radio stations, 137
  and tier pricing, 239
network marketing, 28
newsletters
  business-related, 14
  electronic, 146, 156, 159–160
  for licensing, 216
  publicity in, 12
newspapers, 65, 107
news syndicates, 125–126
niche markets, 99–101, 107, 259

objections, handling, 85
organizations
  industry, 30

organizations *(continued)*
  nonprofit, 7–23
out of stock items, 242

packages, 75
patents, 211
payment, 82–83
persistence, 255–259
personalization, 13, 57, 69, 72
point-of-sale, 20
postcards, 63, 67, 68, 74
prequalification, 93–94, 95, 248–249
press kits, 115–116
press releases, 110–115, 117–118, 157–158
pricing
  and direct mail, 80
  and fund raising, 16–17
  tier, 239
  and value, 225
printing
  barter for, 22
  discount cards, 20
  postcards, 63
  sales call example, 52
print media
  ad anatomy, 121–122
  campaigns, 57
  and charity, 10
  classified ads, 107, 108–109, 112, 122
  columns, 110, 119–120
  display ads, 109
  magazines, 107
  newspapers, 107, 124–126, 125–126
  per-inquiry basis, 124
  press releases, 110–118, 157–158
  weekly shoppers, 107, 109

privacy, 206
profit, 259
promotions, 243
prospecting, 47–53
publicity
  cable TV, 130
  charity donations, 10
  newsletters, 12
  press releases, 110–118, 157–158
  relationships, 108–109
  sponsorships, 21

quality, 228–231
queues, 243

radio
  business spotlight shows, 142
  costs, 138
  effective use, 137
  reaching producers, 110
  talk programs, 137–141
Radio-TV Interview Report, 110
referrals
  acknowledgment, 30
  benefits, 27, 42–43
  from businesses, 38–40
  centers of influence, 28–29, 32, 34–37
  from competitors, 40–42
  from customers, 31–33
  prospecting, 47–48
  relationships, 43–44, 45–46
  requesting, 26, 44–45
  source types, 29–31
restrooms, 238–239
risk, 6

Index

sales calls, 48–49, 52–53
sales techniques, 226–231
samples, free, 9, 10, 57, 97–98
satisfaction, 100–101, 146, 259
schools, 8–11, 13, 34–37
SCORE, 132
scripts
   association director approach, 203, 205
   brochure for nonprofit, 15
   direct mail follow-up, 84–85
   discount card, 16–18, 18–20
   endorsement follow-up, 183
   informed prospecting, 48–52
   nonprofit contact, 11
   press release follow-up, 118
   PTO president call, 10–11
   referral approach, 46
   referral gathering, 32, 35, 36
   school call, 9–10
   selling technique, 230
   for talk show sponsor approach, 139
   telemarketing, 97, 99, 100
   for uninformed prospecting, 52–53
search engines, 152–154
senior citizens, 76, 99, 166, 168
service bureaus, 77–79
signs, 237–238, 242–243, 244
special orders, 242
special promotions, 243
Spielberg, Steven, 255–257
sponsorships, 20–21, 129, 138–139, 158–159
sports
   fund raising, 9, 13
   sponsorships, 20–21
stationery, 176–177, 201, 204, 206
   envelopes, 69–70, 74

success, 6, 255–259
surveys, 31, 74, 96, 100
syndicates, 125–126
syndication, 110, 120, 122

talk shows, 137–139
target markets, 59–62, 99–101, 107, 167–173
telemarketing
   for appointments, 99
   attitude, 97–99, 102
   inbound calls, 94
   irresistible words, 98
   niche markets, 99–101
   reciprocal efforts, 102–103
   and satisfaction, 100–101
   three-step, 101–102
   and TV promotions, 133
telephone contact
   with association director, 203
   attitude, 241–242, 244
   directory listing, 250
   follow-up, 95, 100
   with labor unions, 197–198
   and mailings, 63, 83, 84–86, 98, 174
   with nonprofit decision-makers, 8–11
   and prospecting, 48
   time and temperature, 121
   yellow pages, 197, 250, 251
telephone lines, 176
television
   costs, 129
   and direct mail, 57
   reaching producers, 110
   self-production, 127–132
testimonials, 115, 116
three-step programs, 83–87, 101–102

tier pricing, 239
time and temperature phone, 121
timing
  discount cards, 20
  expiration dates, 82
  fund raising, 13
  referrals, 44
  three-step program, 85
tips
  advertising agency, 117
  attitude, 249
  barter, 22, 37
  cooperative advertising, 89
  customer relations, 240, 242, 245, 248
  decision makers, 13
  direct mail, 64, 67, 68, 69, 70, 72, 74, 81, 83
  donations, 10, 11
  endorsements, 180, 182
  home-based business, 234
  knowledge resources, 14
  mailboxes, 176
  mailing lists, 174, 175, 180
  marketing, 133
  personal names, 184
  press releases, 113
  pricing, 226, 231, 246
  print media, 107, 120, 124
  publicity, 12
  radio advertising, 137
  referrals, 30, 37, 38, 40, 53
  sports teams, 13
  stationery, 204
  target market, 62, 173
  telemarketing, 84
  television, 129, 130
  unions and banks, 188, 190, 191, 192
  Web sites, 153, 162
training, 244
turnkey programs, 12
two-step program, 82–83

value, 228–231

warranties, 239–240, 251–252
Web sites
  attracting visitors, 148, 152–155, 156–161
  banner ads, 155, 161–163
  customer information, 31
  design, 149–152, 155
  exchange links, 155
  for freebies, 161
  profiting from, 147–148
  and stationery, 201
  for target market, 62
  U.S. post office, 76
  uses, 145–147, 149–150
  visitor information, 146, 156–157
  yellow pages, 197
weekly shoppers, 107, 109, 120
words, influential, 73–74, 98, 121, 154

yellow pages, 197, 250, 251
youth market, 146

Zen of Selling, 245